MASTERING THE GRADE 8 SOCIAL STUDIES TEKS

Revised: Streamlined TEKS Edition

MARK JARRETT, Ph.D.

STUART ZIMMER

JAMES KILLORAN

JARRETT PUBLISHING COMPANY

EAST COAST OFFICE
P.O. Box 1460
Ronkonkoma, NY 11779
631-981-4248

SOUTHERN OFFICE
50 Nettles Boulevard
Jensen Beach, FL 34957
800-859-7679

WEST COAST OFFICE
10 Folin Lane
Lafayette, CA 94549
925-906-9742

www.jarrettpub.com
1-800-859-7679   Fax: 631-588-4722

About our Cover. (Top) A painting by the American artist John Ward Dunsmore of Betsy Ross and the first Stars and Stripes. The flag's early design of red-and-white striped fields with 13 white stars, represent the original 13 colonies, against a blue background.
(Bottom) A painting of the Battle of Chattanooga by an unknown artist. In 1863, Union forces led a series of successful engagements against Confederate soldiers. With Chattanooga in Union hands, the door was open for General Sherman to attack Alabama and Georgia.

The authors wish to thank the following educators for their comments, suggestions, and recommendations which proved invaluable to this manuscript.

Greg Byers
K–12 Social Studies Coordinator
Alief ISD, Alief, Texas
Former President, Texas Social Studies
Supervisors Association (TSSSA)

Montra Rogers
Secondary Social Studies Specialist
Curriculum Dept., Houston ISD
Houston, Texas

Polly Schlosser
Instructor of Curriculum and Instruction,
University of Texas at Dallas
Former Secondary Social Studies
Coordinator, Plano ISD
Former President, Texas Council for the
Social Studies (TCSS) and TSSSA
"Supervisor of the Year"

Layout, maps, graphics, and typesetting: Burmar Technical Corporation, Sea Cliff, N.Y.

This book is dedicated...
    to Malgorzata, Alexander, and Julia   — *Mark Jarrett*
    to Joan, Todd, and Ronald
    and my grandchildren Jared and Katie   — *Stuart Zimmer*
    to Donna, Christian, Carrie, and Jesse
    and my grandchildren Aiden, Christian, and Olivia   — *James Killoran*

Copyright 2019 by Jarrett Publishing Company

ISBN 1-935022-15-6   [978-1-935022-15-2]
Printed in the United States of America
Streamlined TEKS Edition
10 9 8 7 6 5 4   21 20 19

ALSO BY JARRETT, ZIMMER, AND KILLORAN

Mastering the TEKS in World Geography
Mastering the TEKS in World History
Mastering the TEKS in United States History Since 1877
Mastering the Grade 8 TAKS Social Studies Assessment
Mastering the Grade 10 TAKS Social Studies Assessment
Mastering the Grade 11 TAKS Social Studies Assessment
Texas: Its Land and Its People
Mastering New York's Intermediate-Level Social Studies Standards
Mastering New York's Grade 7 Social Studies Standards
Mastering New York's Elementary Social Studies Standards: Grade 5 Edition
The Key to Understanding U.S. History and Government
Mastering U.S. History
A Quick Review of U.S. History and Government
Learning About New York State
The Key to Understanding Global History
Mastering Global History
A Quick Review of Global History
Ohio: Its Land and Its People
Ohio: The Buckeye State
Mastering Ohio's Grade 5 Social Studies Achievement Test
Mastering World Regions and Civilizations
Mastering Ohio's Grade 8 Social Studies Achievement Test
Mastering Ohio's 9th Grade Citizenship Test
Mastering World Regions and Civilizations
Mastering Ohio's 12th Grade Citizenship Test
Mastering Ohio's Graduation Test in Social Studies
North Carolina: The Tar Heel State
Michigan: Its Land and Its People
Mastering the Social Studies MEAP Test: Grade 5
Mastering the Social Studies MEAP Test: Grade 8
Mastering Michigan's High School Test in Social Studies
Mastering the Grade 5 MCAS History and Social Science Test
Mastering the Grade 5 CRCT in Social Studies
Mastering the GHSGT in Social Studies
Historia y gobierno de los Estados Unidos
Claves Para La Comprension de historia universal

ABOUT THE AUTHORS

Mark Jarrett has served as a test writer for the New York State Board of Regents, and has taught at Hofstra University. He was educated at Columbia University, the London School of Economics, the Law School of the University of California at Berkeley, and Stanford University, where he received a Ph.D. in history. His dissertation analyzed British foreign policy in the aftermath of the French Revolution. Dr. Jarrett has received several academic awards including the Order of the Coif at Berkeley and the David and Christina Phelps Harris Fellowship at Stanford. As an attorney at the world's largest international law firm, he was an eyewitness to globalization and helped draft some of its first joint venture agreements for foreign investment in China.

Stuart Zimmer is a former Social Studies teacher. He has written *Government and You* and *Economics and You*. He served as a test writer for the N.Y. State Board of Regents in Social Studies, and has written for the National Merit Scholarship Examination. In addition, Mr. Zimmer has published numerous articles on teaching and testing in Social Studies journals. He has presented many educational workshops at local, state, and national teachers' conferences. In 1989, Mr. Zimmer's achievements were recognized by the New York State Legislature with a Special Legislative Resolution in his honor.

James Killoran is a former Assistant Principal. He has written *Government and You* and *Economics and You*. Mr. Killoran has extensive experience in test writing for the N.Y. State Board of Regents in Social Studies and has served on the Committee for Testing of the N.C.S.S. His article on social studies testing has been published in *Social Education*, the country's leading social studies journal. In addition, Mr. Killoran has won a number of awards for outstanding teaching and curriculum development, including "Outstanding Social Studies Teacher" and "Outstanding Social Studies Supervisor" in New York City. In 1993, he was awarded an Advanced Certificate for Teachers of Social Studies by the N.C.S.S. In 1997, he became Chairman of the N.C.S.S. Committee on Awarding Advanced Certificates for Teachers of Social Studies.

TABLE OF CONTENTS

PART 3

Name _____

WELCOME TO GRADE 8 SOCIAL STUDIES

It is no secret that social studies tests are demanding. How can you be expected to learn and remember so much information about American history? With this book as your guide, you should enjoy studying history and also find the *Grade 8 Social Studies STAAR Test* less difficult to master.

The philosophy of this book can best be expressed by an ancient Chinese adage: "Give a person a fish, and you feed that person for a day; teach that person *how* to fish, and you feed that person for a lifetime." The focus of *Mastering the Grade 8 Social Studies TEKS* will be on teaching you all of the content as well as showing you *how* to learn and apply what you know.

Abraham Lincoln delivering the Gettysburg Address.

THE GRADE 8 SOCIAL STUDIES TEST

This year, you will need to pass the *Grade 8 Social Studies STAAR Test*. **STAAR** stands for State of Texas Assessment of Academic Readiness. The **STAAR Test** consists of 52 multiple-choice questions, each with four possible choices. Many of the questions will provide a map, table, graph, illustration or written document as part of the question. The test will assess the same four categories as other Texas social studies tests:

Reporting Categories	
Category 1: History	**Category 3:** Government and Citizenship
Category 2: Geography and Culture	**Category 4:** Economics, Science, Technology, and Society

The test will examine your knowledge of the recently streamlined student expectations in the Grade 8 Social Studies TEKS (*Texas Essential Knowledge and Skills*). Some of these student expectations, known as "**Readiness Standards,**" are essential for a successful understanding of social studies, and often address broad and deep ideas. Other expectations, known as "**Supporting Standards,**" play a less central role and will be tested less often. All of the TEKS will be tested at some time on the test, so you should learn them all to perform your best.

HOW THIS BOOK WILL HELP YOU

This book will help you to learn every one of the streamlined Grade 8 Social Studies TEKS. These TEKS have been organized in a way to make them easier to learn. At the beginning of each chapter, you will see the TEKS covered in that chapter. Some TEKS may appear in more than one chapter. The first part of the book will help you learn how to answer test questions, how to read and interpret different types of data, how to conduct research, and how to make decisions and solve problems.

THE ORGANIZATION OF CONTENT CHAPTERS

Each content chapter has several unique features designed to help you learn important concepts more easily.

IMPORTANT IDEAS

Each chapter is introduced by a list of *Important Ideas*. This is an advanced organizer that summarizes the main ideas and concepts you will learn in the chapter.

KEY TERMS AND PEOPLE IN THIS CHAPTER

At the start of each content chapter, there is also a list of important historical terms and individuals that are discussed in the chapter.

ESSENTIAL QUESTIONS

At the beginning of each content chapter, you will find several *Essential Questions*. These questions establish overarching themes for each chapter. They pose interesting questions that the chapter will answer.

APPLYING WHAT YOU HAVE LEARNED

Each section of the text includes one or more *Applying What You Have Learned* activities. These activities encourage you to think about what you have read. You can complete and research these activities alone or in a small group.

ACTING AS AN AMATEUR HISTORIAN

These "hands-on" activities will ask you to think and act like a historian as you investigate and research various topics related to the text. These activities give you an opportunity to learn about aspects of early American history that may interest you.

LEARNING WITH GRAPHIC ORGANIZERS

These exercises ask you to complete a graphic organizer summarizing the major ideas and concepts in the chapter.

CHAPTER CONCEPT MAPS

Just as a road map shows the locations of towns with respect to one another, a concept map shows how concepts and people are related. Each chapter concludes with a *Concept Map*, which visually represents, the most important information and relationships in that chapter.

STUDY CARDS

Study Cards identify the major ideas and facts at the end of each chapter. You can use these cards alone to quiz yourself, or with a group of classmates. You should expand the number of *Study Cards* by adding additional cards of your own.

CHECKING YOUR UNDERSTANDING

Each content chapter also ends with practice test questions. The answer to the first question is always fully explained. All questions are in a format similar to those on the **STAAR Test**. In addition, every question is identified by its appropriate Social Studies TEKS.

IMPORTANT TOOLS FOR REMEMBERING INFORMATION

History concerns conditions and events in the past. You will learn about people's lifestyles, beliefs, and systems of government. You will also learn about the events that influenced the development of the United States, from colonial times to Reconstruction. With so much information, it is sometimes hard to identify what is important. This section will help you to do that.

IMPORTANT TERMS AND PEOPLE

In social studies, you will learn about many terms, people and concepts. **Terms** refer to specific things that actually happened or existed — such as particular features, places, or groups. When you learn a new term, you should focus on its main features. These include:

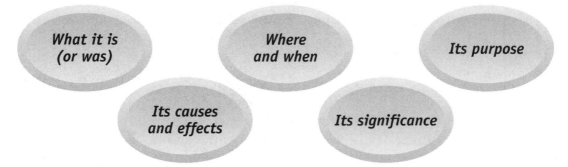

What it is (or was)   *Where and when*   *Its purpose*

Its causes and effects   *Its significance*

As you work your way through this book, you will come upon the names of important people. When you read about these people, think about their background — such as when they lived and their position — and what they accomplished during their lifetime.

KEY CONCEPTS

Concepts are words or phrases that refer to categories of information. They allow us to organize large amounts of information. For example, the American Revolution, the War of 1812, and the Civil War all share certain common characteristics.

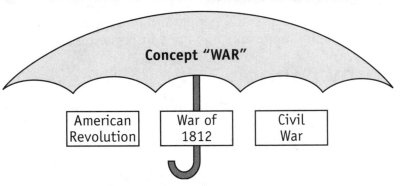

The concept "war" acts as an umbrella, grouping these specific examples together by identifying what they have in common. Questions about concepts usually ask for a definition or an example of the concept. Thus, when you study a concept, you should pay careful attention to:

Its definition   *Examples of the concept*

HOW TO USE YOUR STUDY CARDS

At the end of every content chapter there are two to six *Study Cards*. These *Study Cards* highlight the most important information you should know about a particular term, concept or person in the chapter. You should make a habit of building a collection of these cards by copying by hand or photocopying them.

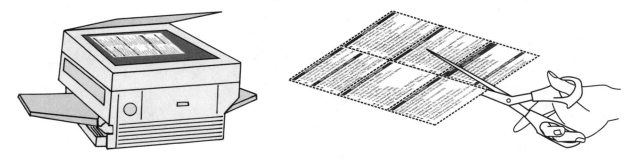

After you duplicate the cards, use the back of each card to create your own illustration. Why should you draw your own illustration? Turning written information into a picture can help you to better understand the term or concept. You may be a visual learner. By "seeing" the term or concept, you can create an impression in your mind that will help you to remember the term better. In drawing these illustrations, do not be concerned with your artistic ability. It is not that important. What is important is that your illustration captures the essence or spirit of the term or concept.

There are many ways to use *Study Cards* to recall information, especially for a test. One method is to sort your cards into two stacks, based on how well you recall the information on each card.

First, gather your cards into one pile. Try to recall the information on the card at the top of the stack. If you can recall it, place the card in the "Know It" stack. If you have trouble recalling the information, place the card in the "Don't Know It" stack.

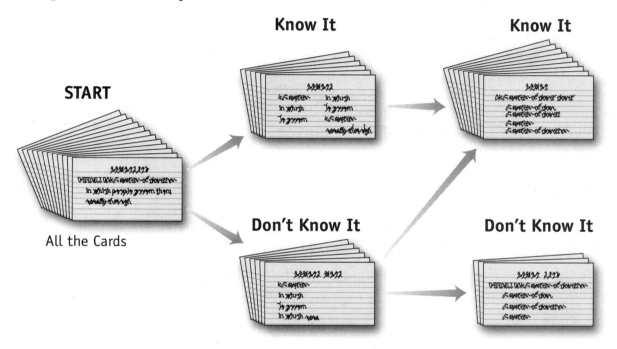

Review the cards in the "Don't Know It" stack every time you study. Study the cards in the "Know It" stack every other time you study. As you move closer to the day of the **STAAR Test**, you should see the number of cards in the "Don't Know It" stack shrink. This will give you even more time to study the ones you know the least.

THE ART OF NOTE-TAKING

In this chapter, you have already learned some effective strategies for remembering information, such as how to create and use study cards. Another strategy for recalling information is by taking notes.

One valuable form of note-taking is to take notes directly in the book itself. This is actually the method preferred by most college students. If you were given this book by your school, first check with your teacher to see if you have permission to write in the book. If you can, then get in the habit of using your own note-taking system as you read. Distinguishing the information that is the most important from what is less important is a skill that improves with practice and that will keep you engaged as you read.

Most history books, like this one, give you main ideas accompanied by supporting details. Here are four popular strategies for note-taking that will help you to recall the main ideas and important details supporting them:

Underlining. One of the easiest ways to take notes in a book is just to <u>underline</u>, in pencil or pen, anything you think is important. Or you could star * important terms and people and **<u>underline</u>** <u>supporting details</u>.

Highlighting. Most college students highlight as they read. With a yellow, blue, or pink highlighter, you can highlight the main ideas in each paragraph. Often, this is the topic sentence found at the beginning or end of the paragraph. Also try to highlight individual names, dates or events that you think are important. Then review the text a second time by just reading the sentences and terms you have highlighted. See if you can remember what they are about. When you study for a test, just re-read the highlighted portions again. If you do not recall what something means, then re-read the entire paragraph.

Color Coding. Color coding is a form of highlighting used to distinguish different types of information. To color-code, you need highlighters of different colors. For example, you might highlight main ideas in yellow, important people in pink, and key dates or events in blue. When you look back at a page, you can instantly find information you might need or want to learn. The process of identifying and highlighting information in this manner helps to keep you engaged while reading. Then read over the highlighted portions several times.

Notes in the Margin. One of the most effective ways of taking notes is to write in the space between the text and edge of the page, known as the margin. Write a label describing what the text says — like "Ratification Debate" or "Transatlantic Slave Trade" — or even more detailed notes — "Hamilton's financial plan opposed by Jefferson." These can serve as a summary of the text. Then re-read your marginal notes after you have completed the section or the chapter. If you come across something in your marginal notes you do not recall, then reread that part of the text next to your notes. To study for a test, re-read your marginal notes. You can combine using marginal notes with underlining, highlighting or color-coding.

Need to write in margins

Suppose you cannot write in your book? You can still take notes on a separate sheet of paper. One way to take notes is to outline the information you read. The idea is to "shrink" the text down to its essence — the most essential terms, people and events. Often, a topic sentence or a summary at the end of each paragraph will help you to identify main ideas.

At the beginning of each chapter is a list of important ideas that can be used as a starting point for your notes. Another way to take notes in social studies is to create a timeline as you read. Make a timeline for each chapter with the most important events and people. Summarize key causes and effects next to each event, or key ideas next to each individual or development. The practice of note-taking will help you when it is time to study for a class test or to prepare for the STAAR test at the end of the school year.

This book will provide you with all you will need to know about early American history, geography, government, economics and culture. With this book as your guide, you should be very well prepared to face the challenges presented by the **STAAR Test**.

Name _____

HOW TO ANSWER MULTIPLE-CHOICE QUESTIONS

- **Social Studies Skills 29B** Analyze information by sequencing, categorizing, identifying cause-and-effect relationships, comparing, contrasting, finding the main idea, summarizing, making generalizations and predictions, drawing inferences and conclusions.

TEKS COVERED IN CHAPTER 1

All of the questions on the **STAAR Assessment in Grade 8 Social Studies** will be multiple-choice questions. A **multiple-choice question** is one in which there is a question followed by several possible answers. Your job will be to choose the **best** answer to the question. This chapter will help you learn how to approach these kinds of questions. You can return to this chapter whenever you want as you work your way through this book.

RECALLING IMPORTANT INFORMATION

One common type of multiple-choice question tests your ability to recall important information. These questions test your knowledge of important terms, concepts, and people. Here is an example of how such questions may be asked:

> **1** Which practice was characteristic of mercantilism?
> **A** buying raw materials from colonists and selling them finished goods
> **B** prohibiting colonists from fishing and trading in furs
> **C** shipping large amounts of gold and silver from Europe to the colonies
> **D** increasing the use of slave labor to manufacture goods in Europe

As you can see, this question tests your ability to recall specific information about a term.

UNLOCKING THE ANSWER

🗝 What do you think is the answer to **Question 1**? _____

🗝 Explain, or justify, why you selected that answer. _____

_____

_____

HOW TO USE THE "E-R-A" APPROACH

Whatever type of multiple-choice question you are asked, we recommend you follow a three-step approach to answer it. We call this the "E-R-A" approach:

EXAMINE the Question	**R**ECALL What You Know	**A**PPLY What You Know

Let's look at each of these steps to see how they can help you select the right answer.

STEP 1: EXAMINE THE QUESTION

Start by carefully reading the question. Be sure that you understand any information it provides. Then make sure you understand what the question asks for.

This question asks you to identify which practice was characteristic of mercantilism. Which answer choice describes a practice that was typical of mercantilism?

STEP 2: RECALL WHAT YOU KNOW

Next, you need to take a moment to think of what you can remember about the subject of the question. Mentally review the most important concepts and facts associated with that topic.

Here, you should think about what you can recall from your study of mercantilism. You might recall that mercantilism was a policy of European rulers during the 17th and 18th centuries. The goal of mercantilism was to bring gold and silver into the Mother Country's treasury. The colonies of the Mother Country served as places to obtain raw materials and markets in which to sell manufactured goods.

STEP 3: APPLY WHAT YOU KNOW

Finally, take what you can recall and apply it to the question. Sometimes it helps to try to answer the question on your own **before** you look at the answer choices.

Then look to see if any of the answer choices are what you thought the answer should be. Review all the answer choices to be sure you have identified the best one. Eliminate any answer choices that do not make sense or that are obviously wrong. Then select your final answer.

This question asks you to identify which practice was characteristic of mercantilism.

★ *Choice B, preventing colonists from fishing and trading furs, is wrong. Mercantilists encouraged colonists to sell their fish and furs to Europe.*

★ *Choice C, shipping large amounts of gold and silver from Europe to the colonies, is wrong. Mercantilists actually encouraged the opposite.*

★ *Choice D, increasing the use of slave labor to manufacture goods in Europe, is also wrong since slaves were mainly used in the colonies.*

✪ *Therefore, Choice A is the best answer. It is the only choice that correctly describes a characteristic of mercantilism — buying raw materials from the colonists and selling them as manufactured goods.*

UNDERSTANDING A GENERALIZATION

Some questions will test your ability to draw a conclusion or to make a **generalization** — a general statement identifying what several specific examples have in common. Often, a generalization identifies a feature or relationship found in each of several examples. The question below illustrates this type of question:

---

2   Which generalization best applies to the American colonists?
  F   They all lived along the Atlantic coastline.
  G   They all came to America to find religious freedom.
  H   They were all loyal to the British king.
  J   They all lived in areas with a degree of self-government.

USING THE "E-R-A" APPROACH

◆ **Step 1: E̲XAMINE the question.** First, read the question carefully. Be sure you understand that the question asks for the generalization that best applies to the American colonists.

◆ **Step 2: R̲ECALL what you know.** Think about what you know about the colonists. Americans colonists came to the colonies for many different reasons, including religious freedom, the desire for economic opportunity, and the need to escape political oppression.

CONTINUED

◆ **Step 3: A**PPLY **what you know.** Now apply your knowledge of the colonial period to find the correct answer. Examine the choices and eliminate any answers that are obviously wrong or that make no sense.

★ **Choice F is wrong.** Although the majority of colonist lived along the Atlantic coastline, many of them did not. Some colonists lived on the frontier or on farms in the western areas of the British colonies.

★ **Choice G is wrong.** Many did come to the colonies for religious reasons, but this was not true of all colonists.

★ **Choice H is also wrong.** Again, although many of the colonists were loyal to the British king, this was not true of many of the colonists.

✪ **Choice J is correct.** Since the British government was across a vast ocean, all the colonies developed some forms of self-government. This was seen in their creation of the Virginia House of Burgesses and the Fundamental Orders of Connecticut.

COMPARING AND CONTRASTING

We often compare two or more things to understand them better. To compare, we look at similarities and differences. Items are similar when they have characteristics in common. Items are different when they have features that are not shared. Such questions might use words such as *compare*, *contrast*, *similar*, or *different*. A *compare-and-contrast question* might appear as follows:

3	Jamestown in 1607 and Massachusetts Bay Colony in 1630 were similar in that both settlements were located —
A at the base of a mountain range	C on the Great Lakes
B near the Atlantic Ocean	D on dry islands

Now try answering this question by applying the "E-R-A" approach.

APPLYING THE "E-R-A" APPROACH

◆ **Step 1: E**XAMINE **the Question**

What does the question ask you to do? _____

_____

_____

APPLYING THE "E-R-A" APPROACH

◆ **Step 2: R**ECALL **What You Know**

What do you recall about the characteristics of Jamestown? _____

_____

_____

_____

What do you recall about the characteristics of Massachusetts Bay Colony?

_____

_____

_____

◆ **Step 3: A**PPLY **What You Know**

Based on what you know, which answer choice is the best? _____

IDENTIFIYING CAUSE-AND-EFFECT

History consists of a series of events leading to still other events. Understanding *why* an event came about gives history much of its meaning. *Cause-and-effect questions* test your understanding of the relationship of a condition or event to its causes and its effects.

Causes. A **cause** is what made something happen. For example, if you turn the switch of a light, you *cause* the light to go on. Often, important developments in history have more than one cause. For example, Parliament's placing new taxes on the American colonists was just one cause of the American Revolution.

Effects. An **effect** is what happens because of something. An effect is the result of an event, action or development. For example, when you turn a light switch, the *effect* of your action is that the light goes on.

Important historical developments often have multiple effects. For example, two effects of the American Revolutionary War were the Declaration of Independence and the British loss of the thirteen colonies.

Many questions on social studies tests ask about cause-and-effect relationships. In answering *cause-and-effect questions*, be sure you understand what the question is asking for — is it the *cause* or the *effect*? Then think about the causes or effects of the event you are being asked about.

---

4   Why were the English successful in taking New Netherland in 1664?

   F   Dutch colonists rebelled against Stuyvesant. | asks for a cause |
   G   The English had a superior military force.
   H   The Dutch colonists were weakened by a smallpox epidemic.
   J   The Dutch population in New Netherlands had become ungovernable.

USING THE "E-R-A" APPROACH

This question asks you why the English were successful in taking New Netherland in 1664.

◆ EXAMINE **the question.** You can see that this question asks for a cause.

◆ RECALL **what you know.** How did New Netherland become New York? You may remember that the English sent a fleet of ships with powerful cannons to New York Harbor. Their purpose was to end the Dutch presence in America by conquering New Netherland and ending the Dutch competition in trade. When his fellow citizens refused to fight the invaders, the governor of the colony surrendered without a fight.

◆ APPLY **what you know.** Choice F is wrong, since the Dutch colonists never rebelled. Choices H and J are also incorrect, since the Dutch were not weakened by smallpox nor had their population become ungovernable. The best answer to this question is **Choice G**, since the English fleet, with its powerful guns, was superior to the Dutch. The governor surrendered, fearing that the English would completely sack the colony if he resisted.

Now try answering a *cause-and-effect question* on your own by using the "E-R-A" approach.

---

5   Which result of the French and Indian War contributed to the American Revolution?

   A   The British lost control of Montreal and all of Canada. | asks for a effect |
   B   The British decided to make the colonists help repay their war debt.
   C   Native American Indians were sold lands east of the Appalachian Mountains.
   D   French colonies expanded along the Atlantic seacoast.

USING THE "E-R-A" APPROACH

◆ **E**XAMINE **the question.** This question asks you to find a *result of* the French and Indian War that helped bring about the American Revolution.

◆ **R**ECALL **what you know.** You should recall that the French and Indian War was fought between France and Great Britain. It lasted between 1754 and 1763. It was fought in part for rule over American territories and for control of the growing markets in North America.

◆ **A**PPLY **what you know.** Choice A is wrong since the victorious British gained control of Canada in the treaty ending the war. Choices C and D are also incorrect. Neither situation described in the choices ever occurred. The best answer to this question is **Choice B**. British attempts to get the colonists to repay debts led to colonial protests and contributed to the American Revolution.

IDENTIFYING PURPOSE

Some questions may ask you to identify the **purpose** behind some action — why it was done. Such questions may ask for the "purpose" of a law, or what it was "designed" to do. This is a special type of *cause-and-effect question*, since it focuses on the intentions of the individual or group that brought about a change.

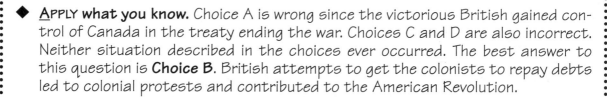

6	What was the British government's aim in passing the Stamp Act of 1765?
F	to unite the colonists against the Spanish
G	to lower the cost of tea in the British colonies
H	to raise money to help pay the cost of British troops in North America
J	to reduce conflicts between the colonists and Native American Indians

USING THE "E-R-A" APPROACH

◆ **E**XAMINE **the question.** This question asks for the purpose of the British government in passing the Stamp Act.

◆ **R**ECALL **what you know.** You should remember that the Stamp Act was imposed by the British Parliament on the American colonies. The act required that printed materials carry a tax stamp. The British passed this act to raise money to help pay for soldiers stationed in North America after the British victory in the French and Indian War. The British believed that the colonists were the main beneficiaries of this military presence and should help to pay for part of this expense.

CONTINUED

◆ Aᴘᴘʟʏ **what you know.** Choice F is wrong. The British did not want to unite colonies against the Spanish. Choice G is incorrect. The Stamp Act had nothing to do with the cost of tea. Choice J is wrong. It was never the intention of the Stamp Act. The best answer is **Choice H.** The Stamp Act's primary aim was to raise money from the colonists to pay for their protection.

DETERMINING SEQUENCE

Some questions may ask you about the sequence of events. Sequence questions test your ability to recall the correct chronology, or time order, of important historical events. Such questions might appear as:

> **7**   Which set of events is in the correct chronological order?
> **A**   French and Indian War, Stamp Act, Boston Tea Party
> **B**   Declaration of Independence, Boston Massacre, French and Indian War
> **C**   John Peter Zenger Trial, Jamestown founded, Mayflower Compact signed
> **D**   Declaration of Independence, Boston Massacre, Boston Tea Party

USING THE "E-R-A" APPROACH

◆ Eˣᴀᴍɪɴᴇ **the question.** This question asks you to identify which answer choice lists events in correct chronological order.

◆ Rᴇᴄᴀʟʟ **what you know.** You need to recall the sequence of several events. If one event in the group is out of order, eliminate that choice.

◆ Aᴘᴘʟʏ **what you know.** Choice B is wrong because the French and Indian War took place *before* the Declaration of Independence. Choice C is wrong since Jamestown was founded *before* Zenger's trial. Choice D is also wrong. The Declaration of Independence came *after* the other two events. The best answer is **Choice A.** The French and Indian War preceded the Stamp Act. These were followed by the Boston Tea Party.

DISTINGUISHING FACT FROM OPINION

Some social studies questions ask you to distinguish between **facts** and **opinions**.

★ A **fact** is a statement that can be proven to be true. For example, the following is a factual statement:

"Abraham Lincoln was elected President on November 6, 1860."

To see if something is a fact, ask yourself if this statement can be proved. We often check the accuracy of a factual statement by looking at several different sources — textbooks, encyclopedias, and almanacs.

★ An **opinion** is an expression of someone's belief. It cannot be checked for accuracy. To check for opinions, ask yourself if the statement would be true all of the time or if the statement tells a thought or feeling. Often, opinions have words expressing feelings, such as *happy*, *best*, or *most*. An example of an opinion would be:

"Abraham Lincoln was the best American President."

There is no way for someone to check the statement that Abraham Lincoln was "the best." This judgment is a matter of personal preference or opinion.

Questions that ask you to distinguish fact from opinion might be phrased as:

---

8   Which statement is a fact rather than an opinion?
F   The "Columbian Exchange" had a positive effect on the Americas.
G   The "Columbian Exchange" benefited England more than Spain.
H   The "Columbian Exchange" brought new foods and products to Europe.
J   The "Columbian Exchange" was one of history's great turning points.

Now answer this *fact-and-opinion question* using the "E-R-A" approach.

APPLYING THE "E-R-A" APPROACH

◆ **Step 1: EXAMINE the Question**

What does the question ask? _____

_____

◆ **Step 2: RECALL What You Know**

What do you recall about the "Columbian Exchange"? _____

_____

_____

_____

◆ **Step 3: APPLY What You Know**

Applying what you know, which is the best answer? _____

CHAPTER 2

HOW TO INTERPRET
DIFFERENT TYPES OF DATA

TEKS
COVERED IN
CHAPTER 2

- **Social Studies Skills 29C** Organize and interpret information from outlines, reports, databases, and visuals, including graphs, charts, timelines, and maps.
- **Social Studies Skills 29H** Use appropriate mathematical skills to interpret social studies information, such as maps and graphs.
- **Social Studies Skills 29I** Create thematic maps, graphs, charts, models, and databases representing various aspects of the United States.
- **Social Studies Skills 29J** Pose and answer questions about geographic distributions and patterns shown on maps, graphs, charts, models, and databases.
- **Social Studies Skills 30C** Transfer information from one medium to another, including written to visual and statistical to written or visual ....
- **Social Studies Skills 30D** Create written, oral, and visual presentations of social studies information.

Part social studies "literacy" is knowing how to interpret different types of data — information often represented in the form of a map, graph, or chart. This skill is also important for succeeding on the **STAAR Grade 8 Social Studies Test**. In this chapter, you will review different kinds of data you should know:

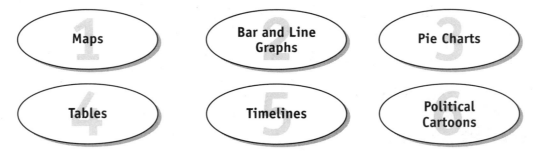

Maps

Bar and Line Graphs

Pie Charts

Tables

Timelines

Political Cartoons

INTERPRETING MAPS

A **map** is a drawing of a geographic area. There are many kinds of maps. For example, a political map shows the major boundaries between countries or states, while a physical map shows the physical characteristics of a region, such as its rivers, mountains, vegetation, and elevation (*height above sea level*).

STEPS TO UNDERSTANDING A MAP

The **title** of this map tells you that it shows the slave trade routes across the Atlantic from 1500 to 1800. A **legend**, or **key**, may list the symbols used in a map and tell you what those symbols represent. In this map, there is no legend. Instead, the thickness of the lines indicates the number of enslaved people sent along these different routes in the Atlantic Slave Trade.

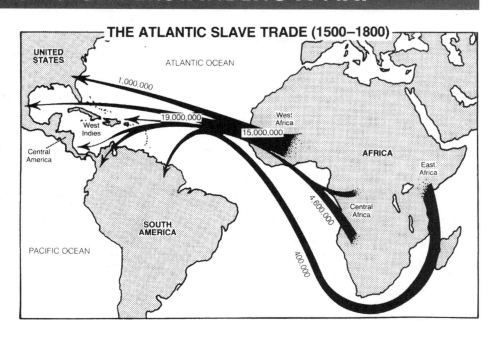

THE ATLANTIC SLAVE TRADE (1500–1800)

LOCATING INFORMATION ON A MAP

To find specific information, you have to use the legend or other map features. For example, if you wanted to find out which area in Africa the largest number of enslaved peoples came from, here is what you need to do:

★ Examine the map to determine where enslaved peoples came from in Africa. The map shows locations from three different parts of Africa — east, central, and west.

★ Examine the thickness of each of the three lines coming from Africa. You can see that the thickest line comes from West Africa. This also has a number — 15,000,000 people — far larger than the numbers for the other regions. Thus, West Africa was the area where most of the enslaved peoples came from.

APPLYING WHAT YOU HAVE LEARNED

Use the map above to answer the following questions:

★ To which areas did most of the enslaved peoples from Africa go?

★ What conclusions can be drawn about the forced migration of Africans to North America?

TESTING YOUR UNDERSTANDING

1   Based on information in the map, which conclusion can best be drawn about the migration of Africans to the Americas between 1500 and 1800?

  A   Most Africans came seeking new economic opportunities.
  B   Most enslaved Africans in the Americas came from West Africa.
  C   Africans came seeking political freedom in the United States.
  D   Enslaved Africans mainly came from areas in East Africa.

INTERPRETING BAR AND LINE GRAPHS

There are many types of graphs. A **bar graph** is made of parallel bars of different lengths. It is used to compare two or more things. Another type of graph is a **line graph**. It is composed of a series of points connected by a line. Line graphs are often used to show how something has changed over time. A key often identifies what the various bars or points in the graph represent.

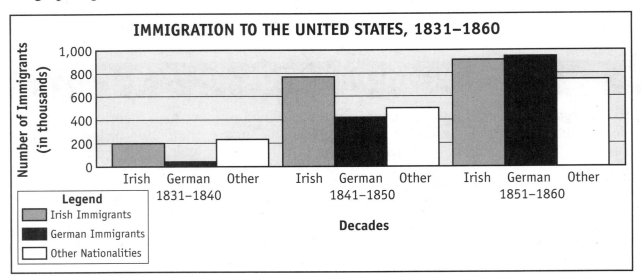

STEPS TO UNDERSTANDING A GRAPH

The title of the bar graph above tells you that it shows the number of Irish, German and other nationalities that migrated to the United States between 1831 and 1850. The **key** identifies what each bar represents.

Most graphs have a vertical and horizontal axis. The **vertical axis** runs along the left-hand side. It measures the length of the bars, or points available on a line graph. In this bar graph, numbers of immigrants are listed along the vertical axis, from 0 to 1,000. Since "(*in thousands*)" is stated, we know that each number represents a thousand: for example, 100 represents 100,000. The **horizontal axis** runs along the bottom of the graph. It often identifies the bars on a bar graph, or the passage of time or some other variable on a line. Here, the horizontal axis indicates the three decades being compared — 1831–1840; 1841–1850; and 1851–1860.

LOCATING INFORMATION ON A GRAPH

To find specific information on a bar or line graph, examine the graph's features. For example, to find out how many immigrants came to the United States from Germany in the decade 1831–1840, here is what you must do:

★ On the horizontal axis, locate the decade *1831–1840*. Choose the bar that represents *German* immigrants. According to the key, it is the black bar.

★ Now, look at the top of that bar, and then glance to the left. See where the top of the bar falls along the vertical axis. You will find it is about a quarter of the way between *0* and *200*. Thus, the number of immigrants from Germany in the decade 1831–1840 was about 50,000.

APPLYING WHAT YOU HAVE LEARNED

Use the same bar graph to answer the following questions:

★ Based on information in the graph, did more immigrants to the United States between 1831 and 1860 come from Ireland or Germany?

★ In which decade did most immigrants from Ireland come to the United States?

★ Use the information in the bar graph on page 18 to create a line graph. Your vertical axis should show the number of immigrants, while the horizontal axis will show the decades. Create a key or legend to show the differences between the information in each of the three lines.

TESTING YOUR UNDERSTANDING

2   Which conclusion is best supported by information in the graph?
   F   Irish and German immigration to America declined from 1830 to 1860.
   G   Irish immigration to America remained constant from 1830 through 1860.
   H   After 1840, German immigrants were prohibited from entering the U.S.
   J   Irish and German immigration to America increased from 1831 to 1860.

INTERPRETING PIE CHARTS

A **pie chart**, also called a circle graph, is a circle divided into sections of different sizes. Data is presented in a pie chart to make an immediate visual impact. Pie charts are used to show relationships between a whole and its parts. The entire circle, or pie, represents the whole. Pie charts are often used to make comparisons and draw conclusions.

STEPS TO UNDERSTANDING A PIE CHART

The title of this pie chart indicates that it shows trade between Britain and her American colonies in 1770. The first pie represents all goods shipped from Britain to the colonies. The pie is divided into different pieces or slices. Each slice represents a region of the colonies that goods were shipped to and is proportional

in size to the amount of British goods the region received. If you add all the slices together, they total 100% of the trade from Great Britain to its colonies. The second pie represents all the goods shipped by the three colonial regions to Britain.

LOCATING INFORMATION ON A PIE CHART

To find specific information, you must examine each piece and see how it is relates to the entire pie chart. For example, if you wanted to find if the New England Colonies shipped more goods to Britain than the Southern Colonies, here is what you must do:

★ Begin by examining the second pie chart carefully. First find the pieces of the pie for New England and the Southern Colonies. Next, compare the two pieces.

★ You can see that 11% of the goods shipped to Britain from the colonies came from New England and 67% came from the Southern Colonies. Therefore, more goods were shipped to Britain from the Southern Colonies than from New England.

APPLYING WHAT YOU HAVE LEARNED

Use the same pie charts to answer the following questions:

★ Based on the information in the pie charts, which region of the colonies imported the *least* goods from Britain?

★ State one conclusion that can be drawn from these pie charts. Explain your answer.

TESTING YOUR UNDERSTANDING

3   Based on the pie charts, which statement is most accurate?

A   New England had a higher percentage of British imports to the colonies than it had of colonial exports to Britain.

B   The Middle Atlantic Colonies were the largest exporters of goods to Britain.

C   The Southern Colonies imported more British goods than New England and the Middle Atlantic Colonies together.

D   The Southern Colonies exported a lower percentage of goods to Britain than they imported British goods into the colonies.

INTERPRETING TABLES

A **table** is an arrangement of words or numbers in columns and rows. It is used to organize large amounts of information so that individual facts can be easily located and compared.

STEPS TO UNDERSTANDING A TABLE

The title of the table below indicates that it provides information about the number of African Americans living in the thirteen English colonies from 1690 to 1730.

AFRICAN-AMERICAN POPULATION IN THE BRITISH COLONIES, 1690–1740

Year	New England Colonies	Middle Atlantic Colonies	Southern Colonies
1690	905	2,472	13,307
1700	1,680	5,361	22,476
1710	2,585	6,218	36,063
1720	3,956	10,825	54,058
1730	6,118	11,683	73,220
1740	8,541	16,452	125,031

In this table, information is organized under four headings, or categories: *Year*, *New England Colonies*, *Middle Atlantic Colonies*, and *Southern Colonies*. The rows show information for each of these categories by decade.

LOCATING INFORMATION ON A TABLE

For specific information, you need to find where the columns and rows intersect. For example, if you want to find the number of African Americans living in the Middle Atlantic Colonies in 1720, you need to:

★ Look for the column marked *Middle Atlantic Colonies*. This column shows information about number of African Americans living the Middle Atlantic Colonies. Next, look for the column marked *Year*. Look down the column until you reach the row for 1720.

★ Finally, look across the "*1720*" row until you reach the column under "*Middle Atlantic Colonies*." Here you can see there were 10,825 African Americans living in the Middle Atlantic Colonies in 1720.

APPLYING WHAT YOU HAVE LEARNED

Use the table on the previous page to answer the following questions:

★ Based on the information in the table, which region of the thirteen colonies had the largest number of African Americans?

★ What factors might explain why there were more African Americans living in this region than in the other two regions?

TESTING YOUR UNDERSTANDING

4   Based on information in the table, which statement is most accurate?

    F   New England had the largest African-American population among the colonies during the period 1690–1730.

    G   The Southern Colonies consistently had the largest African-American population throughout this period.

    H   Before 1730, there were more African Americans living in New England than in the Middle Atlantic Colonies.

    J   During this period, the African-American population in the Middle Atlantic Colonies was in decline.

INTERPRETING A TIMELINE

A **timeline** shows a group of events arranged in **chronological order** (*order in which events occurred*) along a line. The first event to occur is the first event that appears on the timeline, usually on the far left. Distances between events represent the passage of time between them. A timeline can span a short period or several thousand years. The purpose of a timeline is to show how events are related.

MILESTONES LEADING TO THE AMERICAN REVOLUTION

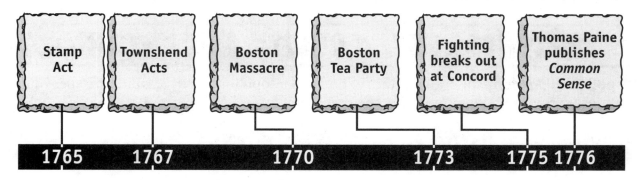

| Stamp Act | Townshend Acts | Boston Massacre | Boston Tea Party | Fighting breaks out at Concord | Thomas Paine publishes *Common Sense* |

| 1765 | 1767 | 1770 | 1773 | 1775 | 1776 |

STEPS TO UNDERSTANDING A TIMELINE

In this example, the title indicates that the timeline lists key milestones, or events, leading to the American Revolution. Timeline events should be related to the title. Here, each event was a key development leading to the American Revolution.

To understand timelines, you should also be familiar with some special terms. A **decade** is a ten-year period; a **century** represents a 100 years; and a **millennium** spans a period of 1,000 years. Identifying centuries is often confusing. For example, the 20th-century refers to the 1900s: the 100 years from 1901 to 2000. This numbering system came about because Western societies start counting centuries from the time it is believed Jesus Christ was born. Thus, the first one hundred years after this event were the years 1–100. This was the first century. The second century covered 101–200, and so on.

APPLYING WHAT YOU HAVE LEARNED

Use the same timeline to answer the following questions:

★ In which century did all of the events on this timeline occur?

★ Create your own timeline for this period. Research and then identify five other events that can be added to your own timeline. Be sure that your title is related to the events and time period.

ANSWERING A TIMELINE-BASED QUESTION

5   Which conclusion can be drawn from the information on the timeline?
   A   Most events in the American Revolution occurred in the Southern Colonies.
   B   The American Revolution was inevitable.
   C   The publication of Paine's *Common Sense* led to the start of the American Revolution.
   D   Disagreements between the colonists and Britain led to fighting in 1775.

INTERPRETING A POLITICAL CARTOON

A **political cartoon** is a drawing that expresses an opinion about a topic or issue. Many political cartoons are humorous, but the point they make is often serious.

STEPS TO UNDERSTANDING A POLTICAL CARTOON

Most political cartoons have a title or a caption that provides some idea of the message the cartoonist is trying to get across. Cartoonists often want to persuade readers to adopt their viewpoint. Sometimes a cartoonist simply wants to draw attention to a particular issue.

Cartoons sometimes use **caricatures** (*exaggerated or distorted pictures of a person or object*) to represent opinions, express concerns, draw attention to problems, or describe people and events. Cartoonists also rely on the use of **symbols** (*objects that represent something else*).

For example, an elephant is a popular symbol for the Republican Party, while a donkey often represents the Democratic Party. Historians and social scientists examine political cartoons for insights into the public mood, underlying beliefs, or attitudes towards past events.

To understand a cartoon, it usually helps to know something about the situation it depicts. For example, read the following background information about conditions relating to the cartoon on page 24:

★ After winning independence, each former colony became an independent state. They soon realized the need for some form of central government. Because of their experience with British rule, however, they were afraid of creating a central government that would be too powerful.

★ In 1781, the states adopted the Articles of Confederation, creating a weak central government in which the state governments could cooperate. The Confederation Congress could declare war and settle disputes, but it could not collect its own taxes or raise its own army. There was no President or national courts. Some believed that the new government had too little power to do its job properly.

APPLYING WHAT YOU HAVE LEARNED

Use the information above and the cartoon on previous page to answer the following questions:

★ What symbols does the cartoonist use in this cartoon?

★ What is the cartoonist's view concerning the balance between the national and state governments under the Articles of Confederation?

★ If you had to write a caption for this cartoon, what would it be?

TESTING YOUR UNDERSTANDING

6   What is the main message of the cartoon?
    F   The colonists must use their power to fight the British.
    G   Powerful state governments are to be feared.
    H   State governments have the real power over the central government.
    J   The Articles of Confederation did not need a President or court system.

INTERPRETING DOCUMENTS

You will learn how to interpret documents in the next chapter.

CHAPTER 3

HOW TO INTERPRET HISTORICAL SOURCES

■ **Social Studies Skills 29** The student applies critical-thinking skills to organize and use information acquired from a variety of valid sources, including electronic technology.

- **Social Studies Skills 29A** Differentiate between, locate, and use valid primary and secondary sources such as computer software, databases, media and news services, biographies, interviews, and artifacts to acquire information about the United States.
- **Social Studies Skills 29B** Analyze information by sequencing, categorizing, identifying cause-and-effect relationships, comparing, contrasting, finding the main idea, summarizing, making generalizations and predictions, and drawing inferences and conclusions.
- **Social Studies Skills 29D** Identify points of view from the historical context surrounding an event and the frame of reference which influenced the participants.
- **Social Studies Skills 29E** Support a point of view on a social studies issue or event.
- **Social Studies Skills 29F** Identify bias in ... written material.
- **Social Studies Skills 29G** Evaluate the validity of a source based on language, corroboration with other sources, and information about the author.
- **Social Studies Skills 30A** Use social studies terminology correctly.

Historians attempt to understand and explain past events. The study of history helps a society remember what it is and where it is going. Just as your own life would become quite meaningless if you had no memory of who you were or what you had done, each society looks to its history for a sense of identity.

— IMPORTANT IDEAS —

A. Historians help us answer questions about the importance of past events, their causes, and their effects. They help us to connect the world as it was with the world as it is today.

B. Historians use primary and secondary sources to study the past. All of our knowledge about the past can eventually be traced back to primary (*original*) sources.

C. To analyze a document, historians consider its historical context, the author's point of view and the frame of reference.

D. To judge the validity of information in a document, historians look at its language, compare it with other texts, and consider information about its author.

KEY TERMS AND PEOPLE IN THIS CHAPTER

- Primary Source
- Secondary Source
- Historical Context
- Point of View
- Frame of Reference
- Bias

ESSENTIAL QUESTIONS

How do historians learn about the past?

PRIMARY AND SECONDARY SOURCES

In a sense, a historian acts like a detective gathering clues. To find information about the past, historians rely on two kinds of sources: primary and secondary.

PRIMARY SOURCES

Primary sources are original records or first-hand testimony of an event under investigation. They include eyewitness reports, official records from the time of the event, letters by people involved in the event, diaries, speeches, photographs, oral histories and surviving **artifacts** (*objects*). Artifacts include buildings, clothing, furniture, jewelry, and pottery. All historical knowledge about past events can eventually be traced back to primary sources.

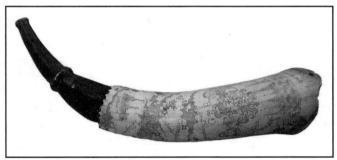

A powder horn used to insert gunpowder in a musket — an artifact from the French and Indian War.

SECONDARY SOURCES

Secondary sources are the writings and interpretations of later writers and historians who have reviewed the information in primary sources. Essentially, secondary sources are one step removed from the original event. Secondary sources interpret, evaluate and draw conclusions from primary sources and other secondary sources.

Secondary sources, such as textbooks and encyclopedia articles, often contain convenient summaries of the information found in primary sources. These summaries also often reveal a writer's interpretation or special viewpoint. Secondary sources include reviews analyzing a play, poems or short stories, newspaper articles, and articles in scholarly journals.

APPLYING WHAT YOU HAVE LEARNED

Suppose you find a website on the Internet about colonial America. Which of the following materials on the website are primary and which are secondary sources?

Website Information	Type Source?	Explain Your Answer
Pictures by a modern artist showing how Jamestown probably looked in the 1600s.	☐ Primary ☐ Secondary	
Coins used during the American Revolution.	☐ Primary ☐ Secondary	
Reproductions of musket bullets being sold to Jamestown tourists.	☐ Primary ☐ Secondary	
Pieces of pottery unearthed at the settlement at Jamestown.	☐ Primary ☐ Secondary	

INTERPRETING WRITTEN SOURCES

To reconstruct the past, historians most often rely on written texts. In interpreting any written document, you must be a critical reader. Sometimes a document will give you information about its writer's background or position.

This information can often help you understand how the writer's position in society or purpose in writing may have affected his or her ideas. The following are questions you should always ask yourself when reading any written document — whether it is a primary or a secondary source:

When and where was the document written?	Why was the document written?	What do I know about the author(s)?
	BEING A CRITICAL READER	
What is the main idea of the passage?	What facts does the writer present to support his or her views?	What is the tone of the passage?

DETERMINING MEANING

Sometimes you may encounter unfamiliar words or phrases, especially in historical documents. People in the past sometimes used words or expressions we no longer use today. Context clues can help you figure out what they mean. The surrounding words and sentences often provide clues to help you discover meaning. Here are some types of clues to help you figure out the meaning of a word or phrase that might be unfamiliar to you:

Part of Speech. From the words in the sentence, can you guess what part of speech the unfamiliar word is — adjective, noun, verb, or adverb?

Substitute Words. Can you guess the meaning of the word from the tone or meaning of the rest of the passage? What other words would make sense if you substituted them in place of the unfamiliar word?

USING CONTEXT CLUES TO FIND THE MEANING

Related Familiar Words. Is the word similar to any other words you already know? Does that help you to figure out what the word means? Can you determine what the word is by breaking it up into parts — such as a prefix, word stem, or suffix?

Bypass the Word. Can you understand the main idea of the sentence without knowing the meaning of the unfamiliar word? If so, it may not be important to spend time trying to figure out its meaning.

For example, read the primary source below. It discusses a boycott or "non-importation" agreement of trade with Britain. The authors agreed not to import, use, and export goods from Britain.

We, His Majesty's most loyal subjects, the delegates of the several colonies, held in the city of Philadelphia, on the 5th day of September, 1774, avow our allegiance to His Majesty, find that the present unhappy situation of our affairs is occasioned by a ruinous system of colonial administration, adopted by the British ministry. In furtherance of this system, acts of Parliament have been passed for raising revenue in America, for depriving American subjects of their constitutional trial by jury, exposing their lives to danger by directing a new and illegal trial beyond the seas, for crimes alleged to have been committed in America.

To obtain a redress of these grievances which threaten our lives, liberty, and property of His Majesty's subjects in North America, we are of the opinion that a non-importation, non-use, and non-export agreement will prove the most speedy and peaceable measure. Thus, we, the inhabitants of the colonies, agree as follows:

That from the first day of December, 1774 we will not import into America, from Britain or Ireland, any goods or merchandise whatsoever, or been export to Britain or Ireland; nor will we import any tea from any part of the world ....

Suppose you did not understand the phrase "avow our allegiance" *in the second line* of the first paragraph. Following is a way to unravel the meaning of this phrase:

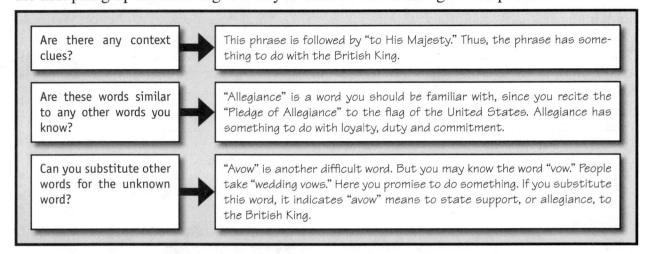

Are there any context clues?	This phrase is followed by "to His Majesty." Thus, the phrase has something to do with the British King.
Are these words similar to any other words you know?	"Allegiance" is a word you should be familiar with, since you recite the "Pledge of Allegiance" to the flag of the United States. Allegiance has something to do with loyalty, duty and commitment.
Can you substitute other words for the unknown word?	"Avow" is another difficult word. But you may know the word "vow." People take "wedding vows." Here you promise to do something. If you substitute this word, it indicates "avow" means to state support, or allegiance, to the British King.

HISTORICAL CONTEXT

Now consider the **historical context** of the document. The **historical context** is the background — the conditions or events taking place at the time the document was written.

The First Continental Congress was called to meet in the city of Philadelphia on September 5, 1774, to organize a response to the British Intolerable Acts. Twelve colonies were represented. It was the start of colonial protests that would eventually lead to independence.

In this document, members of the Continental Congress agreed to an economic boycott of British goods. Samuel Adams sent the document to the "Committees of Correspondence," which was the way critics of the British government in the thirteen colonies kept in touch.

POINT OF VIEW

The **point of view** refers to the author's opinion or view of the subject. Usually, an author's viewpoint is shaped by his or her upbringing, education, or social position. For example, a colonial merchant might look at some events very differently than a British official in India. The point of view expressed in a document often reveals the author's purpose in writing.

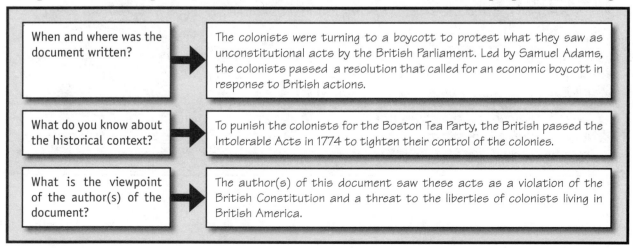

When and where was the document written?	The colonists were turning to a boycott to protest what they saw as unconstitutional acts by the British Parliament. Led by Samuel Adams, the colonists passed a resolution that called for an economic boycott in response to British actions.
What do you know about the historical context?	To punish the colonists for the Boston Tea Party, the British passed the Intolerable Acts in 1774 to tighten their control of the colonies.
What is the viewpoint of the author(s) of the document?	The author(s) of this document saw these acts as a violation of the British Constitution and a threat to the liberties of colonists living in British America.

FRAME OF REFERENCE

Historians sometimes consider the **frame of reference** of the document — the assumptions under which a person, action or historical document must be understood. For example, you should understand that at the time this document was written, the proposed boycott was a daring act. People were expected to be obedient to their King and Parliament. A boycott is when someone refuses to buy products as a form of protest.

ACTING AS AN AMATEUR HISTORIAN

Examine a newspaper or magazine article about a current event. Describe the historical context, frame of reference and point of view of the author.

★ Article Title: _____

★ Source: _____

★ Summary: _____

_____

★ Historical Context: _____

_____

_____

_____

_____

_____

_____

★ Frame of Reference: _____

_____

★ Author's Viewpoint: _____

_____

_____

_____

_____

_____

_____

_____

Name _____

DETECTING BIAS IN A SOURCE

Each source is always influenced by the point of view of its author. A **bias** is a point of view based on pre-existing beliefs. Bias is a form of prejudice or opinion, unsupported by facts. Often our biases prevent us from understanding the true nature of events. An author may be biased because of his or her upbringing, experiences, social class, race, religious beliefs, or gender.

To determine the bias or point of view of an author, ask yourself these questions:

What does the author choose to write about?	What does the author leave out or fail to include?	Does the author appear to like or dislike what he or she describes?
Does the author use positive or negative words?	Does the author seem sympathetic to the people or events he or she writes about?	Are there any similarities between the author and the people being described?

APPLYING WHAT YOU HAVE LEARNED

Read the statements below and identify any biases you can detect:

Statement	Possible Bias
"I am a colonial merchant living in America. It is obvious that we colonists are being discriminated against by the British government. Such abuse must stop immediately. If it does not end, neither I nor any of my fellow colonists can tell where this situation will lead."	
"I am a British army officer living in America. I do not agree with all of these rebel rousers who are just trying to stir up trouble. What has happened to their loyalty to the Crown? Do they not realize that we should be loyal British subjects and respect all that the King and Parliament have done for us."	

FINDING THE MAIN IDEA AND SUMMARIZING

When you read a document, be sure to grasp the **main idea** that the author is trying to show. To support the main idea, the author usually provides facts, examples, and other details. To identify the main idea, first determine the **topic** (or *subject*) of the document. Then determine what the author has to say about that topic.

Sometimes it helps to make a **summary**, or short restatement, of a text you are reading. To make a summary, restate the main ideas of the passage while leaving out less important information. Rewrite the text in your own words to make it shorter. Combine sentences expressing the same general idea. Other sentences, with less essential information, can just be omitted.

EVALUATING THE VALIDITY OF A SOURCE

Often historians compare several sources to uncover what happened in the past. They evaluate the validity of each source to determine which descriptions are the most trustworthy or valid. To evaluate the validity of a source, historians consider:

The language of the source	Corroboration with other sources	Information about the author

THE LANGUAGE OF THE SOURCE

The text itself gives hints. Does the author use facts and specific examples to support any general statements? Are the author's points logically connected? A source is less likely to be valid if the author makes unstated assumptions, appeals to emotions, includes irrelevant information, states half truths, or presents opinions as facts.

CORROBORATION WITH OTHER SOURCES

To *corroborate* is to confirm with other sources. One way to check if information in a source is valid is to check for support from other sources. For example, if a source describes a fire at a home but no other sources describe the same event, you might question its accuracy. Maybe the author saw a sunset on the horizon, and mistook it for a fire. If, on the other hand, other sources reported the same fire, then it is more likely that the first account is also accurate.

INFORMATION ABOUT THE AUTHOR

Historians also evaluate the validity of a source based on information they have about its author. Was the author an eye-witness to the event? Was the author qualified to write the document? For example, a reader might find an engineer's report about the collapse of the World Trade Center in 2001 more reliable than an analysis of that same event by someone without professional training.

APPLYING WHAT YOU HAVE LEARNED

Read the following passages below and then answer the question that follows:

> "The [Continental] Congress [in Philadelphia] derives its power, wisdom, and justice, not from pieces of parchment signed by kings but from the people. A more respectable and fair legislative body never existed. It is founded on the principles of the most perfect liberty. A free man, in honoring the Congress, honors and obeys himself."
>
> — Newspaper editorial, November 1774

> "Suppose we were to revolt from Britain, declare independence, and set up a republic of our own. What might be the consequence of such an action? I fear the prospect; my blood runs chill when I think of the problems, the evils that will ensue, and can be clearly seen. It is impossible for anyone to see them all."
>
> — Rev. Charles Inglis, *True Interest of America*, 1776

These two views differ as to whether or not the colonists were able to rule themselves. Explain what biases each writer held in coming to these different conclusions?

CHAPTER STUDY CARDS

Types of Sources

★ **Primary Source.** Sources created by witnesses at the time of an event.
  • a letter from a solider in War of 1812.
  • an ancient map of a battle plan
★ **Secondary Sources.** These are sources that are based on interpreting and analyzing primary sources.
  • a recent history book on the War of 1812.
  • a biography of a famous person

Examining Historical Sources

★ **Historical Context.** The background (time, place, beliefs, events) behind the creation of the source.
★ **Point of View.** The author's opinion about the subject. An author's point of view is often shaped by the author's education, life experiences, or social position.
★ **Frame of Reference.** These are generally-held assumptions at the time that the source was created.

Characteristics of a Reliable Source

★ Opinions, general statements, and conclusions are supported by facts.
★ Facts can be corroborated by the use of other sources.
★ The source was created at the time of the event it reports.
★ The author is recognized as being knowledgeable and impartial about the subject.

Validity of a Source

People evaluate a source's validity based on:
★ **Language of the Source.** Is it objective, factual and logical, or emotional and contradictory?
★ **Corroboration with other Sources.** Do other sources confirm the same facts?
★ **Information about the Author.** Is the author an eye-witness? Does the author have special qualifications? Does the author seem objective or biased?

CHECKING YOUR UNDERSTANDING

Directions: Circle the letter that best answers the question.

Use the passages below and your knowledge of social studies to answer the following question.

"I see [great] causes for weakness that will prevent America from becoming a powerful state. In short, such are the differences of character, manners, religion, and interest of the different colonies that if they were left to themselves, there would soon be a civil war from one end of the continent to the other." — Andrew Burnaby, British clergyman, 1775	"Let us view America as it now is, an independent state that has taken an equal station amid the nations of the earth. It is a vitality [living thing] liable, indeed, to many disorders, many dangerous diseases, but it is young and strong, and will struggle against those evils and overcome them, and its strength will grow." — Thomas Powell, former Governor of Massachusetts, 1780

1 How did Andrew Burnaby and Thomas Powell differ in the points of view expressed in these accounts?

  A Burnaby marveled at the colonists' abilities, while Powell focused on America's shortcomings.   `SSS 29(C)`

  B Burnaby felt the colonies would not survive, while Powell believed they would fall short of being able to overcome their diseases.

  C Burnaby described events he actually witnessed, while Powell had many facts from others to support his beliefs.

  D Burnaby thought America would be unable to survive, while Powell believed the young nation would overcome the dangers it faced.

EXAMINE **the question.** This question asks how the views of Andrew Burnaby and Thomas Powell differed. RECALL **what you know.** Burnaby was a British clergyman writing in 1775 — before colonial independence, while Powell was writing shortly after American independence. Burnaby was quite pessimistic about an independent America, thinking there would be civil war. Powell thought the nation would overcome its obstacles as its strength continued to grow. APPLY **what you know.** **Choice D is the best answer.**

Now try answering some additional questions on your own:

2 Which document would be considered a primary source?

  F an encyclopedia article about George Washington   `SSS 29(B)`

  G modern textbook with a chapter on Colonial America

  H a recent biography of Samuel Adams

  J a letter written by Abraham Lincoln

CHAPTER 4

PROBLEM-SOLVING AND DECISION-MAKING

TEKS COVERED IN CHAPTER 4

- ■ **Social Studies Skills 31** The student uses problem-solving and decision-making skills, working independently and with others, in a variety of settings.
  - **Social Studies Skills 31A** Use a problem-solving process to identify a problem, gather information, list and consider options, consider advantages and disadvantages, choose and implement a solution, and evaluate the effectiveness of the solution.
  - **Social Studies Skills 31B** Use a decision-making process to identify a situation that requires a decision, gather information, identify options, predict consequences, and take action to implement a decision.

In this chapter, you will learn how historians approach problems and make decisions.

— IMPORTANT IDEAS —

A. To solve problems, historians first identify the problem. Then they gather information, consider options, weigh the advantages and disadvantages of each option, try a solution, and evaluate how well it works.

B. To make decisions, historians identify a situation requiring a decision, gather information, identify options, predict consequences, and take actions to put the decision into effect.

KEY TERMS AND PEOPLE IN THIS CHAPTER

- ■ Problem-Solving
- ■ Options
- ■ Brainstorming
- ■ Criteria
- ■ Decision-making
- ■ Implementation

ESSENTIAL QUESTIONS

○— How do historians approach problems and make decisions?

PROBLEM-SOLVING

A knowledge of history can help us better understand many problems faced in the world today. For example, people throughout history have sought to create governments that were effective but not too oppressive. Suppose you wanted to know how to make such a government. You could look at history for help in solving this problem. Historians also sometimes look at specific historical problems. They want to understand specific developments in history. For instance, could Americans have abolished slavery peacefully without the Civil War?

STEPS IN PROBLEM-SOLVING

In order to solve problems, historians and social scientists follow a logical process:

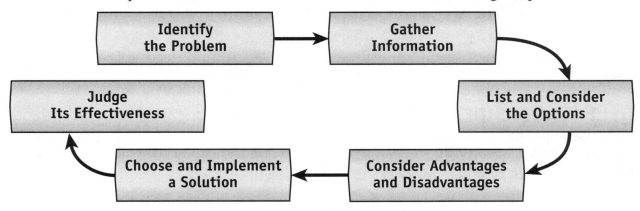

STEP 1: IDENTIFY THE PROBLEM

The first step is to identify a problem. For example, you might have to give advice to a new democracy. You want to help them create a central government that is effective without being too tyrannical.

STEP 2: GATHER THE INFORMATION

Next, you must gather information about the problem. To study forms of government, you might want to study the British monarchy, the Articles of Confederation, the U.S. Constitution, and the Confederacy during the Civil War. You can often find some of this information on the Internet or in your school or local library.

STEP 3: LIST AND CONSIDER OPTIONS

Now you need to explore all the **options** you can think of to solve the problem. (*Here, how to make an effective central government.*) Look through the sources you found for helpful ideas and information. Then you can "brainstorm" ideas with others — listing as many possible solutions as you can. When **brainstorming**, people suggest as many ways of solving the problem as they can think of.

The excitement of hearing other people's ideas often helps the members of a group think of new ideas on their own. For example, during its early history, Americans created several forms of central governments with various degrees of power. Your study of history may lead you to consider the following options for a central government:

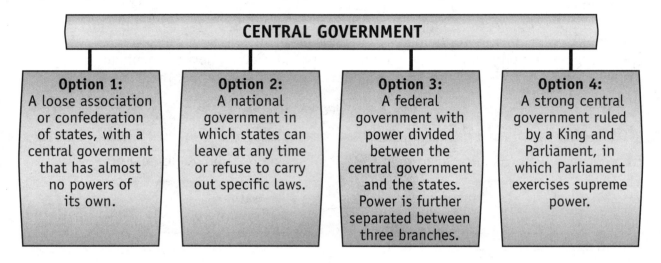

CENTRAL GOVERNMENT

Option 1:
A loose association or confederation of states, with a central government that has almost no powers of its own.

Option 2:
A national government in which states can leave at any time or refuse to carry out specific laws.

Option 3:
A federal government with power divided between the central government and the states. Power is further separated between three branches.

Option 4:
A strong central government ruled by a King and Parliament, in which Parliament exercises supreme power.

STEP 4: CONSIDER ADVANTAGES AND DISADVANTAGES

Next, you should consider the advantages and disadvantages of each option you have thought of. What would be the benefits of each? Would it solve the problem? What would be the costs, risks, or other drawbacks of each option?

STEP 5: CHOOSE AND IMPLEMENT A SOLUTION

Now you are ready to make your own choice. Compare the proposed options to come up with your own solution. There is usually no simple or perfect answer to most major problems. You must decide which advantages are more important, based on your own values. Your solution will depend on what you value and think is "good." People value different things and therefore often disagree about what should be done. Once you have chosen your solution, think about how you can **implement** it (*put it into effect*). Usually you must explain your solution to others in written form or in an oral presentation.

STEP 6: JUDGE ITS EFFECTIVENESS

Once a possible solution has been adopted, you need to develop **criteria** to judge its effectiveness. Criteria are standards for judging something. You need to develop specific criteria to measure how well your proposed solution actually works. The criteria for evaluating the effectiveness of a solution usually include the following:

| Does it solve the problem? | What does it cost? | Have people agreed to carry it out? | Does it create new problems? |

A solution is usually **effective** if it solves the problem at minimal cost without creating other new problems.

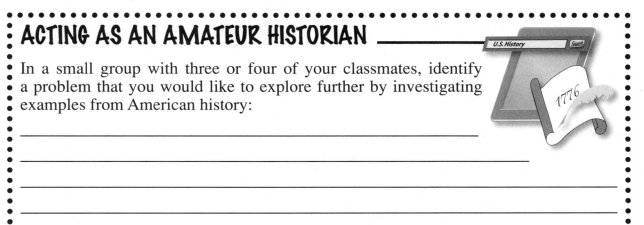

ACTING AS AN AMATEUR HISTORIAN

In a small group with three or four of your classmates, identify a problem that you would like to explore further by investigating examples from American history:

_____

_____

_____

_____

MAKING A DECISION

Historians and other social scientists sometimes make decisions or help others to make decisions. The steps for making decisions are similar to those you previously learned for solving problems:

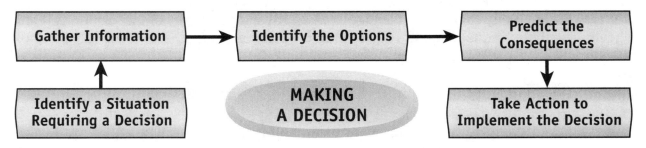

IDENTIFY A SITUATION

Many times, public leaders have to make a decision. For example, what form of government should the countries that rose up against their existing governments during the "Arab Spring" of 2011 now adopt? As you can see, identifying a situation that calls for a decision is very similar to identifying a problem that needs to be solved. It simply means identifying a problem or issue where some action will have to be taken.

GATHER INFORMATION

The next step is to gather information from a variety of sources, just as you would for solving a problem. You need to analyze this information by evaluating its validity, just as you learned earlier in Chapter 3.

IDENTIFYING OPTIONS

The next step is to consider what possible options there are for the decision-maker. Usually, the options range from doing nothing to taking extreme action of some kind. For example, American leaders might consider some the following options in advising countries in the Middle East:

| Not give any advice at all. | Give limited advice when asked by Middle Eastern leaders. | Confer with Middle Eastern leaders to answer their requests and make recommendations. | Apply economic pressure to make sure new governments act more democratically. | Advise Middle Eastern leaders how to write their new constitutions. | Use force to make sure Middle Eastern governments meet American desires for democratic government. |

PREDICT CONSEQUENCES

The decision-maker then has to predict the consequences of each of these options. In other words, what are likely to be the advantages and disadvantages of any of these options if and when it is actually implemented? To help predict such consequences, it often helps to look at historical examples for guidance.

TAKE ACTION

The final step in the decision-making process is to take action. This is really the same as implementing a solution. As with problem-solving, it is often useful to evaluate afterwards the effectiveness of any decision that was implemented.

APPLYING WHAT YOU HAVE LEARNED

American government leaders have been asked to advise several countries in the Middle East how to make their governments more democratic. List those steps American leaders should follow in reaching a decision about how to respond to this invitation.

_____

_____

_____

_____

_____

EUROPEAN EXPLORATION AND COLONIZATION

TEKS COVERED IN CHAPTER 5

- **History 1A** Identify the major eras in U.S. history through 1877, including colonization, ... and describe their causes and effects.
- **History 1B** Explain the significance of the following dates: 1607, founding of Jamestown; 1620, arrival of the Pilgrims and signing of the Mayflower Compact ....
- **History 2A** Identify reasons for English, Spanish and French exploration and colonization of North America.
- **History 2B** Compare political, economic, religious, and social reasons for the establishment of the 13 English colonies.
- **History 3B** Analyze the importance of the Mayflower Compact [and] the Fundamental Orders of Connecticut to the growth of representative government.
- **Geography 10A** Locate places and regions directly related to major eras and turning points in the United States during the 17th [and] 18th centuries ....
- **Government 15A** Identify the influence of ideas from historic documents, including the Mayflower Compact ... on the U.S. system of government.

In this chapter, you will learn about how Europeans first explored and colonized the Americas.

KEY TERMS AND PEOPLE IN THIS CHAPTER

- New Spain
- Encomiendas
- New France
- New Netherland
- Jamestown
- Williamsburg
- Pilgrims
- Puritans
- Mayflower Compact
- Roger Williams
- Anne Hutchinson
- William Penn
- Quakers
- Lord Baltimore
- James Ogelthorpe
- Indentured Servant
- Fundamental Orders of Connecticut

ESS(ENT)IAL QUESTIONS

- Why did Europeans explore the world's oceans and colonize the Americas?
- What political, economic, religious, and social reasons led to the establishment of the thirteen English colonies?
- Which historic documents and colonial practices contributed to the growth of representative government?

— IMPORTANT IDEAS —

A. New advances in technology allowed Europeans to explore the oceans. They were motivated to find an all-water route to Asia.

B. European rulers sponsored exploration to increase their wealth and power.

C. **Christopher Columbus** unexpectedly "encountered" the Americas when he sailed west in search of an all-water route to Asia.

D. The encounter between Europe and the Americas led to the **Columbian Exchange**. Europeans benefited from new foods and products. New plants and animals were also introduced to the Americas.

E. Millions of Native American Indians died from new diseases, such as smallpox and measles, unintentionally introduced into the Americas by European explorers and settlers.

F. Spain conquered the West Indies, Mexico, and Peru and established colonies. It grew rich from shipments of American gold and silver sent back to Spain.

G. France, Holland, and England grew envious of Spain's power and wealth, and sought to establish their own colonies in the "New World."

H. The first permanent English colonies were established at **Jamestown** (1607), **Plymouth** (1620), and **Massachusetts Bay** (1630).

I. England established thirteen colonies along the Atlantic coast. These colonies were established for political, economic, religious, and social reasons.

J. The **Mayflower Compact** and the **Fundamental Orders of Connecticut** encouraged the growth of representative government in the colonies.

THE AGE OF EXPLORATION

EUROPE EXPLORES THE "NEW WORLD"

By the fifteenth century, Europeans were aware of places as distant as Africa, India and China. However, they had no idea of the existence of the Americas. Yet by 1650, most of the Atlantic coastline of the Americas would be under the control of European powers. How did such a rapid change occur?

REASONS FOR EUROPEAN EXPLORATION

The Growth of Trade. In the Middle Ages, a Venetian merchant, **Marco Polo** (1254–1324), returned from China and wrote about the marvelous things he had witnessed there. His writings encouraged an increase in trade. Europeans used spices from the East Indies to preserve their food, drank Chinese tea, prized Chinese porcelain, and wore Asian cottons and silks.

Marco Polo

Name _____

CHAPTER 5: European Exploration and Colonization   **43**

European merchants and rulers were anxious to find a sea route to reach China and the Spice Islands of the East Indies. This would allow them to ship these luxury goods more easily back to Europe.

Advances in Technology. Europeans had benefited from contacts through trade with China, which had invented gunpowder and the magnetic compass. From Arabia, Europeans learned how to make better sails. Europeans also developed the moveable rudder, so they could steer larger ships more easily. These technological improvements in navigation made it possible for Europeans to sail farther than ever before. European sailors began to use the sun's angle to determine their location, allowing them to judge distances. These innovations allowed them to sail into the open ocean instead of hugging the coastline.

Exploration was fanned by the Renaissance spirit of inquiry and a desire to find an all-water route to the East. In Portugal, **Prince Henry the Navigator** (1394–1460) sponsored the exploration of the Atlantic coast of Africa by Portuguese sailors. He developed a new, lighter ship better suited for distant oceanic exploration. Many historians believe Prince Henry played a key role in encouraging European exploration and maritime trade with other continents.

Emergence of Powerful European Rulers. In the early fifteenth century, the sea-faring countries of Europe hoped to extend their influence through exploration. Strong rulers had established power over unruly nobles. These rulers built large armies and amassed great wealth by collecting taxes.

Desire for Profits. Italian city-states had once profited by shipping goods across the Mediterranean, but routes to Asia were cut-off by the Turkish capture of Constantinople in 1453. The capitalist economy was just emerging. People were seeing new wealth from investment and trade. Some hoped to increase their profits through exploration.

Religious Enthusiasm. European missionaries, especially from Spain and Portugal, sought to spread the Christian religion. Christian missionaries believed they not only had a superior religion, but also a superior culture.

APPLYING WHAT YOU HAVE LEARNED

★ What impact did Marco Polo's travels have on European exploration?

★ What economic, social, and political factors motivated Europeans to explore oceans?

EUROPE ENCOUNTERS THE AMERICAS

An Italian sea captain, **Christopher Columbus** (1451–1506), believed he could reach China and the Spice Islands by sailing westwards. After courting several rulers, he finally found support from Queen Isabella of Spain. Columbus set sail in 1492. He never reached Asia, but surprisingly landed in the West Indies, where he established Spain's first settlements in what became known as the "New World." Other explorers, missionaries, and colonists soon followed.

Columbus lands in the Americas.

THE "COLUMBIAN EXCHANGE"

The "**Columbian Exchange**" was one of the most significant events in world history. This term identifies the exchange of plants, animals, and diseases between the Eastern and Western Hemispheres that occurred after 1492. Europeans learned about new foods, such as corn, tomatoes, potatoes, and chocolate. Meanwhile, Europeans introduced sugar, wheat, oranges, grapes, and onions to the Americas.

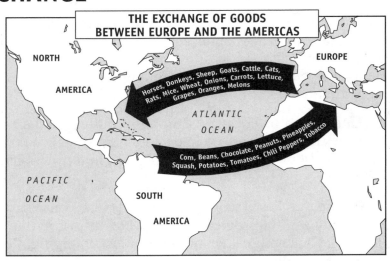

Europeans also introduced many new animals to the Western Hemisphere, including horses, sheep, goats, cows, cats, and rats. This exchange of plants and animals transformed ways of life in both hemispheres. The European encounter with the Americas also spread germs. Europeans brought diseases like smallpox, typhus, cholera, and measles. Over centuries, Europeans had developed resistance to these diseases, but Native Americans had no such immunity. Estimates range from 2 to 18 million Native Americans died from these diseases.

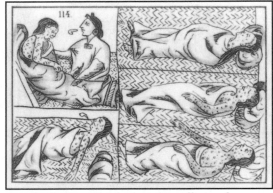
An Aztec artist depicts the suffering from smallpox, a disease introduced by Europeans.

APPLYING WHAT YOU HAVE LEARNED

★ Make your own drawing of one of the inventions that aided navigation.

★ Use the Internet to find and read excerpts from the journal of Columbus.

★ Make a chart of the positive and negative effects of the Columbian Exchange for both Native American Indians and Europeans.

EUROPEAN COLONIAL EMPIRES

By 1494, news of the "New World" was in print throughout Europe. This greatly stimulated the appetite of European monarchs for overseas exploration. The establishment of **New Spain** in the Caribbean, Mexico, Florida and South America further heightened the interest of Spain's chief rivals: France, Holland, and England. The rulers of these nations sent their own explorers to claim lands in the Americas. Where each nation explored and settled was affected by many factors, including ocean currents, weather patterns, and where rival powers had claims.

NEW SPAIN

Spanish conquistadors (*conquerors*) like Hernando Cortés and Francisco Pizarro used horses and superior weapons, such as cannons and crossbows, to conquer the powerful Aztecs of Mexico and the Incas of Peru. Cortés allied with other Native American peoples, who had been conquered by the Aztecs, to achieve his victory. In Peru, the Incas had been weakened by civil war shortly before the arrival of Pizarro.

Spanish conquistadors used horses and superior weaponry to defeat the Aztecs and Incas.

The Spanish conquerors murdered the ruling classes of Mexico and Peru, and destroyed their temples and palaces. **New Spain** was ruled by the viceroys of the king. The Spanish monarchy became enriched by shipments of gold and silver. One fifth of all the gold and silver from the New World went to the king. When the Spanish first arrived in the New World, they brought with them a set of customs and traditions from Spain. Spaniards took large tracts of land for mining, ranching, and farming, known as **encomiendas**. Although the encomienda system was introduced with the idea of caring and providing for Native Americans, it quickly became a highly abusive and destructive system.

Native Americans were used as forced laborers to mine silver and to grow sugar cane or tobacco. Missionaries came from Spain to convert them to Catholicism. As you know, the Spanish used religion to justify their domination over the Native Americans. Millions of Indians died from overwork and new diseases. The Spaniards replaced them by importing enslaved Africans, starting the Atlantic slave trade. Indians and slaves endured terrible conditions in mines and on plantations and ranches.

NEW FRANCE

Other European rulers were envious of Spain's power in the Americas. They sent their own explorers to the "New World." **New France** was established in Canada along the St. Lawrence River, Great Lakes, and Mississippi River. New France never became as populous as the Spanish or English colonies. It consisted of a handful of towns and a series of trading outposts. French missionaries came to convert the Indians to Christianity. French explorers found that the region contained valuable fur-bearing animals, especially beavers. This prompted French colonists to engage in an active fur trade with the Native Americans.

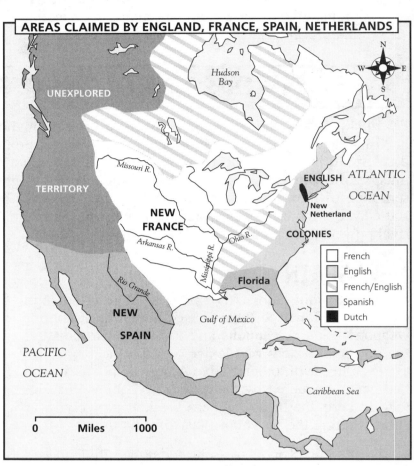

AREAS CLAIMED BY ENGLAND, FRANCE, SPAIN, NETHERLANDS

APPLYING WHAT YOU HAVE LEARNED

Compare and contrast the Spanish and French colonies by making a chart showing their political, economic, and social similarities and differences.

NEW NETHERLAND

Henry Hudson (1565–1611), an English sea captain, was hired by Dutch merchants looking for a Northwest Passage to Asia. In 1609, Hudson reached New York Harbor. Based on Hudson's explorations, the Dutch claimed control of this region. They set up a successful fur trade with the native peoples of the Hudson River Valley, and called their colony **New Netherland**.

At first, New Netherland was a company owned and operated business, run by the Dutch West India Company. The intent of the company directors was to make a profit for the investors in the company. New Netherland became active in trading for furs. Beaver skins and other furs were highly valued by Europeans. The Dutch welcomed people from other countries. They also practiced religious toleration. Walking around the settlement of New Amsterdam in the 1660s, a visitor might have seen Irish, British, German or French people talking in the streets. Others there might be Native Americans or Africans.

The Dutch were active traders of beaver skins and other furs, which were highly valued by Europeans.

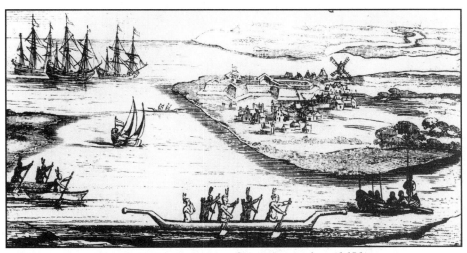

The earliest known view of New Amsterdam (1651).

APPLYING WHAT YOU HAVE LEARNED

★ Which European countries established colonies, and where did they settle?

THE THIRTEEN ENGLISH COLONIES

The colonization of America shifted wealth and power away from the Mediterranean region to the countries of Western Europe. Spain was greatly enriched by American gold and silver. Protestant England became engaged in a series of wars against Catholic Spain. England's rulers desired to stake a claim for lands and riches in the New World, so that they could match Spain's wealth. England's colonies were established for political, economic, religious, and social reasons.

THE FIRST ENGLISH COLONIES

The adventurer **Sir Walter Raleigh** persuaded Queen Elizabeth to found a colony. This first English colony in the "New World," at Roanoke, North Carolina originally consisted of 100 householders. Founded in 1585, this settlement lasted only ten months and then mysteriously failed. The colony had disappeared without a trace. None of the colonists could be found. All personal belongings were left in place as if the people had disappeared into thin air. Although two first attempts at English colonization were failures, it brought attention to the dangers of creating a new society in the far off distant land.

JAMESTOWN (1607)

The first permanent English colony in the "New World" was established by the Virginia Company for economic reasons. This private company hoped to profit from gold and other resources. 104 English men and boys built a settlement of cabins surrounded by a stockade fence near the James River at Jamestown, Virginia in 1607. The river and settlement were named after England's King James I.

Model based on evidence found by APVA Preservation Virginia archaeologists at historic Jamestown

These first settlers were men who came in search of gold. What they found in the area was a swamp plagued by mosquitoes that caused malaria. Half the group were artisans, soldiers, and laborers. The other half were "gentlemen" who did not care to work. They quickly used up their supplies, and many later died from a lack of food.

After their leader, **Captain John Smith**, returned to England in 1609, the colonists at Jamestown endured a second winter of starvation and death. Having failed to plant or store enough grain for their needs, the settlers became desperate for food. The "Starving Time," the winter of 1609, saw only 60 of the first 214 settlers at Jamestown survive.

Captain John Smith (1580–1631

ACTING AS AN AMATEUR HISTORIAN

Captain John Smith recorded what he later learned in his history of the colony — *The Generall Historie of Virginia*, published in 1624.

> "These miserable and poor creatures were [kept alive] for the most part by roots, herbs, acorns, walnuts, berries, and fish, even the skins of horses. So great was our famine, that when an Indian was killed, and buried, the poor dug him up and [ate] him, and others boiled and stewed with roots and herbs: One amongst us killed his wife, powdered her, and ate part of her before it was known, for which he was executed."

★ What hardships did the first settlers at Jamestown face?

★ How did some of the Jamestown colonists survive the "Starving Time"?

Despite these initial setbacks, the colony at Jamestown became profitable by growing tobacco for sale in Europe. By 1619, Jamestown was exporting tons of tobacco to England for the new fashion of smoking. Jamestown's new tobacco economy created a labor shortage. The need for laborers was so great that early settlers attempted to enslave the area's Native American Indians. However, these Indians were unwilling to be used as forced laborers and often escaped into the surrounding forests. The first enslaved people from Africa arrived in the colony in 1619, as well as the first women. As the success of tobacco planting and the cultivation of other cash crops spread, the use of African slaves grew to become the foundation of the Southern agrarian economy.

Later, the area of colonial settlement spread from Jamestown to other parts of Virginia. The capital of the colony was moved to **Williamsburg**. Virginia eventually had both rich plantation owners and smaller farmers, and grew to become one of the wealthiest colonies.

THE IMPACT OF GEOGRAPHY ON HISTORY

In a country without roads, rivers played an important role. The first colonists depended on rivers to ship crops from the farm to the marketplace. The marshy coastal plain along the Chesapeake Bay contained many navigable streams. Landowners constructed their buildings along these streams, while ocean-going ships sailed up these streams for many miles, stopping to load goods at each plantation. These geographic conditions encouraged the development of independent farms and plantations in Virginia and Maryland. At the same time, land away from the rivers remained largely unsettled. These colonies developed few large towns, since buying and selling often took place at a farmer's dock.

THE PILGRIMS AND PURITANS

A second English colony was founded for religious reasons by a group of Protestant Christians known as the **Pilgrims** (*or Separatists*). They were unhappy with the policies of the Church of England. In an attempt to escape persecution, the Pilgrims first fled to Holland. In 1620, a group of Pilgrims sailed to the Americas. They landed at **Plymouth** in present-day Massachusetts. At Plymouth, they established the first permanent European settlement in "New England."

Pilgrims landing in Plymouth.

They committed themselves to a life based on the Bible. Before going ashore, the Pilgrims pledged themselves to self-government by signing an agreement known as the **Mayflower Compact**. They agreed to form their own government and to obey its laws.

ACTING AS AN AMATEUR HISTORIAN

"In the name of God. We who are underwritten, the loyal subjects of King James of Great Britain, France and Ireland, having undertaken for the glory of God, and advancement of the Christian faith, and honor of our country, a voyage to plant the first colony in Virginia, do [agree] and combine ourselves together into a body politic *[a community with its own form of government]*, for our better order and preservation and … to enact and frame just and equal laws, ordinances, acts, and constitutions from time to time, as shall be thought most convenient for the general good of the colony, unto which we promise all due submission and obedience.

In witness whereof we sign our names at Cape-Cod, 11th of November [1620]"

★ Based on the Mayflower Compact, why did the Pilgrims decide to establish a colony in North America? Why do they refer to Virginia?

★ How did the Pilgrims promise to act towards laws passed by the community?

Another group of English Protestants, the **Puritans**, landed in nearby Massachusetts Bay in 1630. They also came to practice their own religious beliefs without persecution. They wanted to "purify" the Church. These Puritans planned to establish a more virtuous society, based on what they believed was God's will. One Puritan writer stated that they would establish a "City upon a Hill" — a symbol of goodness and virtuous living for all the world to see.

Unlike the adventurers at Jamestown, the Pilgrims and Puritans sailed to the "New World" as entire families, along with their wives and children. Eventually, their two settlements merged into the single colony of Massachusetts. Early Puritans and Pilgrims lived simple, religious lives. Their clothing was usually black or gray. They believed that hard work was the key to getting into Heaven. Sundays and holidays were strictly observed. Religious leaders played an important role in governing the colony.

Building a settlement in Massachusetts.

THE OTHER ENGLISH COLONIES

Other English colonies were founded for a variety of reasons:

Rhode Island. The Puritans did not ordinarily permit others to practice their religion freely in Massachusetts. In 1636, **Roger Williams** therefore left Massachusetts to start his own new colony at Rhode Island, based on principles of **religious toleration**.

Among those who also fled to Rhode Island was **Anne Hutchinson**. While living in Massachusetts, she had often met with friends after church and held religious discussions. She expressed her belief that God revealed himself to individuals without the aid of clergy. Puritan leaders saw these meetings as acts against God, since they believed that God could only be revealed to ministers. Anne Hutchinson was put on trial, where she claimed God had spoken to her directly. She was found guilty of lying. In 1637, she was banished from Massachusetts. Soon after, she joined Williams and other dissenters in Rhode Island.

Ann Hutchinson (1591–1643)

Connecticut and New Hampshire. Other Massachusetts settlers formed new colonies in Connecticut and New Hampshire. Settlers in Connecticut, led by Thomas Hooker (1586–1647), established self-government in the **Fundamental Orders of Connecticut** (1639). In addition, the Fundamental Orders of Connecticut provided a basis for future governing in the colony.

New York. At one time, New Netherland separated English colonies to the north and south of it. England, at war with Holland in Europe, sent four ships into the harbor of New Amsterdam in 1664. Dutch settlers, fearing British cannons, refused to fight. Governor **Peter Stuyvesant** surrendered the colony. Under British control, New Netherland was renamed **New York**. Fort Orange became Albany, and New Amsterdam became New York City.

Pennsylvania. William Penn (1644–1718) founded Pennsylvania for the **Quakers**, a group of Protestants who opposed war. Elsewhere, colonists had just taken land from the Native American Indians, but Penn negotiated peaceful purchases. He gave Pennsylvania a written constitution that limited the power of government, provided a humane penal code, and guaranteed many fundamental liberties.

William Penn negotiating to buy land from Native Americans.

Maryland. Lord Baltimore started the colony of Maryland, across the Chesapeake Bay from Virginia, as a haven for England's Catholics.

Delaware and New Jersey. These territories were also taken by the English from the Dutch in 1664. Later both became separate colonies.

North and South Carolina. The Carolinas were established for economic reasons. The colony was formed in 1663 when King Charles II gave land to eight nobles. The nobles hoped to make a profit by attracting settlers from Virginia, who would grow tobacco for sale to Europe. In 1712, the Carolinas were divided into North and South Carolina. In 1729, North Carolina was made into a royal colony. It became known for its naval stores — tar, pitch, and turpentine — made from pine trees. South Carolina became a colony of mostly large plantations. Landowners purchased enslaved Africans to serve as field workers. **Charleston** became a major port for shipping rice and indigo (*blue dye*), and for receiving slaves.

Sowing cotton seeds in South Carolina.

Georgia. This colony was established for social reasons. **James Ogelthorpe** formed the colony in 1733 as a place for imprisoned debtors and convicts sent from England.

APPLYING WHAT YOU HAVE LEARNED

Can you classify the thirteen colonies based on why they were established or seized by the British? The first row has been filled in for you. Complete the others.

Reasons	Definition	Examples
Political	Concerns rulers' demands and balance of power between countries. Also concerns government, citizens' rights and responsibilities European countries competed to develop colonies in the New World.	New York, Delaware, New Jersey *New Hampshire*
Economic	Concerns money and wealth. Some colonies were established to make profits.	*North & South carolina virginia*
Religious	Deals with beliefs and practices in the worship of God. Some colonies were established as places where different groups of colonists could worship God in their own way.	*Pennsylvania, Connecticut Rhode Island, Massachussettes Maryland*
Social	Involves how people organize themselves or live together. One colony was founded as a place where a special group of people (debtors) could start a new life.	*Georgia New Hampshire*

ACTING AS AN AMATEUR HISTORIAN

Maps are important tools for both geographers and historians. Sketching your own map of an area can help you better grasp where certain places are located. A "sketch map" is *not* visually identical to the map being sketched. Rather a "sketch map" focuses on the relationships between and among places. It helps you to better understand the various spatial relationships.

Make your own "sketch map" of early colonial America showing the location of these places: Jamestown, Williamsburg, Plymouth, Boston, Baltimore, Philadelphia, New York City, Albany, and Charleston. Use the Internet to find pictures of these cities during colonial times to decorate the outside borders of your map. What do all of these locations have in common?

LEARNING WITH GRAPHIC ORGANIZERS

Complete the graphic organizer below by explaining the primary reason why each colony was founded. The names of the colonies have been filled in for you.

REASONS WHY EACH COLONY WAS ESTABLISHED

Connecticut	Massachusetts	The Carolinas
Established for social reasons and practiced self government	Religious reasons Pilgrims established to pursue God's work.	Concerns money and wealth. Established for profits

Delaware	New Hampshire	Pennsylvania
Territory taken from the Dutch by the English	Established for social reasons and practiced self government.	Established for Quakers and Protestants against war

Georgia	New Jersey	Rhode Island
Made to imprison debtors from England and convicts	territory taken by the English from the Dutch	Freedom of religion

Maryland	New York	Virginia
Safe Haven for catholics	Political reasons involving England takeing New York	Economical reasons

WHY DID COLONISTS COME TO THE NEW WORLD?

The colonists who established the first English colonies braved the dangers of crossing the Atlantic Ocean. The ships they came on were small and crowded. Their destination was a strange and unfamiliar land with primitive living conditions. Why did they come?

POLITICAL REASONS: ENCOURAGEMENT FROM RULERS

British monarchs encouraged the development of colonies as new sources of wealth and power. They granted charters to groups of businessmen, like the Virginia Company, who offered to help colonists settle in the "New World."

ECONOMIC REASONS: HUNGER FOR GOLD AND SILVER

Based on the success of Spain, the first colonists believed that gold and silver existed in great abundance in the Americas. These early adventurers came to the Americas in search of precious metals.

ECONOMIC REASONS: LAND HUNGER

Colonial settlements presented new business opportunities for merchants. The "Proprietors" who owned the Carolinas encouraged people to come. Many colonists came to obtain their own land. Most people in Britain, Ireland, and the rest of Europe were peasants or tenant farmers occupying small, over-worked lands and paying high rents. In America, free land still

The availability of land was a major attraction drawing settlers to Colonial America.

seemed plentiful. The settlers did not recognize the rights of Native American Indians or understand their use of the land. Many of the first settlers were given free land by the colony or were able to purchase land cheaply.

Later many colonists came as "indentured servants." A colonial landowner paid for an indentured servant's passage across the Atlantic, and the indentured servant then promised to work on the landowner's plantation or farm, usually for a period of seven years. Once the debt was paid off, indentured servants obtained freedom and began saving to buy their own land.

ECONOMIC AND SOCIAL REASONS: A BETTER LIFE

Most colonists had faced difficult lives in Britain, Ireland, Scotland, or Germany. The menace of European wars served as an important reason to leave for many settlers. They wanted to get away from the horrors that wars brought to their lives. They also came to the Americas to escape poverty, political turmoil, famine, and disease. These problems in Europe led to the Great Migration. Between 1629 and 1640 thousands of European men, women, and children migrated to the Americas. More than 40,000 of them moved to British colonies in New England and the Caribbean. They believed colonial life offered new opportunities.

RELIGIOUS REASONS

Protestant groups, like the Pilgrims and Puritans, came to the Americas to establish their own communities, where they could worship God in their own way. Catholics, Quakers, and Jews later came to the colonies seeking freedom of worship.

ACTING AS AN AMATEUR HISTORIAN

Use the Internet or your school library to conduct research on one of the thirteen colonies. Then make a report on the people who came to that colony. Where did most of them come from? Why did they come?

LEARNING WITH GRAPHIC ORGANIZERS

Complete the graphic organizer below. Identify each of these reasons why people migrated to the "New World."

Political Reasons		Economic Reasons
Encouragement from rulers	**WHY PEOPLE MIGRATED TO THE "NEW WORLD"**	wealth
Social Reasons		**Religious Reasons**
Better lives		Practicing religion on their own

CHAPTER 5 CONCEPT MAP

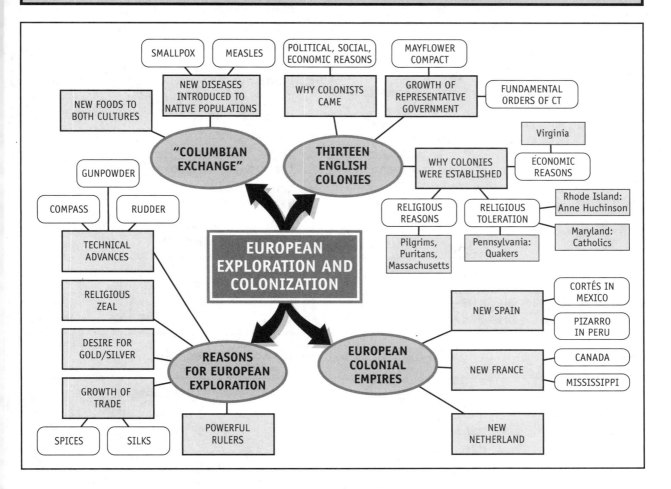

CHAPTER STUDY CARDS

Why Colonists Came to New World

★ **Encouragement from Rulers/Countries.** European rulers sought colonies as new sources of wealth and power.

★ **Mercantilism.** Gold and silver were prized as a source of wealth. Nations measured a nation's wealth by the gold and silver they had.

★ **Religious Reasons.** Groups came to establish their own religious communities.

★ **Better Life.** Most colonists faced hardships in Europe. Saw colonies as a place to escape famine; offered economic opportunities.

Colonization of North America

★ **New Spain.**
  • Mexico, Cuba, Central America.
  • Missionaries sent to convert Indians.
  • Encomiendas: forced labor.

★ **New France.**
  • Canada, Great Lakes, Mississippi River.
  • Wanted to establish trading posts for furs.

★ **New Netherland.** Became NY in 1664.

★ **Thirteen British Colonies.**
  • Established colonies along Atlantic coast.

Key Historic Documents

★ **Mayflower Compact (1620).**
  • Document by Pilgrims at Plymouth
  • Pledged themselves to self-government.
  • They agreed to form their own government and obey its laws.

★ **Fundamental Orders of Connecticut (1639).**
  • Led by Thomas Hooker; settlers in Connecticut established self-government.
  • Although not considered a constitution in the modern sense, the Orders were the basis of Connecticut government from 1639 to 1662.

Key Individuals

★ **Christopher Columbus.** Established Spain's first settlements in the New World.

★ **Robert de LaSalle.** Explored Great Lakes, St. Lawrence River, and Mississippi River.

★ **Henry Hudson.** Reached New York and sailed up river that bears his name.

★ **Hernando Cortés.** Spanish conqueror.

★ **Francisco Pizarro.** Spanish conqueror.

★ **Roger Williams.** Started colony at Rhode Island based on religious toleration.

★ **Lord Baltimore.** Began Maryland colony as a haven for England's Catholics.

★ **William Penn.** Founded Pennsylvania colony as a haven for Quakers.

CHECKING YOUR UNDERSTANDING

Directions: Put a circle around the letter that best answers the question.

1

> When I first went to Virginia, I remember we hung an [an old sail] to four trees to shadow us from the sun; our walls were rails of wood; our seats unhewed trees, till we cut planks; our pulpit a bar of wood nailed to trees. In [bad] weather we shifted into an old, rotten tent. This was our church till we built a homely thing, like a barn. The best of our houses were like this. We had daily prayers morning and evening, two sermons every Sunday, and communion every three months till our minister died.

— *Adapted from John Smith, The Generall Historie of Virginia, (1624)*

Based on this passage from John Smith, what conclusion can be drawn about the lives of colonists in Jamestown, Virginia?

A   The standard of living was similar to most European nations.

B   Religion played an important part in the lives of early colonists.

C   Local Native American Indians were a serious threat to early colonists.

D   Growing tobacco was the main source of income of early colonists to Virginia.

(Hist 2(B))

EXAMINE **the question.** This question tests your ability to draw a conclusion from a reading passage. RECALL **what you know.** You should recall that most of the colonists were quite religious 200 years ago. Religion was a central feature of life in Europe. APPLY **what you know.** You should realize that since most the Smith passage deals with his church, sermons, and praying that **Choices A, C,** and **D** do not really apply to this passage. The best answer is **Choice B.** The passage demonstrates the importance of religion to settlers in early Virginia.

Now try answering some additional questions on your own.

2   Why is the Mayflower Compact considered an important step in the development of American democracy?

    F   It established the principle of separation of church and state.   `Govt 15(A)`

    G   It provided a basis for self-government in the Plymouth Colony.

    H   It defined colonial relations with local Native American Indians.

    J   It outlawed slavery in the Massachusetts Bay Colony.

3   One way in which the settlements at Jamestown (1607) and of New France in Canada (1608) were similar is that both were located —

    A   in the mountains   **C**   next to bodies of water   `Geog 10(A)`

    B   on islands far from fresh water   **D**   in a dry climate

4   The Mayflower Compact and the Fundamental Orders of Connecticut are most closely associated with —

    F   abuses by absolute monarchs   `Hist 3(B)`

    G   establishment of religious toleration

    H   steps toward colonial self-government

    J   adoption of universal suffrage

5   In which region of the United States was the first permanent English settlement located?

    A   Pacific Northwest   **C**   Atlantic Coast   `Geog 10(A)`

    B   Great Plains   **D**   Great Lakes Mountains

6   The need for agricultural workers in the tobacco fields of colonial Virginia led to the —

    F   formation of labor unions   `Hist 2(B)`

    G   decision to industrialize

    H   improvement in farming

    J   use of enslaved people from Africa

7   What was one important result of the encounter between Europeans and Native American Indians?

    A   Native American Indian populations continued to increase.   `Hist 2(B)`

    B   The African slave trade ended.

    C   New diseases were spread to Native American populations.

    D   Spain's empire in the New World declined.

8   Early European explorers who came to the "New World" were looking for a Northwest Passage in order to —

    F   prove the world was round   `Hist 2(A)`

    G   improve trade with Native American Indians

    H   explore the Great Lakes

    J   find a shorter water-route to Asia

9   According the map, which geographic feature along the Atlantic coastline contributed most to the growth of trade in the British colonies?

    A   many offshore islands   `Geog 10(A)`

    B   high, rocky cliffs

    C   natural harbors

    D   barrier reefs

WHERE COLONISTS SETTLED

Legend
- Places where colonists settled
- ◆ Town or village

Fort Orange
Connecticut R.
Exeter
Boston
Plymouth
Providence
Hartford
New Haven
Newport
Hudson R.
Delaware R.
New Amsterdam
Fort Nassau
Fort Christina
Atlantic Ocean
Rappahonnock R.
St. Mary
Williamsburg
James R.
Chesapeake Bay
Jamestown

10   The information on this map suggests that most early colonists —

    F   were unable to achieve political unity   `Geog 10(A)`

    G   were located very close to each other

    H   built their settlements near bodies of water

    J   encountered great difficulties with Native American Indians

11   According the map, which statement is most accurate?

    A   The largest number of people lived in Virginia.   `Geog 10(A)`

    B   Most colonies were located next to the Great Lakes.

    C   Most towns and villages developed in and around areas of settlement.

    D   Areas of settlement tended to avoid nearness to bodies of water.

12

We the Loyal Subjects of King James ... having undertaken ... a voyage to plant the first colony in Virginia; do ... mutually ... combine ourselves together into a civil body politick ...; and shall meet and [convene] for the general good of the Colony; we promise all due submission and obedience. In witness we have subscribed our names at Cape Cod. — *The Mayflower Compact, 1620*	We do therefore associate and connive ourselves to be as one Public State or Commonwealth; and do, for ourselves and our successors ... enter into combination and Confederation ... As also in our Civil Affairs to be guided and governed according to such Laws, Rules, Orders and Decrees as shall be made ... — *Fundamental Orders of Connecticut, 1639*

Based on these excerpts, in what way were these two documents similar?
F   The signers of both documents had only just landed in America.   `Hist 3(B)`
G   In both documents, colonists agreed to establish a community and obey to its laws.
H   In both documents, colonists agreed to obey the British King's decisions.
J   Both documents established a government in which its members chose their own governor.

13   Which colonial settlement is correctly paired with the reason it was founded?
A   North Carolina — haven for Pilgrims and Puritans   `Hist 2(B)`
B   Georgia — place for imprisoned debtors and convicts
C   Maryland — refuge for Quakers
D   Pennsylvania — refuge for English Catholics

14   What was the major reason European rulers sought to colonize North America?
F   They needed people from North America to settle in Europe.   `Hist 2(A)`
G   They sought to learn more about Native American cultures.
H   They sought to expand their power with riches from the "New World."
J   They wanted a place to send their criminal population.

15   One reason for the importance of the Mayflower Compact and the Fundamental Orders of Connecticut was that they laid the foundation for —
A   a two-house legislature in state governments   `Hist 3(B)`
B   the growth of representative government in Colonial America
C   the development of English common law in the colonies
D   social freedom in colonial legislatures

16   The journeys of Christopher Columbus and Robert de LaSalle to the "New World" were made possible because of the —
F   effects of the Atlantic slave trade   `Hist 2(A)`
G   support of exploration by the English Parliament
H   trade connections established by the travels of Marco Polo
J   development of new navigational instruments and technology

CHAPTER 6

LIFE IN COLONIAL AMERICA

TEKS
COVERED IN
CHAPTER 6

- **History 1B** Explain the significance of the following dates: signing of the Mayflower Compact ....
- **History 3A** Explain the reasons for the growth of representative government and institutions during the colonial period.
- **History 3B** Analyze the importance of the Mayflower Compact, the Fundamental Orders of Connecticut and the Virginia House of Burgesses to the growth of representative government.
- **History 3C** Describe how religion and virtue contributed to the growth of representative government in the American colonies.
- **History 4A** Analyze causes of the American Revolution, including ... mercantilism....
- **Geography 10A** Locate places and regions directly relating to major eras and turning points in the United States during the 17th and 18th centuries.
- **Geography 10B** Compare places and regions of the United States in terms of physical and human characteristics.
- **Geography 10C** Analyze the effects of physical and human geographic factors such as weather, landforms, waterways, transportation and communication on major historical events in the United States.
- **Geography 11A** Analyze how physical characteristics of the environment influenced population distribution, settlement patterns, and economic activities in the United States during the 17th and 18th centuries.
- **Economics 12A** Identify economic differences among different regions of the U.S.
- **Economics 12B** Explain reasons for the development of the plantation system [and] the transatlantic slave trade ....
- **Economics 12C** Analyze the causes and effects of economic differences among different regions of the United States at selected times.
- **Government 15A** Identify the influence of ideas from historic documents, including the Magna Carta, the English Bill of Rights [and] the Mayflower Compact ... on the U.S. system of government.
- **Government 15E** Explain the role of significant individuals such as Thomas Hooker ... in the development of self-government in colonial America.
- **Culture 23A** Identify selected racial, ethnic, and religious groups that settled in the United States and explain their reasons for immigration.
- **Culture 23C** Identify ways conflicts between people from various racial, ethnic, and religious groups were addressed.
- **Culture 23E** Identify the political, social, and economic contributions of women to American society.
- **Culture 25A** Trace the development of religious freedom in the United States.
- **Culture 25B** Describe religious influences on social movements, including the impact of the first ... Great Awakening.
- **Culture 26A** Identify examples of American art, music, and literature that reflect society in different eras.

In this chapter, you will learn about Colonial America — when what would later become the United States was still a part of the British Empire. England established thirteen colonies along the Atlantic coast with a variety of lifestyles. Geographic differences led to the emergence of three distinct regions: New England, the Middle Atlantic, and the South.

KEY TERMS AND PEOPLE IN THIS CHAPTER

- New England
- Triangular Trade
- Mid-Atlantic Colonies
- Southern Colonies
- Magna Carta
- Bill of Rights of 1689

- House of Burgesses
- Mayflower Compact
- Fundamental Orders of Connecticut
- John Peter Zenger
- Pilgrims

- Puritans
- Great Awakening
- Mercantilism
- Atlantic Slave Trade
- Cotton Mather
- Phillis Wheatley

ESSENTIAL QUESTIONS

- What differences existed between the main regions of the thirteen colonies?
- What was life like in Colonial America?
- What factors contributed to religious freedom in the thirteen colonies?
- How did the economic system of mercantilism affect the thirteen colonies?

— IMPORTANT IDEAS —

A. Different patterns of life developed in three regions of the colonies, based on differences in geography, climate, settler origins, and economic activities. Variations in weather, landforms, and waterways led these regions to develop differently.

B. In **New England**, a short growing season, cooler climates, rocky soil, and an influx of Puritan settlers encouraged the development of small farms and the growth of fishing, shipping, and handicraft trades.

C. In the **Southern Colonies**, a long growing season and warmer climate, as well as the arrival of mainly Anglican settlers seeking to make their fortune, encouraged the development of larger farms that often grew cash crops for sale to England. Along main water routes, large plantations developed.

D. Part of the Southern Colonies' economy was based on slave labor. Slaves grew cotton, tobacco, rice and indigo. They were taken by force from Africa and faced a horrific "**Middle Passage**" journey across the Atlantic. Most Southerners, however, did not own slaves.

E. The **Middle Atlantic Colonies** had greater ethnic and religious diversity than either New England or the Southern Colonies. Some of these colonies had once been under Dutch rule and were conquered by the English in 1664. The Middle Atlantic Colonies had fertile soil and grew food crops.

— IMPORTANT IDEAS (continued) —

F. The colonists benefited from traditions of political liberty and representative government inherited from England. English subjects gained important rights in **Magna Carta** (1215), England's **Civil War**, the **Glorious Revolution**, and the **English Bill of Rights** (1689). To these rights, the colonists added their own institutions of representative government in the **Virginia House of Burgesses** (1619), the **Mayflower Compact** (1620), New England town meetings, and the **Fundamental Orders of Connecticut** (1639). In the mid-1700s, each colony had its own assembly elected by male property owners in the colony, and a governor appointed by the royal government in London.

G. Religion played an important role in colonial life. **Pilgrims** and **Puritans** first came for religious reasons. Other colonies were also established as homes for England's persecuted or unpopular religious groups — Quakers went to Pennsylvania and Catholics to Maryland.

H. **Roger Williams** and **Anne Hutchinson** left Puritan Massachusetts and established the principle of religious toleration in Rhode Island. New York already had enjoyed religious toleration under Dutch rule. During the **First Great Awakening**, preachers like **Jonathan Edwards** and **George Whitefield** addressed large crowds in open fields and stirred religious feelings. These preachers also supported religious toleration.

I. **Mercantilism** was the policy of using colonies to bring wealth to the "Mother Country." Mercantilists taught that the colonists should sell cash crops to the Mother Country and buy more expensive finished goods in return.

J. Colonists brought sugar from the West Indies, turned it into rum in the colonies, shipped the rum to England or Africa, and obtained manufactured goods from England and slaves from Africa. Historians refer to these exchanges across the Atlantic as the "**Triangular Trades**."

K. The roots of American art, music, and literature reach back to colonial times. Colonial writers included John Smith, William Bradford, Cotton Mather, Anne Bradstreet, Benjamin Franklin and Phillis Wheatley. Painters included Benjamin West, John Singleton, Charles Wilson Peale, and Gilbert Stuart.

DIFFERENCES EMERGE AMONG THE ENGLISH COLONIES

By the mid-1730s, thirteen English colonies existed along the Atlantic coast. New patterns of life developed in three separate regions of the English colonies. Differences were based on the physical characteristics of their environment (such as weather, landforms and natural waterways), religious beliefs, the origins of the colonists, the presence of slaves, and different ways of earning a living.

NEW ENGLAND

The colonies of New England — **Massachusetts**, **New Hampshire**, **Connecticut**, and **Rhode Island** — had rocky soil and less fertile land. Since the New England Colonies were the farthest north, they had longer winters and a colder climate than the other colonies. Many New Englanders had small farms where they grew crops for their own use.

Others used the forests in the region for lumber and building ships. These colonies were located near the ocean where there was an abundance of whales and fish. Large numbers of New Englanders became sailors, fishermen, and merchants. The practice of religion, especially Puritanism, also remained important in New England.

New Englanders frequently owned and manned ships. They carried sugar from the West Indies to New England, where it was turned into rum. The rum was carried to Africa, where it was traded for slaves. New England merchants also carried sugar from the West Indies to England. Their ships were then loaded with manufactured goods and sailed back to New England. You will learn more about these "triangular trades" later in this chapter.

THE 13 ENGLISH COLONIES, 1750

FRENCH

Lake Huron
Lake Ontario
Lake Erie
FRENCH
APPALACHIAN MOUNTAINS
N.H.
NEW YORK
MASS.
CONN.
R.I.
PENN.
NEW JERSEY
MD.
DEL.
VIRGINIA
NORTH CAROLINA
SOUTH CAROLINA
GEORGIA
ATLANTIC OCEAN
SPANISH

New England
Middle Colonies
Southern Colonies

Scale of Miles
0   250   500

THE MIDDLE ATLANTIC COLONIES

The Middle Atlantic Colonies — **New York**, **New Jersey**, **Delaware**, and **Pennsylvania**— were located between New England and the Southern Colonies. Winters were not as harsh as in New England and summers were longer. Uncleared forests and fertile soils attracted many colonists to this area. Most of the settlers came from the Netherlands (*Holland*), Germany, Sweden, France, and Scotland. Settlers first

The first job of the colonial farmer was to clear the land.

focused on cutting down the trees and removing stones and stumps from the soil so that it could be prepared for planting. The forests of the Middle Atlantic Colonies gave birth to an active lumbering and shipbuilding industry.

The Middle Atlantic Colonies were particularly well suited for small farms, and soon became known as the "Bread Basket." It was here that wheat, oats, barley, and rye were often grown. The fertile soil of the area even permitted a large amount of grain to be exported.

People were also attracted to a greater atmosphere of religious freedom. No single church or religion dominated the Middle Atlantic Colonies. These colonies had greater religious diversity than either New England or the South. The main religious groups were Anglicans, Dutch Reformed Protestants, Catholics, and Jews.

THE SOUTHERN COLONIES

The Southern Colonies — **Virginia**, **Maryland**, **North Carolina**, **South Carolina**, and **Georgia** — had a warmer climate than other parts of Colonial America. The land was flat and the soil was well-suited to growing cash crops throughout the year. Southerners were largely English, Scots, and Scotch-Irish settlers who came to America for economic motives. In parts of England, Scotland and Northern Ireland, many poor farmers could not afford to buy their own land. English settlers were usually Anglican (*Church of England*), but Scots and Scotch-Irish settlers were often Presbyterian. In general, German and Scotch-Irish immigrants avoided living in the coastal settle-

Despite many large plantations, most Southerners lived on small farms.

ments where English influence was strongest. They tended to settle farther inland. Southern forests provided lumber, tar and resin. Resin, made from the sap of pine trees, provided some of the best shipbuilding materials in the world.

DEVELOPMENT OF THE PLANTATION SYSTEM

Some Southerners developed plantations along major water routes. Each plantation was a large-scale agricultural operation on which 20 or more slaves worked crops such as tobacco, cotton, rice and indigo (*a blue dye used to color fabrics*) for shipment to England in exchange for manufactured goods. The plantation system began in Virginia and spread to other parts of the Southern Colonies accessible by water.

The plantation system in the Old South.

Large plantations, owned by rich families, depended on the use of enslaved peoples from Africa and their descendants as the main work force. Landowners in South Carolina even learned important techniques used in Africa for growing rice from their slaves.

The main crops planted on a plantation were very labor intensive. A successful harvest depended on slaves working from sunrise to sunset. Women usually worked the same hours as the men. Women were expected to return to the fields not long after giving birth to children. The mortality (*death*) rate among slaves was high. Slave women were encouraged to have large numbers of children to replace slave losses. The great majority of whites did not live on plantations. They often farmed their land on a smaller scale.

APPLYING WHAT YOU HAVE LEARNED

★ How did settlers to the thirteen colonies adapt to their physical environment?

★ How did the Southern plantation system make that region unique?

ACTING AS AN AMATEUR HISTORIAN

A historical map shows the way an area was in the past. The map below provides an outline of the thirteen English colonies. Using the Internet or your local or school library, research the following:

★ Identify each of the thirteen British colonies by name.

★ Use different colors to show the three regions of Colonial America: New England, the Middle Atlantic Colonies, and the Southern Colonies.

★ Add other colors to show the territories claimed by Spain and France.

★ Identify the Appalachian Mountains, St. Lawrence River, Mississippi River, Lake Erie, Lake Ontario, and Long Island.

★ Identify these ports and towns: Savannah (Georgia), Charleston (S.C.), Raleigh (N.C.), Jamestown (VA), Williamsburg (VA), Baltimore (MD), Philadelphia (PA), New York (NY), Boston and Plymouth (MA).

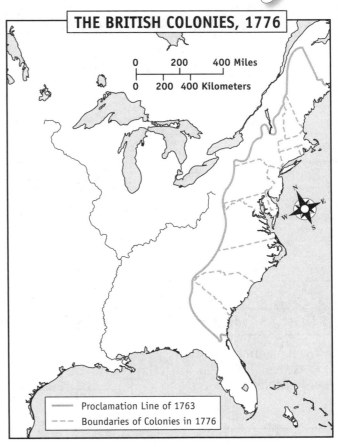

THE BRITISH COLONIES, 1776

0   200   400 Miles
0   200   400 Kilometers

——— Proclamation Line of 1763
- - - Boundaries of Colonies in 1776

LEARNING WITH GRAPHIC ORGANIZERS

Complete the graphic organizer summarizing similarities and differences between the three regions. Parts of the first region have been completed for you.

NEW ENGLAND	MIDDLE ATLANTIC COLONIES	SOUTHERN COLONIES
Colonies	**Colonies**	**Colonies**
New Hampshire, Massachusetts, Connecticut, Rhode Island	New York, New Jersey, Delaware, Pennsylvania	Virginia, Maryland, North carolina, South carolina Georgia
Physical Geography	**Physical Geography**	**Physical Geography**
Rocky soil		
Economic Activities	**Economic Activities**	**Economic Activities**
Other Features	**Other Features**	**Other Features**
Town meetings; Puritan leadership; later non-Puritans began arriving		

COLONIAL GOVERNMENT

The colonists enjoyed several institutions of representative government based on both English political traditions and new practices that emerged in the colonies.

ENGLISH POLITICAL TRADITIONS

During the Middle Ages, England had developed traditions of liberty and limited self-government that were unique in Europe.

MAGNA CARTA

In 1215, the English king was forced by his barons to promise not to take away any free man's property or to imprison any free man without following procedures established by the laws of the land. The "Great Charter" guaranteed individuals the right to a fair trial by their peers and forced the king to obtain the consent of a council of nobles before imposing any new taxes.

ACTING AS AN AMATEUR HISTORIAN

"**Clause 29.** No Freeman shall be taken or imprisoned, or [have] his Freehold, or Liberties [taken away], or be outlawed, or [sent away], or any other wise destroyed; nor will We pass upon him, nor condemn him, but by lawful judgment of his Peers [equals], or by the Law of the land. We will sell to no man, we will not deny or defer to any man either Justice or Right."

★ How did Clause 29 of the Magna Carta help to guarantee the rights of individuals living in England?

★ Why did this become an important feature of political life in the colonies?

THE BRITISH PARLIAMENT

In the Middle Ages, the English king summoned his nobles and representatives from counties and towns to show support for the crown. **Parliament** developed into a national legislature consisting of nobles and elected representatives. New taxes had to be approved by Parliament. After two revolutions in the 1600s, Parliament achieved supremacy over the king.

BILL OF RIGHTS OF 1689

After the Glorious Revolution of 1688, the rights of English subjects were confirmed by the **Bill of Rights of 1689**. England's rulers agreed not to have a standing army or to impose new taxes without the permission of Parliament. The English Bill of Rights also guaranteed trial by jury, the right to petition Parliament, and other personal freedoms, as well as freedom of speech and debate in Parliament.

The Magna Carta, the rise of Parliament, the English civil wars, and the English Bill of Rights all combined to establish important traditions of individual liberty and limited government that were familiar to the English colonists.

THE RISE OF COLONIAL SELF-GOVERNMENT

Unique conditions in the "New World" also played a role in the development of representative government in the colonies.

In colonial times, it took several weeks, or even months, for ships to cross the Atlantic for England and then to return to the colonies. There were no telephone or telegraph lines. It fell to the colonists to solve many of their local problems themselves.

Meeting of the Virginia House of Burgesses.

★ **House of Burgesses.** In 1619, the colony of Virginia established an elected representative assembly known as the **House of Burgesses**.

★ **Mayflower Compact.** The following year, the Pilgrims agreed to self-government in the **Mayflower Compact**.

★ **Town Meetings.** In early colonial Massachusetts, each town was largely self-governing. In Massachusetts Bay, only adult male members of the Puritan Church could hold office or participate in town meetings. The town meeting elected "selectmen" to manage town affairs. After 1634, each town also elected representatives to the **General Court**, the colony's general assembly.

★ **Fundamental Orders of Connecticut.** In 1639, three towns in Connecticut agreed to the **Fundamental Orders of Connecticut**. This document, written by **Thomas Hooker**, stated that government is based on the rights of individual citizens. It also declared that Connecticut would rule itself. Towns would elect representatives each April and September to their "General Assembly" or "Court." These officials, known as magistrates, would then elect the colony's governor.

LATER COLONIAL GOVERNMENT

Eventually, a partnership developed in each colony between an elected colonial assembly and a governor appointed in London by the British government.

Freedom of the Press. The colony of New York played an important role in the development of freedom of the press, an important aspect of representative government. In the 1730s, **John Peter Zenger** published a newspaper accusing the Governor of New York of corruption.

British soldiers burned copies of John Peter Zenger's Weekly Journal.

New York's Governor put Zenger on trial. Zenger won his case when his lawyer, Andrew Hamilton, showed that his statements were true. The case established the right of the press to criticize those in power, so long as the writer told the truth.

APPLYING WHAT YOU HAVE LEARNED

★ What important individual rights and beliefs about government did the colonists bring from England?

★ What additional representative institutions did the American colonists create?

ACTING AS AN AMATEUR HISTORIAN

Select one of the thirteen colonies and conduct research on the Internet or at school or your local library on how that colony's government operated. Include information on who ran the colony, how laws were made, and if the colony had its own court system.

THE GROWTH OF RELIGIOUS FREEDOM IN THE ENGLISH COLONIES

The colonies also saw the growth of religious freedom. The first two English colonies had people of very different religious backgrounds. Virginia was mainly founded by **Anglicans** — those who belonged to the Church of England. Massachusetts was founded by **Pilgrims** and **Puritans** — members of Protestant groups who came to the Americas to worship God in their own way.

Puritans wore simple, plain clothing. Observe the woman carrying a Bible.

In Massachusetts Bay Colony, Puritans originally set high standards for Church membership. They wanted to promote **virtue** (*goodness*). Puritans thought the members of their Church were chosen by God, and that only those "Elected" would go to Heaven. Each Sunday was a day of rest in which the whole community went to church. The minister often gave a sermon threatening sinners with the punishment of damnation after death.

The Puritans believed that a state-endorsed religion would insure a bond between members of society, helping to maintain order and stability. They felt that having more than one religion might threaten social stability. Although they came to America to worship God in their own way, they did not support religious toleration for others.

SALEM WITCHCRAFT TRIALS

The famous **Salem Witchcraft Trials** took place in Massachusetts in 1692 and 1693. A West Indian slave told a group of children tales of voodoo. The girls claimed they were being tortured by witches. Those accused of witchcraft were asked to repent and to name their fellow witches to avoid punishment. Twenty people were hanged before authorities put an end to the hysteria. Some historians argue the trials were an attempt by strict Puritans to maintain their authority. Others point out that by discrediting Puritan prejudices, the witchcraft craze actually weakened the hold of Puritanism on the colony.

THE RISE OF RELIGIOUS TOLERATION

In Massachusetts, some colonists objected to the strict control of the Puritans. **Roger Williams** and **Anne Hutchinson** left to found a new colony in Rhode Island. Rhode Island was the first English colony to establish the principle of **religious toleration** — the recognition that others had the right to practice their own faiths. Dutch New York also practiced religious toleration.

ACTING AS AN AMATEUR HISTORIAN

The passage below was written by Roger Williams, who was banished from Massachusetts Bay Colony after he spoke in favor of freedom of conscience.

> "There is no regularly constituted Church of Christ on Earth, nor any person qualified to administer any church ordinances…. Enforced uniformity [goes against] civil and religious liberty and denies the principles of Christianity and civility. No man shall be required to worship or maintain a worship against his will…. It is the will of God that [freedom of conscience] be granted to all men in all countries."

What is the main point that Roger Williams is making in this passage?

Other English colonies were established to protect members of persecuted religious groups. Catholics were welcomed to Maryland and Quakers to Pennsylvania. With so many different religious groups living in Colonial America, it just made more sense for people to tolerate each other rather than to fight over religion.

Religious beliefs also contributed to the growth of representative government. Many Protestants believed that Church elders or elected members should govern the Church. They applied the same approach of electing representatives to govern the community as a whole.

THE FIRST GREAT AWAKENING

The importance of religion to the colonists was illustrated by the **Great Awakening** of the 1740s. Ministers emphasized the importance of religious feelings. During the Great Awakening, preachers like **Jonathan Edwards** and **George Whitefield** often addressed large crowds in open fields. They told listeners that God was merciful and that people could save themselves from damnation by repenting for their sins. Colonists were told to study the Bible for themselves and many became more emotionally engaged in religion. The Great Awakening emphasized people's equality in the eyes of God. The preachers of the Great Awakening were also strong supporters of religious freedom and toleration. They wanted their listeners to accept Christianity as an act of free will.

Whitefield preaching.

APPLYING WHAT YOU HAVE LEARNED

★ Imagine you are a reporter at the Salem Witchcraft Trials or at a gathering during the First Great Awakening. Write a report about what you witness.

★ Conduct research on the Internet or in your local library about the development of religious toleration in the American colonies. Select one colony and summarize how it treated religious differences and beliefs in a written report.

ECONOMIC AND SOCIAL LIFE IN THE ENGLISH COLONIES

MERCANTILISM

The economy of the British colonies was based on **mercantilism**. Under this economic system, Parliament passed laws controlling the trade of the colonies in order to benefit the "Mother Country." The aim was to get more gold and silver. Under mercantilism, colonists were expected to sell their raw materials, such as tobacco, rice, fur, and fish, at low prices to Britain.

In exchange, the colonists were supposed to buy British manufactured products, such as glass, paper, and tea, which were more expensive. Mercantilists believed this unequal trade would increase the wealth of the "Mother Country."

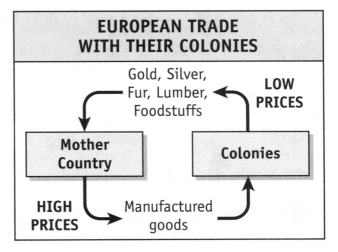

EUROPEAN TRADE WITH THEIR COLONIES

Gold, Silver, Fur, Lumber, Foodstuffs

LOW PRICES

Mother Country

Colonies

HIGH PRICES

Manufactured goods

TRIANGULAR TRADES

England's **Navigation Laws** prevented the colonists from trading directly with the other countries of Europe. Grain and meat from New England and later from the Middle Atlantic Colonies were shipped to the West Indies in return for sugar or cash. New Englanders also sold lumber, dried fish, and rum made from sugar to England. The Southern Colonies sold tobacco, rice, and indigo to England for manufactured goods.

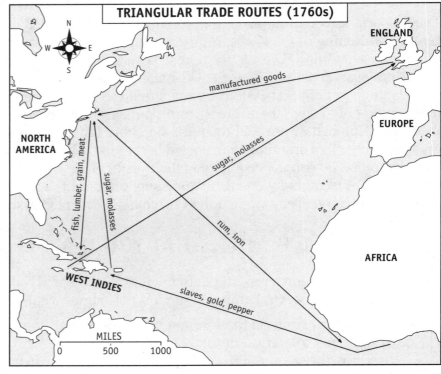

By the 1700s, the colonies had become involved with several trading partners. The most important of these came to be known as the **Triangular Trades** — since each of these routes formed a triangle. (*See map*). The growth in trade encouraged the rise of port towns like Boston, Philadelphia, New York, and Charleston. As the North American colonies grew, their trade became increasingly important to Britain for its own economic well-being. Another important aspect of the triangular trade between Europe, Africa, and the Americas was that it helped disperse African slaves throughout the Western Hemisphere.

EVERYDAY LIFE IN THE THIRTEEN COLONIES

Most people in Colonial America spent their time on farms and in small villages.

ROLES OF MEN, WOMEN, AND CHILDREN

In colonial times, men enjoyed power and authority, while women had few rights, and children had none. The husband spent most of his time farming. The wife did the cooking, weaving, sewing, washing, making candles, churning butter, and other household tasks. Children helped with many chores, like tending livestock.

COLONIAL OCCUPATIONS

Most colonists were farmers, but there were also a large number of people engaged in other occupations, such as blacksmiths, tanners, millers, and carpenters. Other colonists engaged in fishing, whaling, and sailing.

COLONIAL SOCIETY

Colonial society was divided into several social groups. A handful of wealthy landowners and merchants stood at the top of colonial society; then came independent farmers who worked their own land; tradesmen, shopkeepers, and craftsmen working in towns and villages came next; apprentices or servants were below them; and at the very bottom of the colonial social ladder were unskilled laborers and slaves.

SLAVERY AND THE SLAVE TRADE

One of the areas of greatest hardship and profit in colonial society was the slave trade. No concern was given to the feelings or comfort of the victims of this trade. "Slavers" usually bought captured Africans on the West Coast of Africa and put them on slave ships for the voyage to the Americas. Enslaved Africans were treated so harshly that many failed to survive the voyage. Traders were so greedy they sought to carry as many slaves as possible on their ships. Slaves were chained and crammed together below the deck, where sitting or standing room was limited. The air below deck was so stifling that some suffocated. Others tried to starve themselves or to jump over board. When the slaves reached the Americas, they were sold off in auctions. Families were broken up.

Captured Africans experienced horrific conditions on the "Middle Passage."

Enslaved people made up a significant part of the population of Colonial America. The number of Africans in New England grew from under 1,000 in 1700 to about 16,000 in the 1770s. The number of slaves in the South was far greater, reaching 125,000 by 1740. Enslaved men and women were owned by plantation owners, farmers, ministers, doctors, and merchants. They were used to perform household chores and skilled jobs as well as field labor.

ESTIMATED AFRICAN-AMERICAN POPULATION IN THE THIRTEEN BRITISH COLONIES, 1690–1740

Year	New England Colonies	Middle Atlantic Colonies	Southern Colonies
1690	905	2,472	13,307
1700	1,680	5,361	22,476
1710	2,585	6,218	36,063
1720	3,956	10,825	54,058
1730	6,118	11,683	73,220
1740	8,541	16,452	125,031

Source: *Historical Statistics of the United States*

ACTING AS AN AMATEUR HISTORIAN

U.S. History   Search

1776

Dr. Thomas Trotter worked on a slave-ship in 1790. Here was his response when he was asked if the "slaves had room to turn themselves":

> "No. The slaves that are out of irons are locked to one another. It is the duty of the first mate to see them stowed in this manner every morning; those which do not get quickly into their places are compelled by the [whip] when stowed in this manner, and when the ship had much motion at sea, they were often miserably bruised against the deck or against each other. I have seen their chests heaving and observed them draw their breath, with all those laborious and anxious efforts for life which we observe in expiring animals subjected by experiment to bad air of various kinds."

★ What emotions do you think the victims of the slave trade experienced as they crossed the Atlantic in a slave ship?

★ Conduct further research on the treatment of enslaved Africans in the Atlantic Slave Trade during the colonial period. Write a page summarizing your results.

★ Write a short play or skit showing what it was like to live in colonial times.

ART, MUSIC, AND LITERATURE IN THE COLONIES

Benjamin Franklin once remarked that the task of creating a new nation left little time for music and art. Franklin felt that people needed to meet their basic needs before they could turn their attention to creating literature, music, and painting. Few early colonists could manage to spend all their time on artistic activities, and they were distant from the cultural centers of Europe. As a result, it took time for American colonists to develop their own distinct literary and artistic culture.

Early colonists came to America with English or European ways of life. Most relied on artistic and literary tastes based on English or European lifestyles. Early colonists read European books and played and sang European music. The first Americans writers included **Captain John Smith** and **William Bradford**, who wrote histories of their settlements.

In New England, the early Puritans condemned theatre and art. Literature was primarily religious in nature. For example, **Cotton Mather**, a second generation New Englander, was a theologian and historian. In 1688, when his father left for England, he was left in charge of the largest congregation in New England. He ministered to it for the rest of his life, and rose to became one of the most influential men in the colonies. He had much to do with the witchcraft persecution of his day. He devoted his life to praying, preaching, writing, and publishing. Mather wrote and published more than 400 works in his lifetime.

Cotton Mather

ACTING AS AN AMATEUR HISTORIAN

Cotton Mather was instrumental in influencing American religion and in starting the First Great Awakening. His writings gave advice to young ministers on a wide range of topics such as performing virtuous acts, poetry, music, and writing style. This passage deals with educating young people:

> "Where [Godly] schools are not vigorously encouraged, whole colonies will sink into a degenerate and contemptible condition, and become horribly barbarous. You will therefore pardon my freedom with you, if I address you in the words of Luther: *'If ever there be any considerable blow given to the Devil's Kingdom, it must be by youth excellently educated. It is a serious thing, a weighty thing, and a thing that hath much of the interest of Christianity in it, that youth be well-trained, and that schools, and school-masters be maintained. Learning is an unwelcome guest to the Devil, and therefore he would fain starve it out.'"*

★ What did Mather think might happen if colonists failed to educate their youth?

★ Why did Mather choose to quote the words of Martin Luther?

Some of the earliest colonial writers were women, like **Anne Bradstreet** (1612–1672), who wrote poems. Her poetry eloquently expressed the concerns of a Puritan wife and mother. She is considered by many to be the first American poet. Her collection of poems was the first book written by a woman to be published in the United States. She helped lay the groundwork for other female writers in an era when most women tended to family and domestic matters.

Benjamin Franklin (1706–1790) was a printer, publisher, and scientist who became popular with the stories and sayings in *Poor Richard's Almanac*, begun in 1733, and in his *Autobiography* (1777). Franklin openly admitted that many of the sayings in *Poor Richard* were borrowed, rather than coined by himself. Franklin once stated: "Why give my readers bad lines of my own, when good ones of other people's are so plentiful?" Nevertheless, these sayings, taken from "many Ages and Nations," became one of the bases for Franklin's international fame.

Phillis Wheatley (1753–1784), was an African who was kidnapped and brought to the colonies as a slave at the age of seven. She soon learned to speak and write English, taught by the daughter of her owner; within 16 months she could read difficult passages in the Bible. She became a sensation in the 1760s when her poem on the death of the preacher George Whitefield made her famous. A constant theme running through her poetry was that of Christian salvation.

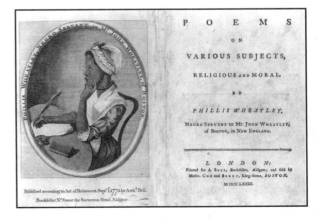

ACTING AS AN AMATEUR HISTORIAN

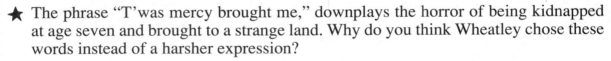

In the poem "On Being Brought from Africa to America," Wheatley tells of her feelings about her condition of enslavement:

> "T'was mercy brought me from my pagan land,
> Taught my benighted soul to understand
> That there's a God, that there's a Saviour too:
> Once I redemption neither sought nor knew.
> Some view our sable race with scornful eye,
> 'Their colour is a diabolic die.'
> Remember, Christians, Negroes, black as Cain,
> May be refin'd, and join the angelic train."

★ The phrase "T'was mercy brought me," downplays the horror of being kidnapped at age seven and brought to a strange land. Why do you think Wheatley chose these words instead of a harsher expression?

★ Wheatley uses "Remember" (line 7) to remind Christian readers of what they should already know. What is it that they should remember?

As urban centers in Colonial America, like New York City, Charleston, Boston and Philadelphia grew in wealth, some colonists developed a taste for paintings. As immigrants to the Americas, people sought to establish their identities in a new land and to bring the benefits of European civilization to their surroundings. Portrait paintings were the primary subject matter for colonial artists. In a time when there were no photographs, colonists desired to be remembered by their descendants. Furthermore, many of these early colonists were self-made people who were proud of their accomplishments. They sought to display their new self-importance to their family, friends, and associates by having their portraits painted. Noteworthy American artists in this period included **Benjamin West**, **John Singleton Copley**, **Charles Wilson Peale**, and **Gilbert Stuart**.

Benjamin Franklin in an oil painting by Benjamin West.

ACTING AS AN AMATEUR HISTORIAN

Research one colonial painter, musician, or writer. Then pretend that you are that artist or writer and give a brief presentation to your class about your work.

ACTING AS AN AMATEUR HISTORIAN

INVESTIGATING COLONIAL AMERICA

In this chapter, you have learned about life in Colonial America. Now you will have an opportunity to study one of the English colonies in greater depth. Your teacher will divide your class into thirteen small groups. Each group will be assigned one colony to research, using classroom resources, the school library or the Internet. For your colony, your group should complete the checklist below. After your checklist is completed, share your results with the other groups for a final overview of Colonial America.

★ Colony name: _Mary land , Southern Colonies_ Year it was founded: _1633_

★ Reasons the colony was founded: _Maryland was founded as a haven for Roman catholics._

★ Its climate, major landforms, and bodies of water: _Climate: Sub tropical Major Landforms: the Atlantic, Plain, Piedmont and the Appalachian Bodies of water: Chesapeake Bay, and Atlantic Ocean._

★ Population of the colony in 1700, 1750, 1775: _Maryland Population:1700: 29,604, 1750 :141073 , 1775 :≈ 202,599_

★ Number of enslaved people in the colony at these select dates: _Maryland slave population 1700: 25,000_

★ Major ethnic groups living in the colony: _Maryland ethnic groups: Paleo - Indians_

★ Main religious groups in the colony: _Maryland religious groups catholics_

★ Major economic activities: _____

★ How the colony was governed: _____

★ Important events in the history of the colony: _____

LEARNING WITH GRAPHIC ORGANIZERS

Complete the graphic organizer below by describing three aspects of Colonial America.

Colonial Government	Everyday Life	Religious Freedom

CHAPTER 6 CONCEPT MAP

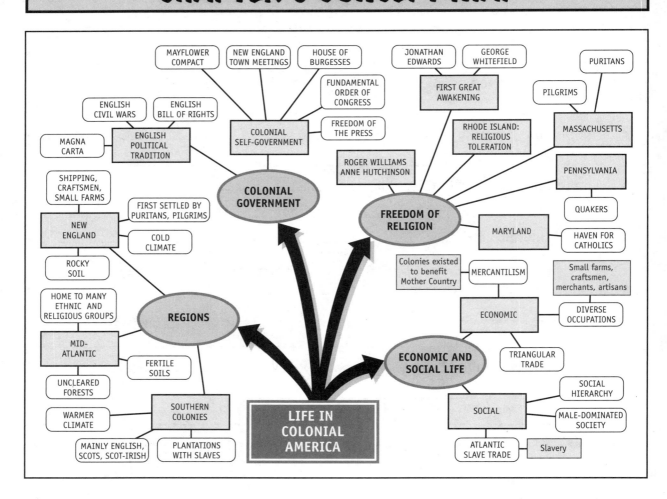

CHAPTER STUDY CARDS

Thirteen Colonies

There were 13 colonies along the Atlantic coast, consisting of three distinct regions:

★ **New England.**
 • Small farms, merchants.
 • Colder climates and rocky soil
★ **Middle Atlantic Colonies.**
 • Fertile soils and uncleared forests
 • People of many ethnic and religious backgrounds
★ **Southern Colonies.**
 • Warmer climates; grew cash crops
 • Included larger plantations with slaves

Economic and Social Life in Colonies

★ **Economy Based on Mercantilism.**
 • Colonists sold raw materials to Britain.
 • Britain sold finished goods to the colonies. This brought wealth to Britain.
★ **Colonial Occupations.** Most colonists were farmers. Many were also craftsmen.
★ **Colonial Society.** Wealthy landowners and merchants stood at the top, independent farmers were next, followed by craftsmen. At the bottom were unskilled laborers and slaves.

Colonial Government

★ **English Political Traditions.**
 • **Magna Carta (1215).** Guaranteed right of trial by jury; king could not impose new taxes without consent.
 • **Parliament.** Included lords and elected representatives in the Commons.
 • **English Civil War.** Parliament established supremacy over the King.
 • **English Bill of Rights (1689).** Guaranteed that Englishmen had certain rights.
★ **Colonial Self-Government.**
 • House of Burgesses (1619)
 • Mayflower Compact (1620)

Freedom of Religion

★ **Massachusetts.** Served as a haven to certain English religious groups:
 • **Pilgrims.**
 • **Puritans.**
★ **Rhode Island.** Established religious toleration.
 • **Roger Williams.**
 • **Anne Hutchinson.**
★ **First Great Awakening.** Emphasized the power of religion in people's lives.
 • **Jonathan Edwards.**
 • **George Whitefield.**

CHECKING YOUR UNDERSTANDING

Directions: Put a circle around the letter that best answers the question.

1   Which region of the thirteen colonies is represented by Cluster A?
   A   frontier region   (Geog 11(A))
   B   Middle Atlantic Colonies
   C   New England Colonies
   D   Southern Colonies

MAIN FEATURES OF THE BRITISH COLONIES

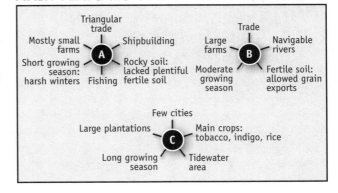

> *First,* EXAMINE **the question.** *This question tests your ability to identify a region of Colonial America based on its geography and economic activities.* RECALL **what you know.** *You should recall that the colonies could be divided into geographic regions: New England, the Middle Atlantic Colonies, and the Southern Colonies. If you* APPLY **what you know** *to these choices, you should realize that the three locations on the diagram identify these same three regions. Cluster A appears to describe characteristics of the New England Colonies. Therefore, the best answer is* **Choice C.**

Now try answering some additional questions on your own.

2   What were among the chief exports produced by colonists in Cluster C?
   F   whale oil and silver   **H**   textiles and tea   `Geog 11(A)`
   G   potatoes and fish   **J**   tobacco and rice

3   The differences between the three clusters in the diagram were mainly due to —
   A   geographic conditions   **C**   political beliefs   `Geog 11(B)`
   B   relations with England   **D**   religious practices

---

4   The Mayflower Compact was an important step in the development of American democracy because it —
   F   established the principle of separation of church and state   `Govt 15(A)`
   G   provided an example of colonial self-government
   H   defined relations with local Native American Indians
   J   outlawed slavery in the Massachusetts Bay Colony

5   Based on the graph, which statement is most accurate?
   A   In 1775, the majority of colonists came from Sweden.
   B   Most colonists could trace their roots to Europe.
   C   Colonists from Germany often faced discrimination.
   D   Few Africans were forced into a life of slavery.
   `Cult 23(A)`

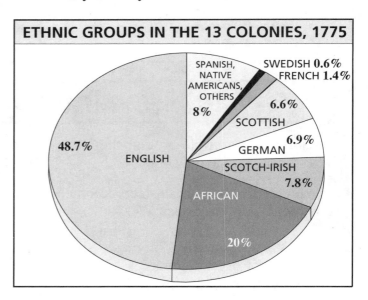

ETHNIC GROUPS IN THE 13 COLONIES, 1775

SWEDISH 0.6%
FRENCH 1.4%
SPANISH, NATIVE AMERICANS, OTHERS 8%
SCOTTISH 6.6%
GERMAN 6.9%
SCOTCH-IRISH 7.8%
ENGLISH 48.7%
AFRICAN 20%

6 With which statement would a Puritan minister in the colony of Massachusetts in 1660 have most likely agreed?

F   "All men and women are created equal."   `Hist 3(C)`
G   "No man should be required to worship against his will."
H   "Differences of opinion are essential for a society to improve."
J   "Both the government and church have a common purpose of promoting virtue."

7 How was the Virginia House of Burgesses important to the development of democracy in the thirteen colonies?

A   It was the first representative assembly in the colonies.   `Hist 3(B)`
B   It created the first written constitution in America
C   It included a bill of rights to protect individual rights.
D   It introduced the principle of electing judges.

8 In which colonial region did good harbors, abundant forests, rocky soil, and a short growing season most influence the economy?

F   Southern Colonies   `Geog 11(A)`
G   Northwest Territory
H   Middle Atlantic Colonies
J   New England Colonies

9

[T]he word of God requires that to maintain the peace and union of a people there should be an orderly and decent government established according to God, to order and dispose of the affairs of the people at all seasons as occasion shall require. [We] do associate … ourselves to be as one Public State or Commonwealth….

This case houses the original Fundamental Orders of Connecticut.

It is Ordered that there shall be yearly two General Assemblies or Courts, one … in April, the other in September following; the first shall be called the Court of Election, [it] shall be yearly chosen from time to time, Magistrates and other public Officers as [needed]: Whereof one [is] to be chosen governor for the year.

This passage from the Fundamental Orders of Connecticut was important to the concept of a democratic society because it represented —

A   an effort by the colonists to use force to resist the king   `Hist 3(B)`
B   a step toward self-government in Colonial America
C   an early attempt to institute voting rights for all colonists
D   an effort by the colonists to establish freedom of religion

10

Cruel Treatment	Poor Sanitary Conditions	Starvation and Disease	Overcrowding and Imprisonment

Using the information above, which group in Colonial America experienced these conditions?

F   Pilgrims on board the Mayflower   `Econ 12(B)`
G   indentured servants hired to work in the colonies
H   enslaved Africans during the "Middle Passage"
J   Native American Indians trading with French fur traders

---

11   Which historic document promised Englishmen the right to a trial by jury?
A   Magna Carta   `Govt 15(A)`
B   Mayflower Compact
C   Fundamental Orders of Connecticut
D   Great Awakening

12   The Fundamental Orders of Connecticut and the Virginia House of Burgesses are most closely associated with —
F   abuses by the British king   `Hist 3(B)`
G   colonial self-government
H   religious toleration
J   voting rights for all

13   What effect did geographic factors have on the economy of New England Colonies?
A   They encouraged the establishment of large plantations.   `Geog 11(A)`
B   They promoted the growth of fishing and shipping.
C   They increased the region's dependence on slave labor.
D   They supported the planting of rice and tobacco farming.

14   Which statement best expresses the religious views of Roger Williams?
F   "I favor the establishment of a state religion."   `Hist 3(C)`
G   "I approve of the persecution of certain religious groups."
H   "I support religious freedom and toleration in the colonies."
J   "I maintain that a colony should be governed by Church officials."

15   According to the theory of mercantilism, the principal purpose of the thirteen American colonies was to provide Great Britain with —
A   raw materials and markets   `Hist 4(A)`
B   naval bases
C   manufactured goods
D   military recruits

16   In which of the thirteen colonies were the towns of Boston, Salem, and Plymouth located?
F   Virginia   **H**   New York   `Geog 10(A)`
G   Massachusetts   **J**   Delaware

17 Which of these events is in the correct order in which they occurred? Hist 3(A)

    A Start of the Virginia House of Burgesses → Magna Carta → Great Awakening → Fundamental Orders of Connecticut

    B Magna Carta → Fundamental Orders of Connecticut → the Great Awakening → start of the Virginia House of Burgesses

    C Fundamental Orders of Connecticut → Great Awakening → Magna Carta → start of the Virginia House of Burgesses

    D Magna Carta → start of the Virginia House of Burgesses → Fundamental Orders of Connecticut → Great Awakening

18 Which statement most accurately describes the people who were allowed to vote in elections of representatives to colonial assemblies in British America?

    F They were colonists of means born in America. Hist 3(A)

    G They were men who owned property.

    H They were women who were able to read and write.

    J They were colonists born in England.

19 Which geographic conditions discouraged the development of a plantation economy in the New England Colonies?

    A a wide coastal plain and an absence of good harbors Geog 11(A)

    B rocky soil and a short growing season

    C numerous rivers and a humid climate

    D flatlands and a lack of forests

20 The painting to the right by John Singleton Copley (1765) shows Dr. Joseph Warren. This painting by Copley is typical of paintings in Colonial America in that it —

    F shows someone in the professions Cult 26(A)

    G is religious in nature

    H is a portrait

    J depicts a government official

21 Which city in the thirteen colonies is correctly paired with a geographic feature that contributed to its growth?

    A New Orleans — Great Lakes Geog 10(B)

    B New York City — Atlantic Ocean

    C Charleston — Mississippi River

    D Boston — Appalachian Mountains

22 Which best explains why colonial farmers settled near oceans or coastal waterways?

    F It was safer since fewer Native American Indians lived there. Geog 11(A)

    G Colonial governments often paid farmers to settle there.

    H The land was easier to clear since it had fewer trees and rocks.

    J Transportation by water of goods and crops was easier.

23 Which best describes an important effect of the First Great Awakening?

    A   Followers put suspected witches on trial.   `Cult 25(B)`

    B   Slavery was abolished in the colonies.

    C   Puritans in England immigrated to settlements in the New World.

    D   People became more emotionally engaged in religion.

24

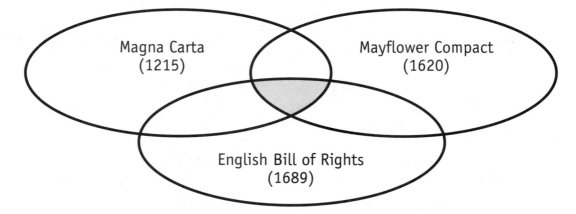

Using the diagram above, what important idea did these three historic documents have in common?

    F   The Parliament has control over the army.   `Govt 15(A)`

    G   English subjects enjoy certain basic human rights.

    H   The king cannot pass new laws without approval from nobles.

    J   The people in the community agree to make their laws and respect them.

25 During the 1700s, the triangular trade routes influenced the economy of the New England colonies by —

    A   encouraging the establishment of large plantations   `Econ 12(A)`

    B   promoting the growth of trade with the West Indies

    C   increasing New England's use of slave labor

    D   selling tobacco, rice and indigo from New England to England

26 Which best explains why colonial settlers first went to Plymouth Colony, Maryland, and Pennsylvania?

    F   to secure freedom from religious persecution   `Cult 23(A)`

    G   to search for gold and silver

    H   to bring spices to the New World

    J   to convert Native American Indians to Christianity

27 Which factor played an important role in the development of the plantation system in the South?

    A   A short growing season prevented the planting of most crops.   `Econ 12(B)`

    B   A lack of fertile soil limited agriculture.

    C   Colonial governments bought all the crops that plantations could produce.

    D   A warm climate permitted the growth of labor-intensive cash crops.

Name _____

THE AMERICAN REVOLUTION: THE ROAD TO INDEPENDENCE

TEKS COVERED IN CHAPTER 7

- **History 1A** Identify the major eras and events in U.S. history through 1877, including [the] revolution ... and describe their causes and effects.
- **History 1C** Explain the significance of the following dates: 1776, adoption of the Declaration of Independence.
- **History 4A** Analyze the causes of the American Revolution, including the Proclamation of 1763, the Intolerable Acts, the Stamp Act, mercantilism, lack of representation in Parliament, and British economic policies following the French and Indian War.
- **History 4B** Explain the roles played by significant individuals during the American Revolution, including Abigail Adams, John Adams, Wentworth Cheswell, Samuel Adams, Mercy Otis Warren, James Armistead, Benjamin Franklin, Crispus Attucks, King George III, Patrick Henry, Thomas Jefferson, the Marquis de Lafayette, Thomas Paine, and George Washington.
- **History 4C** Explain the issues surrounding important events of the American Revolution, including declaring independence; fighting the battles of Lexington, Concord, Saratoga, and Yorktown; enduring the winter at Valley Forge; and signing the Treaty of Paris of 1783.
- **Geography 10A** Locate places and regions directly related to major eras and turning points in the United States during the 18th-century.
- **Geography 10C** Analyze the effects of physical and human geographic factors such as weather, landforms, waterways, transportation, and communication on major historical and contemporary events in the United States.
- **Government 15C** Identify colonial grievances listed in the Declaration of Independence....
- **Government 15E** Explain the role of significant individuals such as ... John Locke in the development of self-government in colonial America.
- **Citizenship 19A** Define and give examples of unalienable rights.
- **Citizenship 20B** Analyze reasons for and the impact of selected examples of civil disobedience in U.S. history, such as the Boston Tea Party....
- **Citizenship 21A** Identify different points of view of political parties and interest groups on important historical issues.
- **Citizenship 22A** Analyze the leadership qualities of elected and appointed leaders of the United States such as George Washington....
- **Citizenship 22B** Describe the contributions of significant political, social, and military leaders of the United States, such as John Paul Jones....
- **Culture 23E** Identify the political, social, and economic contributions of women to American society.

In this chapter, you will study one of the most important events in American history — the American Revolution. You will learn how British colonists in North America objected to new taxes imposed by the British. This dispute, along with other issues such as the Proclamation Line of 1763, eventually brought the colonists into armed conflict with Great Britain. Actual fighting between the British army and the colonists broke out in Massachusetts at Lexington and Concord in 1775. Open warfare finally pushed colonial leaders to declare their independence from England a year later.

— IMPORTANT IDEAS —

A.   Britain defeated France in the **French and Indian Wars**. After the war, the colonists felt more secure, but Britain was left with a large debt in fighting the war.

B.   Some colonists hoped to settle in new western lands, but the British barred settlement west of the Appalachians in the **Proclamation of 1763**.

C.   The British passed the **Sugar Act of 1764**, reducing duties on sugar but enforcing laws against smugglers.

D.   The British imposed a series of new taxes on the colonists: the **Stamp Act**, the **Townshend Duties**, and the tea duty. In each of these, Parliament acted without consulting the colonists. The colonists saw "**taxation without representation**" as tyranny, believing such laws violated their rights as Englishmen. They protested in their colonial assemblies, boycotted British goods, and formed the **Sons of Liberty**.

E.   The British government sent more troops to the colonies to restore order and enforce their measures. A dispute between British solders and colonists in 1770 led to the "**Boston Massacre**."

F.   In December 1773, colonists threw tea overboard in the **Boston Tea Party** to protest the tea duty. Parliament responded with the **Intolerable Acts**, closing Boston Harbor. Most colonists sided with Massachusetts. In Philadelphia, colonial representatives met for the **First** and **Second Continental Congress**.

G.   Fighting broke out in **Lexington** and **Concord** in 1775, starting the **American Revolution**.

H.   The **Second Continental Congress** chose **George Washington** to lead the **Continental Army**. Washington successfully chased the British from Boston. The British went to New York, where Washington was unable to defeat them.

I.   Washington retreated to **Valley Forge** during the first winter of the war. Foreign officers like Steuben, Lafayette and Pulaski trained the colonial troops.

J.   In 1776, **Thomas Paine** argued in *Common Sense* that the colonies should declare independence. In 1776, the Second Continental Congress declared independence. **Thomas Jefferson** wrote most of the **Declaration of Independence**.

K.   In 1777, colonial forces defeated a British army at **Saratoga**, preventing a British plan to divide the colonies. After this victory, France joined on the side of the Americans. In 1781, Washington defeated the British at **Yorktown**, bringing the war to an end.

L.   The British recognized American independence in the **Treaty of Paris** in 1783.

ESS**ENT**IAL QUESTIONS

○— How did the French and Indian War make the colonies ripe for change?

○— Which British policies in the colonies led to disagreement?

○— How did colonial protests against British policies escalate to armed conflict?

○— How did individual leaders influence the course and outcome of the revolution?

KEY TERMS AND PEOPLE IN THIS CHAPTER

- John Locke
- Social Contract
- French and Indian War
- Proclamation Line (1763)
- King George III
- Samuel Adams
- Sugar Act
- Stamp Act
- Boston Massacre (1770)
- John Adams

- Abigail Adams
- Patrick Henry
- Wentworth Cheswell
- Mary Otis Warren
- Crispus Attucks
- Boston Tea Party
- Lexington / Concord
- George Washington
- Valley Forge
- Intolerable Acts

- Marquis de Lafayette
- Benjamin Franklin
- Thomas Jefferson
- Thomas Paine
- Decl. of Independence
- Unalienable Rights
- Battle of Saratoga
- Battle of Yorktown
- John Paul Jones
- James Armistead

THE FRENCH AND INDIAN WAR

By the 1750s, the British claimed control of the Ohio River Valley just across the Appalachians from the British colonies. Meanwhile, the French had built forts along the Great Lakes. They also claimed control of the Ohio River Valley, southwest of their settlements.

The French and Indian War was fought for control of North America.

War between Britain and France broke out in 1754. Because many Indian tribes sided with the French, the conflict became known in North America as the **French and Indian War**. French military bases were located in Quebec and Montreal, while the British had bases along the Hudson River. The area between them became the main battleground. In 1756, the war spread from North America to Europe.

A British force captured the French city of Quebec in 1759. This victory gave the British control of the St. Lawrence River. Under the terms of the peace treaty (1763), France lost most of its colonial empire in North America, including Canada and all lands east of the Mississippi River. These lands became British.

APPLYING WHAT YOU HAVE LEARNED

★ What was the main cause of the French and Indian War?

★ What were the main effects of the British victory in the French and Indian War?

CAUSES OF THE AMERICAN REVOLUTION

In 1763, North America was at peace. Only 12 years later, the colonists would again be at war. To understand the underlying causes of this new conflict, it is important to remember that the colonists had inherited the rights of "freeborn Englishmen" from the Magna Carta, the English Civil War, the Glorious Revolution, and the English Bill of Rights. In America, the colonists had also developed their own representative assemblies — such as the House of Burgesses and the General Court of Massachusetts.

By 1763, the colonists were therefore already used to a large degree of self-government. After the British victory, the colonists felt safer and less in need of British protection without the French threat along their borders. At the same time, the colonists became involved in a series of new disputes with the British government.

PROCLAMATION LINE OF 1763

The first of these disputes concerned the opening of the West. Following the victory in the French and Indian War, many colonists hoped to move to the new lands opened to them by the French defeat. Others hoped their children would find land there. A serious problem for the British, however, was maintaining peace with the Indians on these lands.

King George III issued a royal proclamation: to prevent further Indian attacks, the King declared that the colonists could not settle west of the Appalachian Mountains. The **Proclamation Line of 1763** was greatly resented by those colonists who had hoped to settle on these new western lands. The colonists saw this as an interference in their affairs. In addition, the British continued to keep an army in North America. American colonists saw these troops as further evidence of a British desire to maintain a standing army in the colonies to control them.

THE SUGAR ACT AND MERCANTILISM

Another source of conflict arose when, to enforce their mercantilist policies, the British government passed the **Sugar Act** in 1764. This act reduced the tax on imported sugar in half, but also took steps to enforce it more strictly. **Samuel Adams** (1722–1803), a journalist and politician in Boston, organized protests against the Sugar Act, which was repealed in 1766.

THE ISSUE OF TAXATION

Disagreements quickly arose over the right of the British Parliament to tax the colonists. After the French and Indian War, Britain faced a huge national debt. It also cost money to station British troops in the 13 colonies and the West Indies. In Britain, people already paid higher taxes than the colonists.

The British government therefore proposed a series of new taxes on the colonists. However, these taxes were passed by the British Parliament without first consulting the colonists. British leaders thought this was only right because the colonists were not paying their fair share towards their own defense. Since the colonists lived so far away from London, it seemed impossible for them to participate effectively in the British Parliament.

Taxation without Representation. Wealthy colonial merchants and landowners, used to acting in their colonial assemblies with little British interference, resented these new policies. Colonial leaders were also influenced by Enlightenment writers, like **John Locke** and **William Blackstone**. Locke had written that government was a "**social contract**." He said the purpose of government was to protect individual freedom and property. If a government failed to do this, Locke argued its citizens had the right to overthrow it. Blackstone defined the rights of individuals in English law, as well as property rights that could not be violated, even by the king.

John Locke

Following both Locke and English traditions, **Samuel Adams** and other colonists argued that the British government should not tax the colonists without their consent. These colonists believed that "**taxation without representation**" was "tyranny."

The Stamp Act. The next new British tax was the **Stamp Act** (1765). Parliament ordered that every newspaper, pamphlet, and other public or legal document had to be printed or written on paper with an official stamp, or seal, on it. This was a form of tax, because the British government was to be paid for the official stamp.

The Stamp Act created a firestorm of protests in the colonies. Colonists objected that the British government had imposed this new tax without their consent. Colonists held meetings, **boycotted** (*refused to buy*) British goods, and even attacked British officials in protest. In Virginia, **Patrick Henry** (1736–1799) denounced the Stamp Act, and the House of Burgesses passed resolutions against it. Samuel Adams organized a series of protests in Boston. A "Stamp Act Congress" against the act was held in New York City. Colonists produced petitions to the king and Parliament stating their position on these new taxes. These petitions argued that the colonists could only be taxed by their own consent.

A British tax collector is tied to a pole by an unruly crowd.

OPPOSITION GROWS

In response to colonial protests, the British repealed the Stamp Act, but now introduced the **Townshend Acts** (1767). These acts imposed duties (*special taxes*) on goods used in the colonies, including glass and lead. Again, Parliament passed these taxes without consulting representatives in the colonies. And once again, many colonists bitterly protested against these new taxes. They held rallies and organized into groups like the **Sons of Liberty**. To influence public opinion, they circulated pamphlets, newspapers, and political cartoons criticizing the new taxes.

Yet even in this crisis, most members of the Sons of Liberty continued to remain loyal to King George. They remained confident that the British Parliament would eventually repeal the new taxes.

ACTING AS AN AMATEUR HISTORIAN

This is part of a letter written in 1769 by George Washington to George Mason, a fellow Virginian:

"At a time, when our masters in Great Britain will be satisfied with nothing less than the [denial] of American freedom, it seems highly necessary that something should be done to avert [avoid] the strike, and maintain the liberty, which we derived from our ancestors. But the manner of doing it is the point in question. That no man should hesitate to use arms in defense of so valuable a blessing, on which life depends, is clearly my opinion. Yet arms should be the last resort. Addresses to the throne, and [petitions] to Parliament, we have already proved their inefficacy. How far their attention to our rights and privileges is to be awakened, by starving their trade and manufacturers, remains to be tried."

★ What action does George Washington suggest be avoided if possible?

★ What action does he suggest the American colonists should try next?

THE BOSTON MASSACRE

More British soldiers were sent to the colonies to stop the protests and to prevent further unrest. Eventually, about 4,000 British soldiers, equal to one-quarter of Boston's population, were sent. Their presence added to the growing bitterness between the colonists and the British government. These soldiers were poorly paid. Many worked at part-time jobs to meet their basic needs. In so doing, they were taking jobs needed by the colonists. Bad feelings reached a boiling point in 1770. A group of people in Boston taunted the soldiers and threw snowballs. By accident, the soldiers fired, and several protesters were killed.

Paul Revere's depiction of British soldiers firing on colonists.

Crispus Attucks, a man of mixed African and Native American Indian ancestry, was the first colonist killed. The soldiers were put on trial, but were ably defended by a young attorney, **John Adams** (1735–1826). Adams argued that the soldiers acted in self-defense and they were found to be innocent. Nevertheless, his cousin Samuel Adams and other opponents of British rule called this incident the "Boston Massacre." They circulated pictures and used this tragedy to win public support against the British.

ACTING AS AN AMATEUR HISTORIAN

The following statement was given by Captain Thomas Preston, of the 29th British Regiment, concerning events on March 5, 1770 (the Boston Massacre):

> "… I was soon informed of [a mob of colonists'] intention to carry off a soldier and murder him … I sent an officer and 12 men to protect the sentry and followed myself. The mob became more outrageous, raising their bludgeons and calling out, 'come on you scoundrels, fire if you dare.' I [used] all my power to persuade them to retire peaceably. They continued to advance. [Someone] asked if I intended to order the men to fire. I answered no.… While speaking, a soldier received a severe blow, and instantly fired his gun. Turning to ask him why he fired without orders, I was struck with a club on my arm, which had it been on my head would have destroyed me.…"

How do you think Samuel Adams' description of this event might have differed?

In 1772, Samuel Adams formed the first **Committee of Correspondence** with James Warren and his wife, **Mercy Otis Warren** (1728–1874). Mary wrote a series of pamphlets and satires against the British. The new Committees of Correspondence organized opponents of British polices throughout the colonies. With her husband off fighting, Mercy wrote the first history of the American Revolutionary War using her notes from meetings and conversations. Her ideas and writings convinced many people in the colonies to take up the Patriot cause.

Mercy Otis Warren

The Tea Duty and the Boston Tea Party. In response to colonial protests, the British again canceled all of the new taxes except the duty on tea. In the evening of December 1773, a group of colonists dressed as Mohawk Indians boarded three British ships in Boston Harbor and seized 45 tons of tea. They protested against the tea tax by dumping the tea into Boston Harbor.

Boston Tea Party

The Intolerable Acts. The "**Boston Tea Party**" brought a strong reaction from the British government. The **Intolerable Acts** (1774) closed Boston Harbor until the people of Boston paid for the lost tea. They also restricted the freedom of citizens in Massachusetts by eliminating the elected government council.

ACTING AS AN AMATEUR HISTORIAN

The following passage is from the Boston Port Act (1774), one of the Intolerable Acts:

> "… dangerous commotions and insurrections have been fomented and raised in the town of Boston, in the province of Massachusetts Bay, in New England, by divers ill-affected persons, to the subversion of his Majesty's government, and to the utter destruction of the public peace, and good order of the said town…. [It shall be unlawful to land in Boston] any goods, wares, or merchandise to be brought from any other country, or place, or any other part of the said province, upon pain of the forfeiture of the goods, merchandise, and of the said boat."

★ Restate this part of the Intolerable Acts in your own words.

★ Do you think the British were justified in taking such action? Explain you answer.

The King also now assumed the power to appoint all positions in the government of the colony. Accused officials could be tried in Britain instead of the colonies. These steps greatly increased tensions between the colonists and Great Britain. Lastly, the British government declared the right to "quarter," or house, British soldiers in unoccupied buildings in the colonies.

The Quebec Act. At the same time, the British government passed the **Quebec Act**. This act guaranteed the rights of the French in Canada to follow the Catholic religion. It also gave the

The Quartering Act forced colonists to house and feed British soldiers.

Ohio territory to Quebec and strengthened the power of royal officials in Quebec. These steps only served to further anger the American colonists.

APPLYING WHAT YOU HAVE LEARNED

★ Civil disobedience is a refusal to obey a law we think is unjust. In what way was the Boston Tea Party an example of civil disobedience? Do you think this act of civil disobedience was justified?

★ Make your own poster giving the British or colonial view in these disputes.

LEARNING WITH GRAPHIC ORGANIZERS

Describe each of the milestones along the road to the American Revolution.

French and Indian War (1755–1763)

The British won but at the expense of immense debt. Gained land: Ohio River Valley

Proclamation of 1763

Colonists were prohibited to settle west of Appalachian Mountains.

Sugar Act of 1764

Tax on sugar

Stamp Act of 1765

Tax on stamp, paper and legal documents

Townsend Acts of 1767

Tax on goods such as paint, lead, and glass in order to repay debt from the French-Indian war

Boston Massacre (1770)

Red coats fired at American protestors.

Boston Tea Party (1773)

Sons of Liberty disguised as indians throw over 45 tons of tea into Boston Harbor

Intolerable Acts (1774)

Boston Harbor closed by British until damages from tea were paid for.

THE AMERICAN REVOLUTION

LEARNING WITH GRAPHIC ORGANIZERS

Fill in the following chart by listing some of the causes of the American Revolution:

Political Causes
_____
_____
_____
_____
_____

Economic Clauses
_____
_____
_____
_____
_____

Social Causes
_____
_____
_____

THE ROAD TO INDEPENDENCE

The First Continental Congress. In 1774, representatives from the colonies met in Philadelphia to discuss their common concerns in the growing crisis. This assembly, known as the **First Continental Congress**, decided to continue protesting British taxes. They felt the British government had failed to **redress** (*remedy*) colonial grievances.

Lexington and Concord. Then in April 1775, open warfare finally broke out between British soldiers and colonial militia, known as "**Minutemen**." It began when British soldiers were sent to Lexington and Concord in Massachusetts to arrest several Patriot leaders and to capture a suspected storehouse of weapons. No one is sure who fired the first shots, but it was the "Shot Heard 'Round the World." This event marked the start of the **American Revolutionary War**.

Minutemen at the Battle of Concord.

THE STRUGGLE SPREADS

In May 1775, colonial representatives met again in Philadelphia for the **Second Continental Congress**. All of the colonies sent delegates to Philadelphia. Delegates included **John** and **Samuel Adams** from Massachusetts, **Benjamin Franklin** from Pennsylvania, and **Thomas Jefferson** from Virginia. The delegates quickly voted to join Massachusetts in its fight. In Williamsburg, Virginia, **Patrick Henry** (1736–1799) considered the finest orator in America, convinced the House of Burgesses to support the war with his stirring speech,

Patrick Henry, "The Voice of the American Revolution."

"Give me liberty or give me death." Although the Second Continental Congress lacked the legal authority to govern, it boldly assumed that responsibility.

The Continental Congress appointed **George Washington**, a Virginian who had fought in the French and Indian War, to lead the Continental Army. The selection of a Virginian helped to unify the colonies. Washington proceeded directly to Boston. In March 1776, using cannons captured by Ethan Allen at Fort Ticonderoga in upstate New York, Washington drove the British out of Boston. The British retreated to New York City.

APPLYING WHAT YOU HAVE LEARNED

Imagine that you and your classmates are representatives meeting in the Continental Congress. Hold an imaginary session in which you discuss: (1) complaints of the colonists against Great Britain; and (2) possible solutions to the crisis.

THOMAS PAINE'S *COMMON SENSE*

A variety of colonial viewpoints developed in response to the outbreak of war. **Loyalists** still wanted to remain under British rule. In the provinces of Canada, colonists stayed loyal to the Crown. There were also many Loyalists in the thirteen colonies. Some wanted to stay a part of the British Empire, but with more rights for the colonists. The Iroquois sided with the British, as did many black slaves, who were promised their freedom for helping the British in the war.

Thomas Paine, an Englishman living in the colonies, published a pamphlet, *Common Sense*, early in 1776. Paine believed it was ridiculous for America to be governed by a small, distant island across the vast ocean. He said the colonists derived no benefit from British rule. In fact, the British had dragged the colonists into European wars. Many **Patriots** (*supporters of the Revolution*) began to demand complete independence.

ACTING AS AN AMATEUR HISTORIAN

The passage below comes from Thomas Paine's pamphlet *"Common Sense."*

> "This new world hath been the asylum for the persecuted lovers of civil and religious liberty from every part of Europe. [Here] have they fled, not from the tender embraces of the mother, but from the cruelty of the monster; and it is so far true of England, that the same tyranny which drove the first emigrants from home, pursues their descendants still.… I challenge the warmest advocate for reconciliation to show a single advantage that this continent can reap by being connected with Great Britain. Why is it that we hesitate? From Britain we can expect nothing but ruin…. Everything that is right or reasonable pleads for separation. The blood of the slain, the weeping voice of nature cries, 'tis time to part.'"

★ What arguments does Paine use to support American independence?

★ If you were a Loyalist who supported the British cause, what arguments might you offer to counter those put forth by Paine?

THE DECLARATION OF INDEPENDENCE

Representatives of the **Second Continental Congress** began discussing the issue of American independence early in 1776. John Adams played an important role as leader of the movement for separation from England. A Virginian, Richard Henry Lee, proposed that the colonies declare their independence. Adams seconded the motion.

After much debate, the delegates decided to declare their independence from Britain. **Thomas Jefferson**, working as part of a small committee that included John Adams and Benjamin Franklin, wrote most of the **Declaration of Independence**. John Adams led the debate in the Continental Congress.

Much of our knowledge about the debates in the Continental Congress comes from the stream of letters between Adams and his wife, **Abigail Adams**. Her letters reveal a woman of keen intelligence with strong opinions. Her writing reveals a commitment to voting rights for women and African Americans, and fierce support for American independence.

Abigail Adams (1774–1818)

Major Ideas of the Declaration. This document, issued on **July 4, 1776**, explained the reasons why the colonists sought independence from Great Britain. Borrowing from the ideas of **John Locke**, Jefferson explained that government was a "social contract." Its purpose was to protect citizens' **unalienable rights**. These are rights that should not be taken away from citizens, including the right to "life, liberty, and the pursuit of happiness."

This philosophy teaches that each individual is endowed at birth with rights that are "unalienable" because they were given to us by our Creator. This idea of "unalienable rights" became a basic belief of American government — that some rights are derived from nature and may not be taken or violated by the government.

ACTING AS AN AMATEUR HISTORIAN _____

Jefferson argued that citizens had the right to overthrow an oppressive government to protect these unalienable rights. This argument is found in the most important paragraph of the Declaration:

> "We hold these truths to be self-evident, that all men are created equal, that they are endowed by their Creator with certain unalienable rights, that among these are Life, Liberty and the pursuit of Happiness — That to secure these rights, Governments are instituted among men, deriving their just powers from the consent of the governed, — That whenever any form of Government becomes destructive of these ends, it is the right of the People to alter or to abolish it, and to institute new Government...."

★ Briefly summarize this paragraph in your own words.

★ What justification did this paragraph give for the revolution against King George III?

The Declaration of Independence went on to list the grievances of the colonists against King George III and his ministers. Most of these grievances related to the belief that the British Crown was threatening the colonists' rights in favor of tyrannical rule.

The King imposed taxes on the colonists without their consent.	He made the military superior to the civil government.	He refused to answer colonial petitions for the redress of grievances.

GRIEVANCES AGAINST THE KING IN THE DECLARATION OF INDEPENDENCE

He asked citizens to give up their rights of representation.	He quartered large numbers of soldiers among the colonists.	He deprived the colonists of trial by jury.
He dissolved the colonists' representative assemblies.	He protected his soldiers against trial for murders of colonists.	He waged war against the American colonists.

THE ROAD TO VICTORY

In the first years of the war, the colonial army barely managed to escape disaster. Washington and the Continental Army occupied New York City in 1776. However, the British drove Washington and his army out of New York after the Battle of Long Island. British troops then occupied New York City.

The British next defeated Washington at the **Battle of White Plains**. He managed to keep his army intact and retreated across the Delaware River. In December 1776, hoping to catch Hessian mercenaries (*German hired troops*) by surprise, he re-crossed the Delaware at night and defeated them at the **Battle of Trenton**. This victory assured Washington's continued command as head of the Continental Army and raised morale among the colonists.

ACTING AS AN AMATEUR HISTORIAN

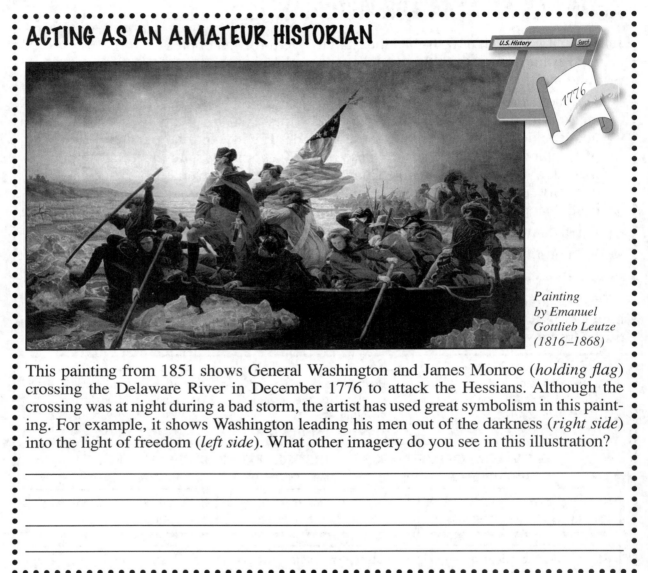

Painting by Emanuel Gottlieb Leutze (1816–1868)

This painting from 1851 shows General Washington and James Monroe (*holding flag*) crossing the Delaware River in December 1776 to attack the Hessians. Although the crossing was at night during a bad storm, the artist has used great symbolism in this painting. For example, it shows Washington leading his men out of the darkness (*right side*) into the light of freedom (*left side*). What other imagery do you see in this illustration?

_____

_____

_____

_____

THE BATTLE OF SARATOGA

While the colonists were debating their future independence, British troops remained in New York City. The British had a plan to win the war by dividing the colonies in two through New York. A divided America would be easier to defeat. Three British armies were to meet in the middle of the colony. However, British General Howe delayed the plan when he first left New York City to attack Philadelphia instead of marching directly north. The second British force turned back instead of marching along the Mohawk River.

The plan then failed entirely when the largest army, commanded by General **John Burgoyne**, was defeated at Saratoga in 1777 by General **Horatio Gates**. General Burgoyne was unprepared because, like many British generals, he held the erroneous belief that the rebels were ignorant farmers who could easily be swept away by highly trained British regulars.

One of those fighting in Saratoga was church leader, historian, and judge **Wentworth Cheswell** (1746–1817). Cheswell is considered the first African American elected to public office in America.

The **Battle of Saratoga** marked a turning point in the war. The victory at Saratoga helped Ben Franklin and John Adams, who had been sent overseas to persuade the French government to supply military assistance to the Americans.

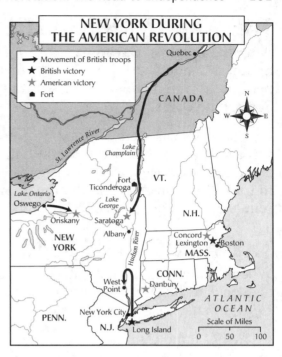

NEW YORK DURING THE AMERICAN REVOLUTION

→ Movement of British troops
★ British victory
☆ American victory
■ Fort

THE WINTER OF 1777–1778 AT VALLEY FORGE

Despite the victory at Saratoga, the war was far from over. The Continental Congress had to leave Philadelphia, which was occupied by British troops. Washington and his battle-weary army spent the winter at **Valley Forge** in Pennsylvania. Here, Washington faced the problem of feeding his 12,000 troops, and even faced threats to his leadership from some of his officers. Long marches had destroyed the soldiers' shoes, and warm blankets were scarce. There were desertions, and many suffered from diseases such as typhus, typhoid, and pneumonia. Although no battle was fought at Valley Forge, it represented a major test for the new Continental Army.

Washington at Valley Forge

Washington used his time at Valley Forge to train and discipline his troops. Foreign volunteers, like Baron von Steuben from Germany and the **Marquis de Lafayette** (1757–1834) from France, helped train the soldiers of the Continental Army. Although the French King forbid him from going to America because France was not at war with England, Lafayette purchased a ship and gathered a group of French officers to help in the struggle. His volunteer service was seen as a major triumph for the American cause.

THE WAR IN THE SOUTH

After the **Battle of Saratoga**, most of the fighting moved to the South. The British thought Southern landowners would be sympathetic to England. The American Revolution also became an international war. Not only France but also Spain allied with the colonists against the British.

The colonists were assisted by **James Armistead** (1760–1830), an African-American slave who acted as a spy. General Lafayette was in desperate need of reliable information about enemy movements. Armistead began posing as an escaped slave, which allowed him to travel freely between both armies. He acted as an orderly and guide to the British, then sent back what he learned to Lafayette.

THE WAR ON THE SEAS

When the war began, the British enjoyed complete naval superiority. The American colonists lacked their own navy. Instead, the colonists relied mostly on **privateers** (*private ships*) to attack British shipping.

In 1775, the Continental Congress provided funds to create a small navy of warships. In 1779, **John Paul Jones** (1747–1792) became America's first naval hero. Commanding the *Bonhomme Richard*, he faced a larger British warship with more firepower. During the battle, when Jones was asked to surrender, he replied "I've not yet begun to fight!" Jones managed to win the battle — the first victory for an American warship. Jones' victory served to boost the morale of the colonists.

Battle between the Bonhomme Richard and the Serapis, 1779.

THE BATTLE OF YORKTOWN (1781)

After several more years of fighting, General Washington managed, with French help, to force General Charles Cornwallis and the main British army into a corner at **Yorktown**, Virginia. The French fleet blocked their escape by sea. After a few days of combat, Cornwallis and his 8,000 British soldiers were forced to surrender in October 1781.

Cornwallis surrenders to Washington.

The Battle of Yorktown turned out to be the last major battle of the war. Occasional fighting continued after the surrender at Yorktown, and Washington feared the war might still drag on for another year. However, when word reached England of the defeat at Yorktown, the Prime Minister was forced to resign and the new government decided to give up the fight.

INDEPENDENCE RECOGNIZED

The **Treaty of Paris of 1783** formally ended the American Revolutionary War. Under its terms, the British recognized the independence of the colonies. The British promised to remove all of their troops from the country. In addition, they gave all the land between the Mississippi River and the Atlantic, from the Great Lakes to the border with Florida, to the new United States. This move gave the new nation twice the area of the former colonies.

A variety of factors were responsible for the American victory over Great Britain, then the world's richest and most powerful empire:

THE AMERICAN VICTORY WAS DUE TO MANY FACTORS

Fighting for their Homeland. The colonists were defending their own soil. The British were fighting a war thousands of miles from their homeland.

Methods of Warfare. Colonial forces used unconventional methods to fight the British. They took advantage of hiding behind trees and other tactics. The British fought in a more traditional manner, with soldiers aligned in a straight formation out in the open.

Local Support. The Continental Army received support from the local population, including women. The British were fighting a war on a hostile terrain. Nevertheless, the British did receive support from Loyalists, and used Canada as a refuge and as a staging ground for attacks against the colonists.

Leadership. Washington was a very capable general. He received help from experienced foreign military leaders, such as Baron von Steuben, Kasimir Pulaski, and Marquis de Lafayette. These European volunteers helped turn the Continental army into a more disciplined fighting force.

The French Alliance. Volunteers, money, troops and naval support from France were essential to the American victory.

LEARNING WITH GRAPHIC ORGANIZERS

Using the spaces below, provide a picture and a brief two or three-line summary for each of these individuals who played a key role in the American Revolution. Use information in the chapter or go on the Internet to find more information.

Abigail Adams: Spouse of John Adams. Mother of John Quincy Adams. Open minded towards women's rights.

Put your picture here

John Adams: Spouse of Abigail Adams. Father John Quincy Adams. Second President of the United States.

Put your picture here

Samuel Adams: American statesman, political philosopher. One of the United States founding fathers. Member of the Sons of Liberty

Put your picture here

James Armistead: Was an enslaved African American. Served in the continental Army during the American Revolution. Was a double agent for the continental Army.

Put your picture here

Crispus Attucks: African and Native American decent. First Man killed in the American Revolution

Put your picture here

Wentworth Cheswell: _____

_____

_____

_____

Put your
picture
here

Benjamin Franklin: _____

_____

_____

_____

Put your
picture
here

Patrick Henry: _____

_____

_____

_____

Put your
picture
here

Thomas Jefferson: _____

_____

_____

_____

Put your
picture
here

Marquis de Lafayette: _____

_____

_____

_____

Put your
picture
here

Thomas Paine: _____

_____

_____

_____

Put your
picture
here

Mary Otis Warren: _____
_____
_____
_____

Put your picture here

George Washington: _____
_____
_____
_____

Put your picture here

ACTING AS AN AMATEUR HISTORIAN

In this chapter you read about some of the British economic policies imposed on the colonists in the decade after the French and Indian War. Notice that the signs are blank. Suppose that these are colonists demonstrating against British policies. Fill in the signs with phrases you think they might have written. Then, in the space below, explain why you picked those particular phrases for your signs.

_____
_____
_____
_____
_____

Name _____

CHAPTER 7 CONCEPT MAP

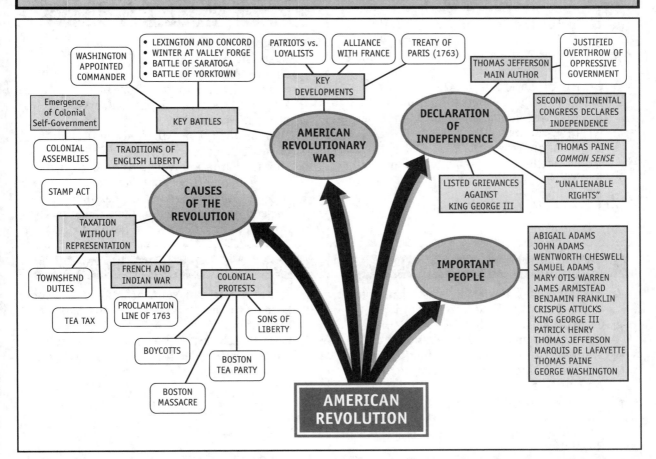

CHAPTER STUDY CARDS

American Revolution

★ **Causes of Revolution.** British wanted to tax colonies to repay debts from the French and Indian War; Colonists felt they were not being represented in British Parliament.
  • Proclamation Line of 1763
  • Stamp Act (1765)
  • Townshend Acts (1767)
  • Tea Act (1773)
  • Boston Tea Party (1773)
  • Intolerable Acts (1774)

★ **Effects of Revolution.**
  • Declaration of Independence (1776)
  • British recognized American independence.

Declaration of Independence, 1776

★ Issued by the Second Continental Congress on **July 4, 1776**.
★ Written primarily by Thomas Jefferson.
★ Stated to the world the reasons why the colonies were declaring their independence.
★ Announced the purpose of government was to protect the people's unalienable rights — life, liberty, and the pursuit of happiness.
★ It declared the right of people to overthrow a government that oppresses its people.
★ Included a list of grievances by the colonists against the British King George III.

Key Revolutionary Battles and Events

★ **Lexington and Concord (1775).** Marked the start of the American Revolutionary War.
★ **Winter at Valley Forge (1776).** General Washington spent winter regrouping.
★ **Battle of Saratoga (1777).** British were beaten. The battle marked the turning point in war. The French concluded an alliance with the colonists afterwards.
★ **Battle of Yorktown (1781).** Marked the last major battle of the American Revolution; British surrendered to General Washington in Virginia.
★ **Treaty of Paris (1783).** Ended the war.

Important Individuals in the American Revolution

★ **Benjamin Franklin** – Statesman; writer; scientist.
★ **Samuel Adams** – A radical leader who organized resistance to British taxes.
★ **King George III** – Supported attempts to discipline colonists.
★ **Thomas Jefferson** – Drafted the Declaration of Independence.
★ **Thomas Paine** – Advocate for independence in his pamphlet, *Common Sense*.
★ **George Washington** – Successfully commanded the Continental Army against the British during the American Revolution.

Other Important Individuals (2)

★ **Abigail Adams.** Her letters were a main source of life during the American Revolution.
★ **John Adams.** Led the debate for independence; became the Second President of U.S.
★ **Wentworth Cheswell.** He fought at the Battle of Saratoga; became the first elected African American.
★ **Mercy Otis Warren.** Stirred colonists against British policies with her writings; she is considered "First Lady" of the American Revolution.

Other Important Individuals (3)

★ **James Armistead.** An African American who became the first double spy in the American Revolution.
★ **Crispus Attucks.** African American who was the first person killed at the Boston Massacre.

CHECKING YOUR UNDERSTANDING

1

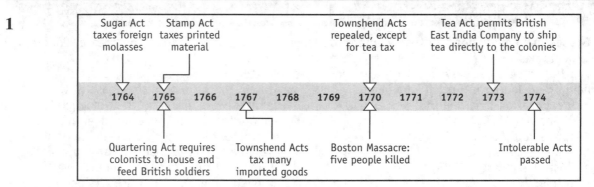

Sugar Act taxes foreign molasses | Stamp Act taxes printed material | Townshend Acts repealed, except for tea tax | Tea Act permits British East India Company to ship tea directly to the colonies

1764 1765 1766 1767 1768 1769 1770 1771 1772 1773 1774

Quartering Act requires colonists to house and feed British soldiers | Townshend Acts tax many imported goods | Boston Massacre: five people killed | Intolerable Acts passed

Which title most accurately describes this timeline?
A   Forms of Colonial Protest
B   The Effects of British Navigation Acts
C   British policies leading to the American Revolution
D   The Abuse of Power by American Colonial Legislatures

[Hist 1(A)]

First, E̲XAMINE **the question.** This question tests your ability to identify what is common among a group of events along a time-line. R̲ECALL **what you know.** Each of these events are tied together by being related in some way to the American Revolutionary War. A̲PPLY **what you know** to the choices. **Choices A, B,** and **D** are all related to the American Revolution but they are too narrowly defined to include all of the events on the timeline. You should realize that only **Choice C** would be an appropriate title that ties all of these events together under one title.

Now try answering some additional questions on your own.

2   The economic system illustrated by this cartoon was opposed by later American colonists because it —

F   supported colonial manufacturing   `Hist 4(A)`
G   took gold and silver from American mines
H   required colonists to sell their raw materials to and buy their finished goods from England
J   prohibited colonists from fishing or trading in furs

3

The Boston Gazette	The London Gazette
• April, 1775 •	• April, 1775 •
The British Redcoats came in sight just before sunrise. The British commanding officer spoke to our militia: "Disperse, you rebels, throw down your arms and disperse." Upon which American troops gave a yell, and immediately one or two British officers discharged their pistols, followed by gun fire from four or five British soldiers.	Six companies of light infantry at Lexington found a body of the country people under arms. The King's troops marched up to them to ask the reason of their being so assembled. Several guns were fired on the King's troops from behind a stone wall, and from other houses. As a result, the troops returned fire and killed several of them.

These two accounts relate to the firing of the first shots of the American Revolution at Lexington, Massachusetts. Based on these accounts, what conclusion can be drawn?

A   American militia men fired the first shots at Lexington.   `Citi 21(A)`
B   The British fired the first shots of the American Revolution.
C   Secondary sources are more accurate than primary sources.
D   The point of view of the writer may lead to some bias in the account.

4   According to the Declaration of Independence, the main purpose of government is to —
F   protect the rights of individuals
G   provide strong military leadership   Hist 4(C)
H   protect a nation from foreign invasions
J   ensure the stability of a country's economy

5   The main purpose for writing the Declaration of Independence was to —
A   declare war on Great Britain   Hist 4(C)
B   force Spain to support the Revolutionary War
C   convince Great Britain to abolish slavery
D   state the colonists' reasons for separating from Great Britain

6

Person A	Person B
Helped start the Committees of Correspondence.	An African American slave.
Wrote pamphlets against the British and an early history of the Revolution.	Spied on British troop movements and reported it to the Americans.

Which two individuals, who played key roles in the American Revolution, are described in columns A and B in the chart above?
F   Mercy Otis Warren and James Armistead   Hist 4(B)
G   Benjamin Franklin and Patrick Henry
H   John Adams and Wentworth Cheswell
J   Thomas Paine and Crispus Attucks

7   The authors of the Declaration of Independence used the phrase "Life, Liberty and the pursuit of Happiness." This phase was used to identify —
A   unalienable rights   Citi 19(A)
B   legal rights
C   states rights
D   economic rights

8   The main reason that Great Britain established the Proclamation Line of 1763 was to —
F   allow Canada to control the Great Lakes region   Hist 4(A)
G   avoid conflicts between American colonists and Native American Indians
H   make profits by selling the land west of the Appalachian Mountains
J   protect the French Catholics of Quebec

9   Which geographic feature served as the western boundary for British colonial settlements prior to the American Revolutionary War?
A   Rocky Mountains   Geog 10(C)
B   Appalachian Mountains
C   Mississippi River
D   Great Plains

10 The American colonists used the slogan, "No taxation without representation," to express their belief in the need for —

    F economic interdependence   Hist 4(A)

    G the consent of the governed

    H mercantilism

    J Parliamentary supremacy

11

> I challenge the warmest advocate for reconciliation, to [show] a single advantage that this continent can reap by being connected with Great Britain. I repeat, not a single advantage is derived. Our corn will fetch its price in any market in Europe, and our imported goods must be paid, buy them where we will….
>
> — *Thomas Paine, 1776*

In this statement, Paine suggested that the American colonies should —

    A negotiate an end to the conflict with England   Hist 4(B)

    B form an alliance with England

    C declare independence from England

    D boycott goods from England

12 Which document included the idea first suggested by John Locke that people have a right to overthrow a government that oppresses them?

    F Mayflower Compact   Citi 20(A)

    G Declaration of Independence

    H Fundamental Orders of Connecticut

    J Proclamation of 1763

13

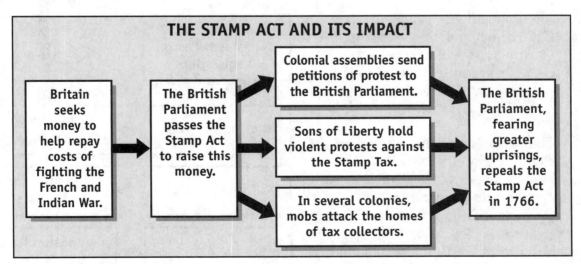

THE STAMP ACT AND ITS IMPACT

Britain seeks money to help repay costs of fighting the French and Indian War. → The British Parliament passes the Stamp Act to raise this money. →

- Colonial assemblies send petitions of protest to the British Parliament.
- Sons of Liberty hold violent protests against the Stamp Tax.
- In several colonies, mobs attack the homes of tax collectors.

→ The British Parliament, fearing greater uprisings, repeals the Stamp Act in 1766.

Based on the chart, what was a major effect of the Stamp Act?

    A The colonists no longer needed British goods.   Hist 4(A)

    B The British refused to sell certain products to the colonists.

    C The law led to a decline in the value of colonial currency.

    D Many colonists participated in actions in opposition to the act.

14 According to the theory of mercantilism, the principal purpose of the thirteen original colonies was to provide Great Britain with —
F workers and manufactured goods   **H** naval bases   Hist 4(A)
G raw materials and markets   **J** military recruits

15 The principles of government that Thomas Jefferson included in the Declaration of Independence were most influenced by
A John Locke's social contract theory   Citi 20(A)
B Cotton Mather's sermons on religion
C King George's belief in divine right
D William Penn's views on religious toleration

16 Which set of events is in the correct chronological order?
F Boston Tea Party → Declaration of Independence → French and   Hist 1(A)
Indian War → Signing of the Magna Carta
G The Fundamental Orders of Connecticut → French and Indian War → Boston Tea Party → Declaration of Independence
H Declaration of Independence → French and Indian War → Boston Tea Party → The Mayflower Compact
J French and Indian War → Declaration of Independence → Start of Town Meetings in New England → Boston Tea Party

17 Which conclusion is best supported by the information in the chart?
A The Stamp Act led to widespread smuggling.
B Colonists raised revenue by imposing new taxes.
C British policies were opposed by many colonists.
D The colonists reacted to British laws in a nonviolent way.
Hist 4(A)

18 The series of events shown in the chart led directly to the —
F surrender of the Dutch in New York to England in 1664
G start of the French and Indian War
H issuance of the Proclamation Line of 1763
J outbreak of the American Revolution
Hist 4(A)

19 Which statement is most consistent with the views of Samuel Adams?

A   Taxation without representation is tyranny.   `Hist 4(B)`

B   Colonists should be grateful to be part of the British Empire.

C   Citizens, under British rule, should support King George III.

D   The English King deserves respect and loyalty from his subjects.

20 Which action by the colonists could be categorized as an act of civil disobedience?

F   colonists throwing British tea into Boston Harbor   `Citi 20(C)`

G   placing restrictions on trade with Spain and France

H   paying the stamp tax to British tax collectors

J   firing guns at British soldiers at Lexington and Concord, Massachusetts

21

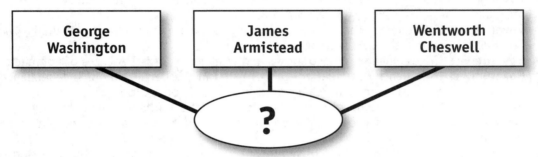

Which title best completes this web diagram?

A   Signers of the Declaration of Independence   `Hist 4(B)`

B   Participants in the Boston Massacre

C   Heroes of the American Revolution

D   Artists of the Colonial Period

22

> I long to hear that you have declared an independency; and by the way in the new code of laws which I suppose it will be necessary for you to make, I desire you would remember the ladies, and be more generous and favorable to them than your ancestors. Do not put such unlimited power into the hands of the husbands. Remember, men would be tyrants if they could. If particular care and attention is not paid to the ladies, we are determined to foment a rebellion....

Whose views are represented in this passage?

F   Benjamin Franklin   H   George Washington   `Hist 4(B)`

G   James Armistead   J   Abigail Adams

---

23 Why were the colonists angered by issuance of the Proclamation of 1763?

A   It took too much land from Canada.   `Hist 4(A)`

B   It gave territory in Florida to France.

C   It limited their freedom to move west.

D   It promoted raids by Native American Indians.

CHAPTER 8

ESTABLISHING A NEW GOVERNMENT, 1777 TO 1788

TEKS
COVERED IN
CHAPTER 8

- **History 1A** Identify the major eras and events in U.S. history through 1877, including the creation and ratification of the Constitution, ... and describe their causes and effects.
- **History 1B** Explain the significance of writing of the U.S. Constitution....
- **History 4D** Analyze the issues of the Constitutional Convention of 1787, including the Great Compromise and the Three-Fifths Compromise.
- **History 6A** Explain how the Northwest Ordinance established principles and procedures for orderly expansion of the United States.
- **Government 15A** Identify the influence of ideas from historic documents, including *The Federalist Papers*, on the U.S. system of government.
- **Government 15B** Summarize the strengths and weaknesses of the Articles of Confederation.
- **Government 15C** Identify colonial grievances listed in the Declaration of Independence and explain how those grievances were addressed in the U.S. Constitution....
- **Government 15D** Analyze how the U.S. Constitution reflects the principles of limited government, republicanism, checks and balances, federalism, separation of powers, popular sovereignty, and individual rights.
- **Government 15E** Explain the role of significant individuals such as ... Charles de Montesquieu in the development of self-government in colonial America.
- **Government 16A** Summarize the purposes for amending the U.S. Constitution.
- **Government 17A** Analyze the arguments of the Federalists and Anti-Federalists, including those of Alexander Hamilton, Patrick Henry, James Madison, and George Mason.
- **Citizenship 21C** Summarize a historical event in which compromise resulted in a resolution....

In this chapter, you will learn how Americans established a new system of government after achieving their independence from Britain. You will also learn how the Articles of Confederation proved too weak to govern the new nation, and how a new Constitution was written in 1787 and adopted in 1788.

KEY TERMS AND PEOPLE IN THIS CHAPTER

- Articles of Confederation
- Northwest Ordinance
- Northwest Territory
- Shays' Rebellion
- Constitutional Convention
- "Great Compromise"
- "Three-fifths Compromise"

- Commerce Compromise
- Republicanism
- Federalism
- Charles de Montesquieu
- Separation of Powers
- Checks and Balances
- Limited Government

- Popular Sovereignty
- Limited Government
- Amendment
- Ratification
- Federalists
- Anti-Federalists
- *Federalist Papers*

— IMPORTANT IDEAS —

A. After declaring independence from Great Britain, each colony became an independent state and adopted its own state constitution.

B. The **Second Continental Congress** enacted the **Articles of Confederation**. This created a loose confederation of states. Each state had one vote in the Confederation Congress, and nine states were needed to pass a law. The Confederation Congress controlled foreign affairs but was unable to raise its own army or collect taxes. It depended on the state governments for support.

C. The Confederation Congress passed the **Northwest Ordinance** in 1787, establishing principles for the orderly future expansion of the United States. Slavery was prohibited in the Northwest Territory.

D. The new nation faced many problems under the Articles of Confederation. States taxed goods from other states, and each state printed its own money, making trade difficult. In 1786, farmers in Massachusetts rose up in **Shays' Rebellion**. Although it was put down by state militia, there was no national army if it had spread.

E. American leaders decided a stronger government was needed. At Annapolis, they decided to invite delegates to Philadelphia to revise the Articles.

F. The **Constitutional Convention** was held in Philadelphia in 1787. The delegates soon decided to abandon the Articles and write a new constitution.

G. The delegates agreed that the new government should be based on the principles of **republicanism, popular sovereignty**, and **limited government**. They also agreed on the need for a stronger national government. They followed the advice of the French writer Montesquieu in establishing a separation of powers with three branches of government.

H. Several important issues divided members of the Convention. Delegates from larger states wanted representation in Congress by size, while smaller states wanted each state to be equal. The **"Great Compromise"** settled the dispute.

I. A second issue divided the delegates over the issue of how slaves would be counted towards a state's representation in Congress. The issue was settled with the **"Three-fifths Compromise."**

J. The new constitution established the principles of **federalism, popular sovereignty, limited government, separation of powers**, and **checks and balances** to make sure the new central government would not become too strong.

K. The **Preamble** of the Constitution stated the purposes of the new government. The delegates also created a process to amend the Constitution.

L. After the Constitution was completed, the country debated whether to **ratify** (*approve*) it. **Anti-Federalists** believed the new government would be too strong and tyrannical. **Federalists** believed a stronger government was needed and that the principles of federalism and separation of powers were sufficient safeguards to protect individual liberties.

M. The Constitution was ratified after its supporters promised a **Bill of Rights**.

Ess(ENT)ial Questions

- What were the Articles of Confederation?
- What conditions led Americans to change their system of government?
- What issues were resolved at the Constitutional Convention?
- How well did the new Constitution embody the principles of the Declaration of Independence?

WHAT IS GOVERNMENT?

By nature, human beings are social. They must live in communities in order to survive. Communities need to make rules, decide disputes, and protect their members from aggressors. The body given the authority to carry out binding decisions for a community is known as its **government**.

In fact, the word *govern* comes from an ancient Greek word for steering a ship. Just as a pilot guides a ship, a government guides the conduct of the members of a community in their dealings with each other and outsiders. The government makes rules that members of the community must follow, and it has the power to enforce those rules. It represents the community in dealing with other communities.

POWERS OF GOVERNMENT

Governments possess three powers to carry out their authority:

- **Legislative Power** (to the make laws)
- **Judicial Power** (to apply the laws to specific situations)
- **Executive Power** (to carry out the laws)

REPRESENTATIVE DEMOCRACY

Once people are in a situation in which they must create a new government, another question immediately arises — *What type of government should they create?* Creating a government is a matter of great concern to each member of society. Why do they give people whom they hardly know power over their lives? And how much power can be given to a government without encouraging it to threaten their liberties?

Americans had many different types of government from which to choose after independence. They could have created a monarchy, a constitutional monarchy, or a **representative democracy** — rule by popularly elected representatives. In **1776**, the colonists chose to establish a representative democracy. Creating a stable democracy proved to be a difficult challenge.

THE ARTICLES OF CONFEDERATION

The first governments of the new United States were actually established at the state, not the national level. After declaring independence, each former colony became an independent state. Colonial charters were rewritten as state constitutions.

Americans also recognized the need for some form of central, or national, government. The Continental Congress itself was inadequate to serve as a permanent form of national government. But because of their recent experiences with British rule, the former colonists were afraid of creating a central government that would be too powerful. The Constitutional Congress drafted the **Articles of Confederation** in 1776 and 1777 to solve this problem.

After the Articles of Confederation were written, the document had to be approved by each state before it could become official. Although the Articles were sent to the states in November 1777, it took almost four years, until March of 1781, for each state to *approve* them in full.

ACTING AS AN AMATEUR HISTORIAN

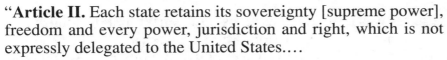

The thirteen new states finally adopted the Articles of Confederation in 1781. Here are some of its major provisions:

> "**Article II.** Each state retains its sovereignty [supreme power], freedom and every power, jurisdiction and right, which is not expressly delegated to the United States.…
>
> **Article III.** The States hereby enter into a firm league of friendship with each other, for their common defense, the security of their liberties, and their general welfare, binding themselves to assist each other against all attacks upon them.…
>
> **Article V.** In determining questions in the United States in Congress assembled, each State shall have one vote.
>
> **Article VI.** No State, without the consent of the Congress, shall enter into any conference, alliance or treaty with any king, prince or state."

★ What were the goals of the new Confederation?

★ Identify one advantage and one disadvantage of one of the articles above.

STRUCTURE OF THE CONFEDERATION GOVERNMENT

Members of the Continental Congress feared that individual freedom might be threatened by the national government if it had too much power. Therefore, the Articles of Confederation deliberately placed more power in the hands of the individual states, making the new national government very weak. It was only a loose association — a "league of friendship," with only one branch of government — the Congress.

POWERS OF CONGRESS

Each state could send several delegates, but had only one vote in the new Confederation Congress. In this way, each state was given equal representation. The powers of the Confederation Congress were extremely limited. It could declare war and settle disputes between states, issue currency, and conduct affairs with Indian tribes and foreign countries. It could also command its own army, but it depended on the states to raise the soldiers for this army. There was no central executive and no national court system in the new government.

The new Congress could not even collect its own taxes. For revenue, each state was given an amount to pay based on the value of its land. This was meant to cover the costs of providing for the nation's "common defense." The Articles of Confederation failed to include a way of requiring a state to turn over its tax monies to the Congress.

The Articles of Confederation

Since the Confederation Congress relied on the states to give it money, it is not surprising that it found itself unable to pay its debts, either at home or abroad. The states failed to supply the Confederation government with enough funds to meet its needs.

The support of nine states was needed to pass most laws, making it difficult for the new Confederation Congress to enact new legislation. The Congress also lacked the power to regulate the national economy. States could even tax goods from other states and issue their own money.

ARTICLES OF CONFEDERATION

Powers of the Confederation Government	Limits on the Confederation Government	Structure of the Confederation Government
• Declare war • Negotiate treaties • Manage foreign affairs • Coin (print) money • Establish a postal system • Establish a military from troops contributed by states	• No power to enforce laws • No national courts to settle disputes between the states • No power to tax • No power to regulate trade: could not put tariffs on foreign goods	• One branch of government: Congress (a one-house legislature) • One vote in Congress for each state • No national executive • No national courts

ACHIEVEMENTS

Despite its shortcomings, the Articles of Confederation created a national government that had some important achievements. It successfully concluded the peace treaty with Britain, ending the American Revolution. It helped develop the concept of **limited government** — a system in which government has only certain powers and cannot act beyond the powers it was specifically given. The Articles of Confederation also developed the idea that American citizenship included both **privileges** and **immunities** (*rights to take certain actions without penalty*). State governments could not deny these privileges and immunities to citizens who came from other states.

The Confederation Congress also passed the **Land Ordinance of 1785** and the **Northwest Ordinance of 1787**. These acts prohibited slavery in the Northwest Territory, encouraged free public education, and guaranteed both religious freedom and trial by jury. Procedures were also established for governing the **Northwest Territory**, which was divided into smaller territories.

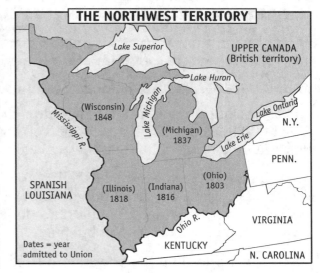

THE NORTHWEST TERRITORY

The Northwest Ordinance introduced a method for admitting these territories into the Union as new states once a population of 60,000 people was achieved within each territory. The new states were admitted on terms of complete equality with the original thirteen states.

ACTING AS AN AMATEUR HISTORIAN

The **Northwest Ordinance of 1787** spurred the westward expansion of the United States. Here is one of the most important provisions of this document:

> "**Article 5.** There shall be formed in the territory, not less than three nor more than five States; And when any of the said States shall have sixty thousand free inhabitants, such State shall be admitted into the Congress of the United States on an equal footing with the original States in all respects, and shall be at liberty to form a constitution and State government: Provided the constitution and government shall be republican, and in conformity to the principles contained in these articles...."

★ What requirements did the Northwest Ordinance have for the admission of a territory into the Union as a new state?

★ Why was this ordinance such a significant achievement?

APPLYING WHAT YOU HAVE LEARNED

★ Make a Venn diagram showing the powers of the Confederation and state governments under the Articles of Confederation.

★ Debate the pros and cons of the Articles of Confederation.

★ Make a chart showing the structural weaknesses and achievements of the Articles of Confederation.

THE NATION ADOPTS A NEW CONSTITUTION

THE CRITICAL PERIOD, 1781–1787

Historians often refer to the years after the adoption of the Articles of Confederation (1781–1789) as the "**Critical Period**" of American history. George Washington described this as a time in which the states were held together by a "rope of sand."

The new government established by the Articles of Confederation suffered from many weaknesses. The Confederation government had no national executive and could not tax. Because it had no way of forcing states to obey it, the decisions of the Confederate Congress were more advisory than binding.

In seeking to limit the powers of the central government, American leaders had gone too far. They had created a national government with too little power to govern effectively. The new system also did not meet the needs of the growing economy. States were allowed to tax goods from other states; no uniform currency existed; there was a shortage of currency; and unemployment was widespread. The Confederation Congress was unable to protect manufacturing and shipping. Land values saw no rise in value because the government could neither defend its borders nor protect settlers living on the frontier.

Shays' Rebellion. A crisis soon arose that brought these weaknesses into sharp focus. Poor farmers — many of them former soldiers in the Continental Army — were upset over their growing debts, falling farm prices, and high state taxes. Failure to repay debts at this time often resulted in imprisonment in debtor's prison. In 1786, an uprising of farmers — known as **Shays' Rebellion** — broke out in Massachusetts.

Massachusetts farmers protesting.

Name _____

The rebels wanted to stop state courts from seizing their property and imprisoning them for unpaid debts. They also wanted the state to issue paper money. There was no national army to put down the uprising if it had spread to other states. Although the state militia was able to put it down, many property-owners across the country now felt the need for a stronger national government.

THE CONSTITUTIONAL CONVENTION

A meeting of representatives at Annapolis in 1786 called for a convention of delegates to revise the Articles of Confederation. Since only five of the 13 states were represented at Annapolis, they agreed to assemble again a few months later in Philadelphia.

In May 1787, representatives from the states met in Philadelphia to revise the Articles of Confederation. George Washington, Benjamin Franklin, and

The signing of the U.S. Constitution at Independence Hall

Alexander Hamilton were among the delegates. The representatives quickly agreed on discarding the Articles of Confederation. Instead, they decided that a new national constitution was needed.

ACTING AS AN AMATEUR HISTORIAN

Although it was agreed that the discussions of the Constitutional Convention were to be kept secret, James Madison wrote down every speech. Madison is known as the "Father of the U.S. Constitution." If not for his notes, little of what took place at the Constitutional Convention would be known. Below is a speech that Madison gave at the Convention:

"In time of war, great powers are given to the Executive. Constant [fear] of war has the same tendency to make the head too large for the body. A standing military force, with an overgrown Executive, will not be a safe [protector] of liberty. The defense against foreign threats has been the instrument of tyranny at home. Among the Romans it was a standing truth to stir fear of a war, whenever a revolt was threatened. The armies were kept on under the [excuse] of defending [the people, but they] enslaved them."

★ What did Madison mean when he said, "the head [is] too large for the body"?

★ What danger was Madison warning against in this speech?

AGREEMENT, DISAGREEMENT, AND COMPROMISE

The delegates at the Constitutional Convention generally agreed on the need for strengthening the national government and for creating a national executive, legislature, and judiciary. But they did not agree on all issues. For example, they could not agree on how states should be represented in the new Congress. Should states be represented according to their size? Another issue concerned slavery. Should the states count their slave populations when determining how many representatives they should have in Congress? A third issue concerned taxes. Should the new national government be able to tax **exports** (*goods sold abroad*)?

Delegates signing the new Constitution.

For a time, it appeared that the Constitutional Convention might even break up over some of these issues, but the delegates finally reached a series of compromises. A **compromise** is an agreement in which each side makes concessions to the other side to resolve the dispute.

The "Great Compromise." The first compromise delegates reached was over state representation. Virginia was a large state. James Madison of Virginia proposed a plan in which each state should be represented in Congress in proportion to its population. Delegates from New Jersey, a smaller state, objected. They proposed equal representation for states, just as they had enjoyed under the Articles of Confederation. Delegates from the large states agreed to a compromise to prevent the departure of the delegates of the small states. Delegates from Connecticut proposed a Congress with two houses to solve the problem.

The "Three-fifths Compromise." A second disagreement concerned the counting of slaves. Southern states wanted slaves to be counted as part of their population for representation in Congress. Northern states, with fewer slaves, opposed this idea. Northern and Southern delegates also disagreed over whether the new Congress should be able to regulate and even outlaw the slave trade. The North wanted Congress to regulate the slave trade, while Southerners opposed this. It also raised the issue of whether slaves would be counted in determining the taxes a state paid the federal government.

THE RISING SLAVE POPULATION

Throughout the colonial and antebellum period, slaves lived mainly in the South. They made up less than one-tenth of the South's population in 1680. By 1790, it had grown to one-third. About 293,000 slaves lived in Virginia alone, making up 42% of all slaves in the nation. North and South Carolina, and Maryland had more than 100,000 slaves each. The South's slave population reached about 1.1 million by 1810.

Year	White	Free Non-White	Slave
1790	1,240,454	32,523	654,121
1800	1,691,892	61,575	851,532

These two disagreements were eventually settled by the following compromises:

MAJOR CONSTITUTIONAL COMPROMISES

Issue: How should states be represented in the national legislature?

Issue: How should slaves be counted?

The "Great Compromise:" Larger states felt they should have a greater say in the national government. Smaller states felt each state should have an equal voice. In this compromise, a two "house" (bicameral) legislature was created — Congress. In the House of Representatives, states were represented according to their population size. This allowed states with a larger population to have a greater number of representatives. In the Senate, each state, no matter what its size, would be represented by two Senators. Senators were elected indirectly. All laws needed the approval of both houses of Congress.

The "Three-Fifths Compromise:" Southern states wanted slaves counted as part of their population, to have more members in the House of Representatives. The states compromised by agreeing to count every five slaves as three free persons for both taxation and representation.

FREE PERSONS = SLAVES

TAXATION AND REPRESENTATION

The "Commerce Compromise." Another dispute involved the taxing of trade. Southern landowners, who sold cash crops to England, feared taxes on exports of their tobacco and other crops. In the "Commerce Compromise," the delegates agreed to prohibit all taxes on **exports** (*goods sold to foreign countries*). Only imported goods could be taxed. The delegates also agreed that Congress could not regulate or limit the slave trade for at least the next twenty years — until 1808.

APPLYING WHAT YOU HAVE LEARNED

★ The delegates to the Constitutional Convention probably agreed on more aspects of the new government than they disagreed on. List several of the questions on which the delegates agreed.

★ Create a poster about the Constitutional Convention. Show what the delegates agreed on, where they disagreed, and what compromises they made.

★ Hold a mock Constitutional Convention in your classroom. Have your teacher assign different roles to members of your class.

ORGANIZATION OF THE NEW GOVERNMENT

As a result of the agreements and compromises reached at the Constitutional Convention, the delegates created a new system of government. The chart on the next page shows the organization of the Constitution itself:

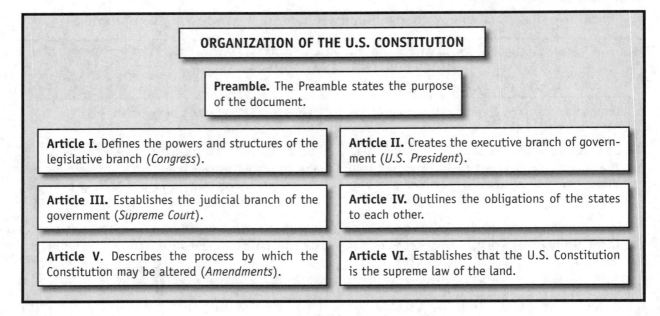

ORGANIZATION OF THE U.S. CONSTITUTION

Preamble. The Preamble states the purpose of the document.

Article I. Defines the powers and structures of the legislative branch (*Congress*).

Article II. Creates the executive branch of government (*U.S. President*).

Article III. Establishes the judicial branch of the government (*Supreme Court*).

Article IV. Outlines the obligations of the states to each other.

Article V. Describes the process by which the Constitution may be altered (*Amendments*).

Article VI. Establishes that the U.S. Constitution is the supreme law of the land.

PREAMBLE TO THE U.S. CONSTITUTION

The **Preamble**, or introduction, to the Constitution began with the words "We the People," emphasizing that the members of the Constitutional Convention were acting as the representatives of the American people as a whole. The Preamble gave six purposes for the new constitution and the government it created. These purposes were to:

"form a more perfect union."

"establish justice."

"insure domestic tranquility (*peace*)."

"provide for the common defense."

"promote the general welfare (*well-being of citizens*)."

"secure the blessings of liberty."

BRANCHES OF THE NEW GOVERNMENT

The Constitution established three branches in the new government:

THE EXECUTIVE BRANCH

The new national executive was the **President**. The President was made Commander-in-Chief of the nation's army and navy. The President was given the power to appoint ambassadors, negotiate treaties, and appoint Supreme Court Justices. As chief executive, the President would also enforce the nation's laws. New laws by Congress also required the President's signature. The President was to be elected for a four-year term.

Because the delegates to the Convention did not entirely trust the common people, they arranged for the President to be chosen by an **indirect election**. Voters would first choose members of the **Electoral College**. Once selected, these electors would then vote to choose the President. Each state is free to choose its electors as it wishes. In the late 1700s, America was largely rural. Most people were farmers who knew little about politics. In this environment, a direct election of the President would probably have been difficult.

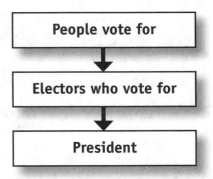

THE LEGISLATIVE BRANCH

The new national legislature was called **Congress**. Based on the "Great Compromise," it consisted of two houses: the **House of Representatives** and the **Senate**. Congress had the power to make laws, declare war, borrow and issue money, pay for military forces, and regulate commerce (*trade*) between different states or with foreign countries.

THE JUDICIAL BRANCH

A new national judiciary was created, consisting of the **Supreme Court** and any lower courts later created by Congress. The **Supreme Court** could rule on cases involving either the new Constitution or laws passed by Congress. Its Justices (*judges*) were to be appointed for life by the President, with the approval of the Senate. Life tenure meant that the Justices would not have to run for election and could be completely independent.

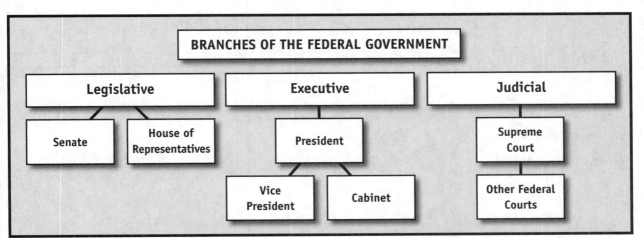

APPLYING WHAT YOU HAVE LEARNED

★ Select one of the goals listed in the Preamble and explain its importance.

★ Make a chart summarizing the powers and duties of the President, Congress, and the Supreme Court. Look in the school library or online for more information about each branch of government.

LEARNING WITH GRAPHIC ORGANIZERS

Compare the features of the Articles of Confederation and the U.S. Constitution:

FEATURES	ARTICLES OF CONFEDERATION	U.S. CONSTITUTION
Powers of Government		Checks and balances
Legislative Branch	Individual State's	Senate House of Representatives
Executive Branch	None	President, Vice President Cabinet
Judicial Branch	None	Supreme Court Federal Court

CONSTITUTIONAL PRINCIPLES

The basic challenge faced by the authors of the Constitution was to create a national government that would be strong, but not so strong that it might undermine individual liberties identified in the Declaration of Independence. To achieve this goal, the new Constitution adopted a number of important principles:

LIMITED GOVERNMENT

One of the most important principles of the U.S. Constitution is the belief that the powers of government should be limited. A self-governing people gives their government leaders only certain specific powers. These are the "just powers" of government mentioned in the Declaration of Independence. Under our system of limited government, our national government has no duties or powers, other than those powers specifically granted to it in the Constitution.

REPUBLICANISM

Americans created a **republican** form of government — a democratic government chosen by the people. A republic describes a government in which decisions are made by elected representatives, not handed down by a king.

POPULAR SOVEREIGNTY

Another key principle of the U.S. Constitution is that the people are **sovereign** — they hold supreme power. The "just" powers of the government come from the consent of the governed. The people exercise their sovereignty by electing representatives to Congress, and by indirectly electing the President.

FEDERALISM

The authors of the U.S. Constitution created a "federal republic." Government powers were divided between the national government and the states. To accomplish this, the writers of the Constitution created a system in which power was shared between the national (or *federal*) and state governments. The federal government treats issues facing the entire nation, while state governments handle local affairs. Because power was divided between the national and state governments, the

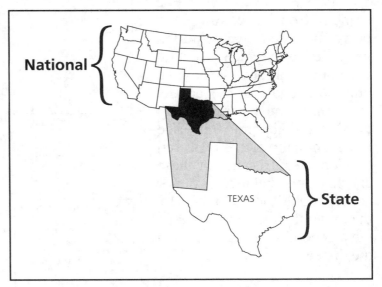

authors of the Constitution believed the national government would not become too strong.

SEPARATION OF POWERS

The framers of the U.S. Constitution sought to change another aspect of the Articles of Confederation. Under the Articles, the national government had just one branch — the Confederation Congress. The framers of the Constitution feared placing too much power in the hands of any one leader or single branch of government. Following the writings of the **Baron de Montesquieu** and the example of most state constitutions, they decided to divide the powers of government among three separate branches: the **Congress,** the **President**, and the **Supreme Court**. As James Madison later explained in the *Federalist Papers*, this separation of powers would act to prevent tyranny and protect liberty.

Charles Montesquieu

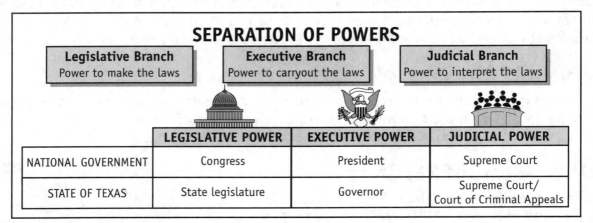

SEPARATION OF POWERS

Legislative Branch	Executive Branch	Judicial Branch
Power to make the laws	Power to carryout the laws	Power to interpret the laws

	LEGISLATIVE POWER	EXECUTIVE POWER	JUDICIAL POWER
NATIONAL GOVERNMENT	Congress	President	Supreme Court
STATE OF TEXAS	State legislature	Governor	Supreme Court/ Court of Criminal Appeals

CHECKS AND BALANCES

To further prevent any one branch from becoming too powerful, the Constitution gave each branch several ways to stop or "check" the other branches. For example, the Senate must approve key Presidential appointments. The President can veto bills passed by Congress. Because of these checks and balances, major actions could not be taken by the federal government without a general agreement among the different branches.

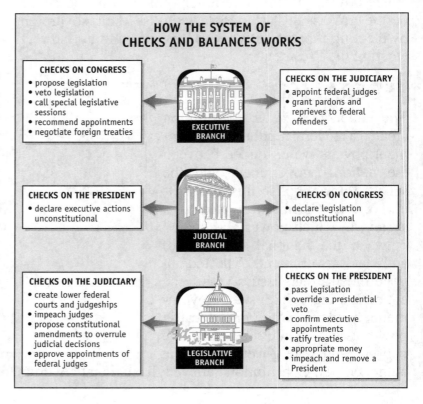

HOW THE SYSTEM OF CHECKS AND BALANCES WORKS

CHECKS ON CONGRESS
• propose legislation
• veto legislation
• call special legislative sessions
• recommend appointments
• negotiate foreign treaties

EXECUTIVE BRANCH

CHECKS ON THE JUDICIARY
• appoint federal judges
• grant pardons and reprieves to federal offenders

CHECKS ON THE PRESIDENT
• declare executive actions unconstitutional

JUDICIAL BRANCH

CHECKS ON CONGRESS
• declare legislation unconstitutional

CHECKS ON THE JUDICIARY
• create lower federal courts and judgeships
• impeach judges
• propose constitutional amendments to overrule judicial decisions
• approve appointments of federal judges

LEGISLATIVE BRANCH

CHECKS ON THE PRESIDENT
• pass legislation
• override a presidential veto
• confirm executive appointments
• ratify treaties
• appropriate money
• impeach and remove a President

INDIVIDUAL RIGHTS

You will learn about the issues surrounding the protection of individual rights in the next chapter.

PROVISIONS FOR CHANGE: THE AMENDMENT PROCESS

The Constitution included provisions for change. The way the U.S. Constitution keeps pace is through the **amendment process**, which allows changes and additions to the text of the Constitution. To prevent changes for unimportant reasons, the amending process was made more difficult than passing an ordinary law. Although over 200 years old, our Constitution has thus kept up with the changing needs of our nation.

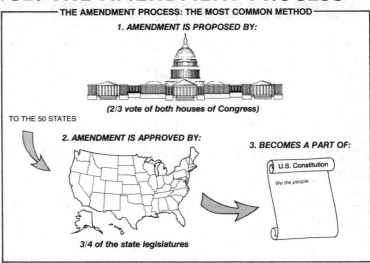

THE AMENDMENT PROCESS: THE MOST COMMON METHOD

1. AMENDMENT IS PROPOSED BY:

(2/3 vote of both houses of Congress)

TO THE 50 STATES

2. AMENDMENT IS APPROVED BY:

3. BECOMES A PART OF:

U.S. Constitution

We the people . . .

3/4 of the state legislatures

A special "**elastic clause**" in the U.S. Constitution further provided Congress with the power to enact any laws they deemed "necessary" to carry out its other powers. These provisions have made our Constitution into a "living document." The "elastic clause" has allowed the powers of Congress to increase dramatically since the early 1800s, due in large part to the decisions of the Supreme Court.

APPLYING WHAT YOU HAVE LEARNED

Many of the principles found in the U.S. Constitution were designed to prevent abuses of power. Select two of the principles discussed in this section and describe how they were attempts to prevent an abuse of power.

ACTING AS AN AMATEUR HISTORIAN

U.S. History   Search

1776

The original U.S. Constitution has undergone numerous changes since it was first approved almost 230 years ago.

★ Look online or in your school library for a copy of the main part of the Constitution. Use a copy that identifies those parts of the original document that have been crossed out and revised.

★ Explain how one of those revisions brought about a change to the *original* U.S. Constitution. Then prepare a two-minute oral presentation to your class, stating whether you agree or disagree with that particular revision to the U.S. Constitution.

LEARNING WITH GRAPHIC ORGANIZERS

Complete the following chart describing the principles of the U.S. Constitution:

Limited Government	Republicanism	Popular Sovereignty
self governing people gives government leaders only certain specific powers.	Democratic government chosen by the people.	The people exercise their sovereignty by electing representatives to congress

CONSTITUTIONAL PRINCIPLES

Federalism	Separation of Powers	Checks and Balances	Provisions for Change
Government powers were divided between national and state	Central government doesn't have too much power so there's a department for each power.	Each power has a "check" on other powers.	Allows Additions to the Constitution

The Declaration of Independence (1776) had listed a series of grievances committed by King George III of England against the colonists. A number of those grievances addressed violations by the King of his duties under the English Bill of Rights. Many of the provisions of the U.S. Constitution were included to prevent a repetition of such abuses:

IMPACT OF COLONIAL GRIEVANCES ON THE CONSTITUTION	
Grievances listed in the Declaration of Independence	**Where each was addressed in the U.S. Constitution**
The King imposed taxes without the consent of the colonists.	U.S. Constitution provides that all taxes must be approved by the House of Representatives.
The King made the military superior to the civil government.	U.S. Constitution provides that the Commander-in-Chief is a civilian — the President.
The King kept a large standing army among the colonists.	Congress has the right to raise and support an army. It determines its size through its control of funds.
The King made judges dependent on his will.	All federal judges are appointed for life.

THE DEBATE OVER RATIFICATION

Members of the Constitutional Convention knew they could not adopt their new plan on their own authority. They decided that before the Constitution could become law, nine states should **ratify** (*approve*) it. Special conventions were held in each state for this purpose.

FEDERALISTS AND ANTI-FEDERALISTS

Opponents of the new Constitution were known as **Anti-Federalists**. They included such patriots as **Patrick Henry** and **George Mason**.

ACTING AS AN AMATEUR HISTORIAN

In this address to the Virginia legislature in June 1788, Patrick Henry objects to scrapping the Articles of Confederation:

> "The Confederation, this same despised government, merits, in my opinion, the highest [praise]: it carried us through a long and dangerous war; it rendered us victorious in that bloody conflict with a powerful nation; it has secured us a territory greater than any European monarch possesses: and should a government which has been that strong and vigorous, be accused of imbecility, and abandoned for want of energy? Consider what you are about to do before you part with this government…. Before you abandon the present system, I hope you will consider not only its defects, but likewise those that of which you are about to substitute for it."

What arguments does Henry raise against abandoning the Articles of Confederation?

The Anti-Federalists found several major problems in the new Constitution. They argued it would create a central government that would be too strong and might threaten individual liberties. Anti-Federalists feared future government leaders might build a strong army and use it to collect unpopular taxes. The Anti-Federalists also pointed out that there was no bill of rights in the new Constitution to protect individual liberties. Finally, the Anti-Federalists felt that the Constitution gave too much power to the central government at the expense of state governments. Without safeguards for the states, the federal government might undermine their rights, especially on the issues of slavery and taxation.

ACTING AS AN AMATEUR HISTORIAN

New York's ratification was crucial. If New York rejected the Constitution, the new nation would be split in two. New York newspapers published essays in an attempt to sway voters. The following essay was written by an opponent of the new Constitution under the pen name "Brutus":

> "Let us inquire whether the thirteen states should be reduced to one republic or not? The territory is vast and has nearly three million [people]. Is it realistic for a country so numerous to elect representatives to speak [for them] without becoming so enormous [it is] unable of carry out public business? A free republic cannot exist in such a large territory. With the population and geographic size of our nation, citizens will have little [familiarity] with those chosen to represent them; many will not even know the character of a majority of those [in] the federal assembly; it will consist of men whose names they have never heard, and whose regard for the public, they are total strangers to."

> — *Brutus*

★ What argument does "Brutus" raise against supporting the proposed new Constitution?

★ Do you agree with "Brutus" on the main point in the passage? Explain your answer.

THE *FEDERALIST PAPERS*

Those favoring the proposed Constitution were called **Federalists**. They argued that a stronger central government was needed to protect the nation from domestic unrest and foreign invasion. They also argued that under the proposed plan, federalism and the separation of powers would prevent any one branch of the new central government from becoming too strong. Therefore, individual liberties would be protected.

New Yorkers Alexander Hamilton and John Jay, along with Virginian James Madison, wrote the *Federalist Papers*. This was a series of 85 essays that sought to convince Americans that the new nation would not last if the proposed constitution were not adopted.

The *Federalist Papers* helped to persuade Americans to approve the new constitution. Thomas Jefferson called them the best explanation ever written about the principles of government. Some have even called these essays the most significant public-relations campaign in history. To obtain the necessary votes for ratification, supporters promised to add a bill of rights. With this assurance, by the end of 1788, eleven states had voted to **ratify** (*approve*) the U.S. Constitution.

Alexander Hamilton, James Madison, and John Jay — authors of the Federalist Papers.

ACTING AS AN AMATEUR HISTORIAN

Many Americans believed, as **Baron de Montesquieu** had written, that liberty was only safe in small societies governed either by direct democracy or by legislatures with small districts. James Madison, in *Federalist No. 51*, argued the opposite. In a large republic, different interests would have to come together to form a coalition (*alliance*) in order to govern the nation. Government was created to prevent politicians or small groups from using government for their own unjust purposes:

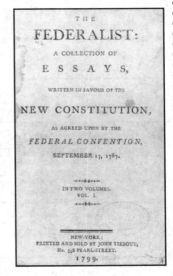

"In republican government, the legislative authority dominates. The remedy for this is to divide the legislature into different branches; and to [make] them, by different [methods] of election and different principles of action, as little connected with each other as their common functions will [allow].... In a single republic, all the power surrendered by the people is submitted to ... a single government; and [misuse of that power] is guarded against by dividing the government into separate departments. In America, the power surrendered by the people is first divided between two distinct governments, and then the power of each is subdivided among separate departments. Hence a double security arises to protect the rights of the people. Different governments will control each other, at the same time that each will be controlled by itself. If a majority is united by a common interest, the rights of the minority might be threatened. There are two ways of providing against this evil: by creating a will in the community independent of the majority of the society; the other, by comprehending in the society so many separate descriptions of citizens as will render an unjust combination of a majority of the whole improbable, if not impractical."

What arguments does Madison make to calm fears of some that the new government could threaten people's liberties?

LEARNING WITH GRAPHIC ORGANIZERS

Complete the graphic organizer below by describing three arguments used by the Federalists and the Anti-Federalists concerning ratification of the U.S. Constitution.

FEDERALISTS vs. ANTI-FEDERALISTS

Federalist Arguments in Support of Ratification
1. Strong domestic government
2.
3.

Anti-Federalist Arguments Against Ratification
1.
2.
3.

CHAPTER STUDY CARDS

Government Under the Articles

★ **Articles of Confederation.** (1777–1778)
- Set up a weak central government.
- Each state had only one vote in Congress.
- **Weaknesses:** lacked power to regulate trade; no national court system; lacked power to tax; lacked a national army.
- **Strengths:** Passed **Northwest Ordinance**, creating procedures to admit new states.

★ **Critical Period.** (1781–1787)
- **Shays' Rebellion.** Massachusetts farmers rebelled against courts foreclosing their farms.
- Showed the weakness of the Articles of Confederation in putting down rebellions.

Constitutional Convention (1787)

★ Convention met in 1787 in Philadelphia.
- Scrapped Articles of Confederation and agreed to draft a new constitution.
- **James Madison** kept notes and is known as the "Father of US Constitution."

★ Delegates agree to create three government branches.
- **Executive Branch:** President, chosen by the Electoral College.
- **Legislature Branch:** two-House Congress.
- **Judicial Branch:** Supreme Court.

★ New national government can raise an army, collect taxes, coin money, regulate commerce between states, and declare war or peace.

The Bundle of Compromises

★ **"Great Compromise."** Dealt with the issue of representation in Congress:
- Large states wanted representation based on population. Small states wanted states to be equal in Congress.
- Compromise established two houses: states were equal in the Senate; the House of Representatives was based on population.

★ **Three-fifths Compromise.**
- Issue of how slaves should be counted for purposes of representation.
- Five slaves would count as three persons for both representation and taxation.

Ratification of the Constitution

★ **Anti-Federalists.** Were opposed to approval of the new Constitution.
- George Mason, Patrick Henry
- Feared central government would be too powerful and threaten individual liberties.

★ **Federalists.** Supported approval.
- Favored a strong central government.
- James Madison, John Jay, Alexander Hamilton wrote the *Federalist Papers*.
- They argued that the Constitution had protections to prevent the rise of tyranny. These included the division of powers between the federal government and the states, and the separation of powers between the branches.

Principles of the U.S. Constitution

★ **Limited Government**
★ **Republicanism**
★ **Popular Sovereignty**
★ **Federalism**
★ **Separation of Powers**
- Legislative Power
- Executive Power
- Judicial Power
★ **Checks and Balances**
★ **Amending Process**

U.S. Constitution (1787)

U.S. Constitution. Was a written plan of government that spelled out the powers and organization of the new national government.

It is important because it:
★ Established the institutions of the national government (separation of powers).
★ Defined the powers of the national government (federalism).
★ Provided a legal basis for the protection of the rights of its citizens.

CHAPTER 8 CONCEPT MAP

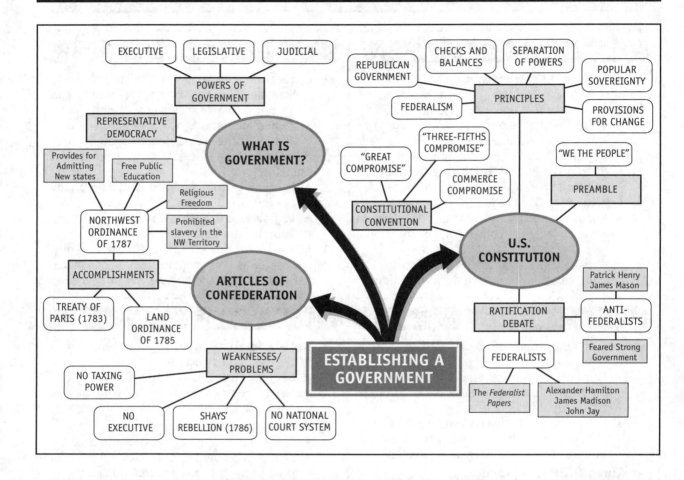

- EXECUTIVE
- LEGISLATIVE
- JUDICIAL

POWERS OF GOVERNMENT

REPRESENTATIVE DEMOCRACY

WHAT IS GOVERNMENT?

Provides for Admitting New states

Free Public Education

Religious Freedom

NORTHWEST ORDINANCE OF 1787

Prohibited slavery in the NW Territory

ACCOMPLISHMENTS

TREATY OF PARIS (1783)

LAND ORDINANCE OF 1785

ARTICLES OF CONFEDERATION

NO TAXING POWER

WEAKNESSES/ PROBLEMS

NO EXECUTIVE

SHAYS' REBELLION (1786)

NO NATIONAL COURT SYSTEM

ESTABLISHING A GOVERNMENT

REPUBLICAN GOVERNMENT

CHECKS AND BALANCES

SEPARATION OF POWERS

POPULAR SOVEREIGNTY

FEDERALISM

PRINCIPLES

PROVISIONS FOR CHANGE

"THREE-FIFTHS COMPROMISE"

"GREAT COMPROMISE"

COMMERCE COMPROMISE

"WE THE PEOPLE"

CONSTITUTIONAL CONVENTION

PREAMBLE

U.S. CONSTITUTION

Patrick Henry James Mason

RATIFICATION DEBATE

ANTI-FEDERALISTS

Feared Strong Government

FEDERALISTS

The *Federalist Papers*

Alexander Hamilton James Madison John Jay

CHECKING YOUR UNDERSTANDING

1 The main idea of this cartoon is that the Articles of Confederation —

A would carry the nation into the future.

B had many serious shortcomings.

C gave the government sufficient powers.

D created a navy strong enough to protect against foreign invasion.

Hist 15(B)

"Rough Sailing Ahead?"

E̲XAMINE **the question.** This question tests your ability to under-stand a political cartoon. R̲ECALL **what you know.** The cartoonist has drawn a large ship representing the Articles of Confederation. It is sailing through rough waters. The waves are high, threatening to sink the ship. These waves symbolize different shortcomings of the Arti-cles — no national army, no power to enforce treaties, and no power to raise an army. The caption raises the question whether the govern-ment under the Articles is in danger of sinking. A̲PPLY **what you know.** You should realize that **Choices A, C,** and **D** do not really define the main idea of the cartoon. The best answer is **Choice B,** since the cartoonist implies the Articles of Confederation had many shortcomings.

Now try answering some additional questions on your own.

2   Why did some of the founders of the American republic consider the lack of a national executive and judiciary under the Articles of Confederation as one of the document's great strengths?

   F   They feared a strong central government.   `Hist 15(B)`
   G   They feared the threat of a foreign invasion.
   H   They were willing to risk tyranny for an effective national government.
   J   They desired to copy the British monarchy.

3   The "Three-fifths Compromise" was included in the U.S. Constitution in order to resolve a conflict over the —

   A   number of votes needed to approve a treaty in the Senate   `Hist 4(D)`
   B   number of states needed to ratify a proposed amendment
   C   reimbursement of plantation owners for runaway slaves
   D   counting of enslaved persons for purposes of taxation and representation

4   One accomplishment of the national government under the Articles of Confederation was the passage of a law establishing —

   F   a central banking system   `Hist 6(A)`
   G   a process for admitting new states into the Union
   H   the President's right to put down rebellions
   J   the ability of Congress to tax the states effectively

5   Which question at the Constitutional Convention was resolved by the "Great Compromise"?

   A   How should the President be elected?   `Hist 4(D)`
   B   Who should control commerce and trade?
   C   What should be the structure of the federal court system?
   D   What formula should be used for Congressional representation?

6

> The proposed Constitution, far from abolishing state governments, makes them an essential part of the national government by allowing them a direct representation in the Senate, and leaves in their possession certain important government powers. This fully corresponds, in every way, with the idea of a federal government.
>
> — *Alexander Hamilton, Federalist No. 9 (1781)*

Based on this passage, which of the following statements would Alexander Hamilton agree with?

F State governments face the threat of being abolished by the federal government under the new constitution.   `Hist 15(A)`

G The states will lack representation in the Senate.

H Under the new Constitution, the states will enjoy important powers.

J State governments should fear the power of the new national government.

7 Which statement describes a characteristic of the national government established by the U.S. Constitution?

A The powers of the national government were limited.   `Hist 15(D)`

B The Supreme Court had the authority to create lower courts.

C The President had exclusive control over all government activities.

D The states kept the most governmental powers.

8 Which grievance in the Declaration of Independence was later addressed by the U.S. Constitution?

F providing that all taxes must be approved by Congress   `Hist 15(C)`

G creating a process for the admission of new states

H enacting a law to allow the President to declare war

J appointing federal judges for a limited term of office

9 The purpose of the amending process in the U.S. Constitution was to —

A allow the Constitution to adjust for changing times   `Govt 16(A)`

B balance power between the state and the national governments

C prevent any one branch of the government from becoming too powerful

D protect the liberties of individuals from the abuses of government power

10 The principle of federalism deals with the division of power between the —

F President and Congress   `Govt 15(D)`

G Senate and House of Representatives

H national and state governments

J three branches of federal government

11

> He [the President] shall have power, with the advice and consent of the Senate, to make treaties, provided two thirds of the senators present concur; and he shall nominate, with the advice and consent of the Senate, ambassadors, [and] other public ministers....
>
> — *Article II, Section 2, Clause 2, U.S. Constitution*

Which principle of the U.S. Constitution is reflected in this passage?

A checks and balances   `Hist 15(D)`
B amendment process
C popular sovereignty
D federalism

---

12 What was a key argument used by the Federalists for ratification of the U.S. Constitution?

F It prohibited the power of the federal government to wage war.
G It provided for construction of a new capital in the South.   `Govt 17(A)`
H It allowed the slave trade to continue for at least twenty more years.
J It had features that prevented the abuse of government power.

13 Which historic document was written in support of ratification of the U.S. Constitution?

A Magna Carta   `Hist 15(A)`
B Mayflower Compact
C Declaration of Independence
D The *Federalist Papers*

14

> The nation deserves and I will select a Supreme Court Justice that Americans can be proud of. The nation also deserves a dignified process of confirmation in the United States Senate, characterized by fair treatment, a fair hearing and a fair vote. I will choose a nominee in a timely manner so that the hearing and the vote can be completed before the new Supreme Court term begins.
>
> — *President George W. Bush, 2005*

Which constitutional principle is discussed in this quotation?

F federalism   `Govt 15(D)`
G checks and balances
H states' rights
J due process

---

15 Why did the framers of the Constitution create three separate branches of the national government?

A to insure that the legislative branch was bicameral   `Govt 15(D)`
B to make sure all laws were approved by the Supreme Court
C to make sure that the President was superior to the legislature
D to prevent any one branch of government from gaining too much power

16 Which conclusion about the ratification of the U.S. Constitution can be drawn from the map?

  F All states were in favor of ratification.

  G Spanish Louisiana strongly favored ratification.

  H Rhode Island was the last state to vote for ratification.

  J Georgia was the first state to ratify the U.S. Constitution.

  Hist 4(E)

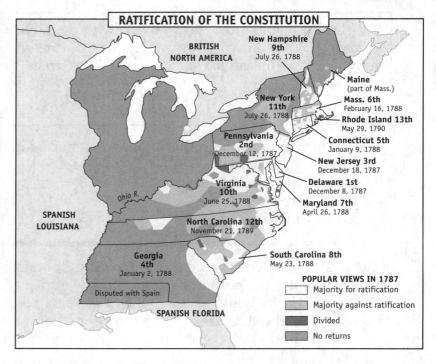

RATIFICATION OF THE CONSTITUTION

BRITISH NORTH AMERICA

New Hampshire 9th
July 26, 1788

Maine (part of Mass.)

New York 11th
July 26, 1788

Mass. 6th
February 16, 1788

Rhode Island 13th
May 29, 1790

Connecticut 5th
January 9, 1788

Pennsylvania 2nd
December 12, 1787

New Jersey 3rd
December 18, 1787

Delaware 1st
December 8, 1787

Virginia 10th
June 25, 1788

Maryland 7th
April 26, 1788

Ohio R.

SPANISH LOUISIANA

North Carolina 12th
November 21, 1789

Georgia 4th
January 2, 1788

South Carolina 8th
May 23, 1788

POPULAR VIEWS IN 1787
- ☐ Majority for ratification
- ☐ Majority against ratification
- ☐ Divided
- ☐ No returns

Disputed with Spain

SPANISH FLORIDA

17 Which action is an example of the system of checks and balances?

  A Texas requires at least 180 school days per year.   Govt 15(D)

  B An individual pays both state and federal income tax.

  C The House of Representatives votes to expel one of its members.

  D The Senate approves the President's nomination to the Supreme Court.

18

THE EVENING POST	The Boston Gazette	THE NEW YORK GAZETTE
New Congress to Have Two Houses	**Slaves to Count as Three-Fifths of a Person**	**No Tax on Goods Sent out of the Country**

Which conclusion about the Constitutional Convention is best supported by these headlines?

  F The President and Congress would have equal powers.   Hist 4(D)

  G The Framers of the Constitution were able to compromise on important issues.

  H States that were small in area lost power in the new Constitution.

  J States with large populations controlled the outcome of the Convention.

19 What is the purpose of the checks-and-balances system in the U.S. Constitution?

A   to expand the President's treaty-making powers   `Govt 15(D)`

B   to divide power between the federal and state governments

C   to prevent any one branch of the government from becoming too powerful

D   to allow each branch of the government to veto those laws it objects to

20

The king is forbidden to introduce most new taxes without the permission of the council of his nobles. — *Magna Carta*	The king is forbidden from imposing taxes on his subjects without the approval of Parliament. — *English Bill of Rights*, 1689	**?** — *U.S. Constitution*, 1787

Which statement best replaces the question mark in the diagram?

F   The U.S. Congress must pass all taxes.   `Govt 15(A)`

G   Each year, the President must submit a budget to Congress.

H   Elections in the House of Representatives occur every two years.

J   The Congress cannot spend more than is provided in its budget.

21

THE EVENING POST	The Boston Gazette
Seventeenth Amendment Passes Requiring U.S. Senators to be Directly Elected	Twenty-Sixth Amendment Approved Giving 18 Year Olds the Right to Vote

Which best describes the purpose of the amending process shown in these two newspaper headlines?

A   The nation's needs change, requiring revisions to the Constitution.   `Govt 16(A)`

B   The national government's power must be limited or it will become tyrannical.

C   The states are the rightful enforcers of the provisions of the Constitution.

D   The Constitution was created by the states to serve the states.

22 Between 1787 and 1789, a major controversy between the Federalists and the Anti-Federalists focused primarily on —

F   expansion of slavery into the territories   `Govt 17(A)`

G   the wisdom of creating a two-house legislature

H   division of power among different levels of government

J   the issue of ratification of the new U.S. Constitution

CHAPTER 9

THE RIGHTS AND RESPONSIBILITIES OF AMERICAN CITIZENS

TEKS COVERED IN CHAPTER 9

- **Government 15C** Identify colonial grievances listed in the Declaration of Independence and explain how those grievances were addressed in the ... Bill of Rights.
- **Government 17A** Analyze the arguments of the ... Anti-Federalists, including ... Patrick Henry and George Mason.
- **Citizenship 19B** Summarize rights guaranteed in the Bill of Rights.
- **Citizenship 19C** Identify examples of responsible citizenship, including obeying rules and laws, staying informed on public issues, voting, and serving on juries.
- **Citizenship 20A** Evaluate the contributions of the Founding Fathers as models of civic virtue.
- **Citizenship 21A** Identify different points of view of political parties and interest groups on important historical issues.
- **Citizenship 21B** Describe the importance of free speech and press in a constitutional republic.
- **Culture 25C** Analyze the impact of the First Amendment guarantees of religious freedom on the American way of life.

In this chapter, you will learn about the Bill of Rights. In 1789, Congress sent to the state legislatures twelve proposed amendments to the U.S. Constitution. Amendments three through twelve were adopted by the states and became the Bill of Rights. This chapter also examines other rights and responsibilities of American citizens.

KEY TERMS AND PEOPLE IN THIS CHAPTER

- ■ Bill of Rights
- ■ First Amendment
- ■ Freedom of Speech
- ■ Right to Petition
- ■ Right of Assembly

- ■ Due Process of Law
- ■ Equal Protection
- ■ Unreasonable Searches
- ■ Eminent Domain
- ■ Search Warrant

- ■ Grand Jury Indictment
- ■ Double Jeopardy
- ■ Self-Incrimination
- ■ Bail
- ■ Responsibilities

— IMPORTANT IDEAS —

A. Anti-Federalists criticized the Constitution for the absence of a "**Bill of Rights**." The first Congress proposed ten amendments. These amendments were added to the Constitution in 1791 as the **Bill of Rights**.

B. The **First Amendment** guarantees freedom of religion, free speech, freedom of the press, the right to assemble, and the right to petition the government. It also states that the Congress shall not establish any religion.

C. These First Amendment rights are crucial to our democracy. They allow us to criticize government officials and debate issues without fear of government reprisals. Few of these rights, however, are absolute. Government can place reasonable limits on these freedoms. For example, we cannot scream fire in a crowded theatre as a joke.

D. The **Second Amendment** guarantees our right to "bear arms." This allows citizens to own guns. The **Third Amendment** prohibits government from quartering troops in our homes without consent. These rights arose out of circumstances that developed during the American Revolutionary War.

E. The Fourth, Fifth, Sixth, and Eighth Amendments protect individuals accused of a crime from unjust accusations and government abuse.

F. The **Fourth Amendment** prevents the police from conducting "unreasonable searches and seizures." Unless a specific exception applies, the police need a search warrant before they can conduct a search.

G. The **Fifth Amendment** states that individuals cannot be tried twice for the same crime, or be forced to incriminate themselves.

H. The **Sixth Amendment** guarantees those accused of a crime a fair and public trial by a jury and the assistance of a lawyer.

J. The **Eighth Amendment** prevents judges from setting bail that is too high, or inflicting "cruel and unusual" punishments.

K. The **Tenth Amendment** reserves powers not granted to the federal government to the state governments and the people.

L. U.S. citizens have additional rights and responsibilities beyond those specified in the Bill of Rights. They are able to vote, to serve on juries, and to hold public office. They should try to remain informed on public issues and to participate actively in public life.

ESSENTIAL QUESTIONS

- What individual rights are guaranteed by the Bill of Rights?
- What are some of the other rights of citizenship?
- What are the responsibilities of citizenship?

THE BILL OF RIGHTS

The original Constitution contained few specific guarantees of individual rights. It stated the Congress could not pass a law punishing someone for an act that was not already a crime at the time it was committed. Nor could Congress condemn a person without a trial. Surprisingly, there were no other guarantees of individual rights. In several states, ratification for the Constitution was only obtained when Federalist supporters promised to add a Bill of Rights. Anti-Federalists like Patrick Henry and George Mason attacked the Constitution for failing to include a Bill of Rights.

ACTING AS AN AMATEUR HISTORIAN

George Mason in his *Objections to the Federal Constitution* feared an overly powerful central government. He believed that the republic should begin with a commitment to unalienable individual rights superior to those of the states. For this reason, he was critical of the Constitution.

> "There is no declaration of rights: the laws of the government being dominant to the laws and constitutions in the states offer no security. Nor are the people secured even in the enjoyment of the benefit of the common law … the laws will be generally made by men [not] concerned with their effects and consequences…. [T]here is no declaration of any kind for preserving the liberty of the press, the trial by jury, nor against the danger of standing armies in time of peace."

What did Mason dislike about the original Constitution?

As soon as the first Congress assembled in 1789, it began deciding which rights to include in the **Bill of Rights**. Eventually, a list of possible rights was reduced to twelve. After three-quarters of the members of Congress approved the proposed amendments, they were sent to the states for approval. Two-thirds of the state legislatures approved ten of these amendments by 1791, when they came into effect.

THE FIRST AMENDMENT

One of the most important amendments in the Bill of Rights was the **First Amendment**:

> *"Congress shall make no law respecting an establishment of religion, or prohibiting the free exercise thereof; or abridging the freedom of speech, or of the press; or the right of the people peaceably to assemble, and to petition the government for a redress of grievances."*

The First Amendment actually covers several rights at the same time:

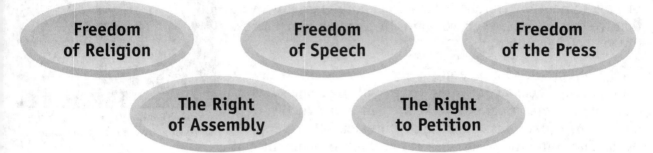

Freedom of Religion   **Freedom of Speech**   **Freedom of the Press**

The Right of Assembly   **The Right to Petition**

Let's look at each of these rights more closely.

FREEDOM OF RELIGION

It is no mistake that a guarantee of religious freedom is stated at the start of the First Amendment. From the very beginning, many people had migrated to the American colonies for the freedom to practice their own religious beliefs.

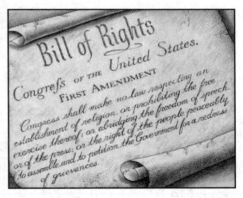

The First Amendment guarantees individuals the right to freely engage in any religious practices that do not directly harm other individuals. In many countries in Europe at that time, there was an established religion supported by the government. The First Amendment states that Congress will not "establish a religion." This is sometimes called the establishment clause. While the ban on government involvement in religion seems clear, there have been instances in which the proper role of government has been debated. For example, it is clear that Congress cannot pass a law saying that a particular religion is the established religion of the United States. Nor can Congress vote to give money to a particular church or religious group. But can public schools have prayers in school? The Supreme Court, which has the role of interpreting these amendments, has said no.

Some limited government activity concerned with religion has been declared "constitutional" by the Supreme Court. For example, the Supreme Court has said that a state can pay for bus transportation to students who choose to go to a full-time religious school. This is to support the expenses of these students' general education. However, because government cannot "establish" a religion, there can be no religious activities, such as prayers, in public schools.

FREEDOM OF SPEECH

Burning the American flag is a right protected by the First Amendment.

In many countries, people are afraid to criticize their government. They fear being fined, jailed, or otherwise punished for what they say. In the United States, the First Amendment protects our freedom to say or write almost anything in public. Americans cannot be put in jail just for criticizing the government or for expressing individual beliefs.

Freedom of speech allows individuals in our society to express themselves in most circumstances without fear of government interference. This does not mean, however, that we can say whatever we want. In some circumstances, our speech can be limited.

The Supreme Court requires the government to give a "compelling" reason for interfering with free speech. For example, a person cannot yell "fire" in a crowded movie theater as a joke, since this might threaten other people's lives. The Supreme Court has ruled that government can limit free speech, if a "clear and present danger" is created by that speech. A person also cannot use the right of free speech to violate other laws — such as deliberately spreading harmful lies, or copying someone else's words without permission.

APPLYING WHAT YOU HAVE LEARNED

In a paragraph, explain why the right of free speech in American society can never be absolute (*complete or total*). Why do there always have to be some restrictions on free speech?

FREEDOM OF THE PRESS

The freedom of the press is also guaranteed by the First Amendment. This freedom is very similar to freedom of speech. It permits people to express themselves through publication. Freedom of the press allows newspapers, radio, and television to write or announce what they want without fear of punishment. This freedom is essential in a democratic republic such as ours. People need to be well-informed to vote and to make other democratic choices. Radio, television and the press must be able to report the news and to help people exchange their ideas and beliefs. Our free press acts as a watchdog that makes sure our government leaders are telling us the truth. Our participation in elections would become meaningless if government officials could control the flow of information or stop the free exchange of ideas.

However, freedom of the press does not give reporters any special rights not already given to citizens in general. For example, a court can compel a journalist to disclose his or her sources. Newspapers also do not have the right to publish deliberate lies in order to harm a person.

Name _____

CHAPTER 9: The Rights and Responsibilities of American Citizens   **147**

THE RIGHT OF ASSEMBLY

In some countries, people cannot peacefully gather to protest against government policies without fear of punishment. If they gather or demonstrate, they fear they might be beaten, arrested, imprisoned, or even killed. The First Amendment states that Congress cannot deny individuals the right to "peacefully assemble." This means that people have a right to gather peaceably with others without fear that the government will use force against them. In a democracy, many groups and organizations often use the right to "peacefully assemble" as a way to get the word out. They gather in parades and demonstrations to show their support for certain ideas and beliefs.

THE RIGHT TO PETITION

Congress also cannot deny individuals the right to write to government representatives or officials, seeking a change in the law. This is known as the right to **petition**. This right is based on the belief that citizens have a right to complain to their representatives about things that they do not like and would like to see changed.

If there is a law or policy that citizens dislike, they gather people's signatures on petitions. These petitions are then sent to government officials.

The right to gather signatures on a petition is protected by the First Amendment.

APPLYING WHAT YOU HAVE LEARNED

Rewrite the First Amendment in your own words. Which rights in the First Amendment do you think are the most important? Explain your reasons.

THE SECOND AMENDMENT

"A well regulated Militia, being necessary to the security of a free State, the right of the people to keep and bear Arms, shall not be infringed."

Americans recognized the important role played by the militia in winning the Revolutionary War. A **militia** is a "citizen's army," a force made up of ordinary citizens who take up arms. The **Second Amendment** states that "a well-regulated militia" is necessary for the security of a free state. For this reason, it says people should have the right to keep and bear arms (*carry weapons*). Because of the Second Amendment, Americans have the right to own guns. In other countries, citizens do not have this right. Some Americans question whether this right is still necessary today and whether it encourages violence.

APPLYING WHAT YOU HAVE LEARNED

Do you think Americans should be allowed to own guns, or should the Second Amendment be changed? Explain your answer.

THE THIRD AMENDMENT

"No Soldier shall, in time of peace be quartered in any house, without the consent of the Owner, nor in time of war, but in a manner to be prescribed by law."

At the time of the American Revolution, the question of quartering troops was a matter of great concern. The British government had "quartered" soldiers in colonists' homes. The **Third Amendment** prohibits the government from placing troops in people's homes without their permission.

BILL OF RIGHTS: RIGHTS OF THE ACCUSED

The Fourth, Fifth, Sixth, Seventh, and Eighth Amendments prohibit government officials from taking away a person's life, liberty or property without following fair and reasonable procedures. These procedures are often referred to as the "**due process of law**." Many of these rights can be traced back to Magna Carta (1215) and the English Bill of Rights (1689). Without these rights, citizens might be subject to unfair accusations or government abuse.

THE FOURTH AMENDMENT

A "search" occurs when a police officer or other government official enters our home, car, or some other place to look for evidence. A "seizure" occurs when a person or property is taken by the government. The **Fourth Amendment** protects individuals from "unreasonable" searches and seizures. If there is a reasonable expectation of privacy, a judge must sign a "**search warrant**" presented by a police officer, before the officer can conduct the search. If the judge believes the search is reasonable, permission for it will be granted.

Recently, new Fourth Amendment issues have arisen — Is it constitutional for the police to track your cell phone calls?

If the person to be searched consents, if the criminal activity is in "plain view," or if there is a pursuit or other emergency, a warrant may not be required. Otherwise, if the police break the rules, they cannot later use the evidence they find in a court.

THE FIFTH AMENDMENT

A citizen cannot be deprived of life, liberty, or property without **due process of law**. This means that certain legal procedures must be carried out according to established rules before a person can be punished.

★ **Eminent domain** refers to the power of the government over property in its territory. Sometimes, the government needs to take over property — such as to build a public highway or construct a school. A person's property cannot be taken away for public use without payment (*"reasonable compensation"*).

★ A person cannot be tried for a serious federal crime, that could lead to imprisonment or execution, without an indictment by a grand jury. An **indictment** is a formal accusation by a court before a person is arrested. A **grand jury** is a group of citizens that meet to review if there is enough evidence available to hold a trial.

★ No person can be subject to **double jeopardy** — being tried twice for the same crime. The government, with all its power and resources, should not be allowed to make repeated attempts to convict an individual for a suspected offense, subjecting him or her to embarrassment and great expense.

★ An accused person cannot be forced to say things that will be used against him or herself (**self-incrimination**). A person's confession of a crime is not valid if he or she was not first informed of the right to have a lawyer.

THE SIXTH AMENDMENT

This amendment guarantees a fair and impartial trial to all persons accused of a crime. They must be told of the charges against them; they have the right to a trial by jury; and they have the right to be represented by a lawyer.

THE EIGHTH AMENDMENT

Federal courts cannot require unusually high bail. **Bail** is the money an accused pays to a court as security so that he or she need not remain in jail while awaiting trial. This amendment also states that no one can be punished in a cruel or unusual way. On this basis, the Supreme Court has ruled that a state cannot pass a law with a mandatory death sentence. Some critics say that capital punishment itself should be prohibited by the Eighth Amendment, but the Supreme Court has yet to agree.

APPLYING WHAT YOU HAVE LEARNED

The freedoms our citizens enjoy because of the Bill of Rights are important to the fabric of life in America. Design and create a poster that showcases these freedoms.

LEARNING WITH GRAPHIC ORGANIZERS

Complete the graphic organizer below by fully describing each of these amendments.

First Amendment

_____
_____
_____
_____
_____

Second Amendment

_____
_____
_____
_____
_____

Third Amendment

_____
_____
_____
_____
_____

KEY AMENDMENTS IN THE BILL OF RIGHTS

Fourth Amendment

_____
_____
_____
_____
_____

Fifth Amendment

_____
_____
_____
_____
_____

Sixth Amendment

_____
_____
_____
_____
_____

Eighth Amendment

_____
_____
_____

OTHER AMENDMENTS

There are three other amendments that were included in the Bill of Rights that are often overlooked. The Seventh Amendment addressed citizen's rights to a jury trial in civil matters, while the Ninth and Tenth Amendment concerned the limits of federal power.

THE SEVENTH AMENDMENT

> *"In suits at common law, where the value in controversy shall exceed twenty dollars, the right of trial by jury shall be preserved, and no fact tried by a jury, shall be otherwise re-examined in any Court of the United States, than according to the rules of the common law."*

The **Seventh Amendment** guarantees our right to a jury trial in most civil cases — lawsuits in which one party sues another for causing a personal injury or for breaking a contract. One concern of the Anti-Federalists about the new constitution was that federal courts of appeals would overturn the findings of juries in the lower courts. The Seventh Amendment guarantees that jury findings of fact will be respected. Because of this amendment we

The Jury by John Morgan (1861)

still enjoy today the right to a jury trial in federal civil cases such as car accidents, disputes over breaking many contracts, and most discrimination or employment disputes.

THE NINTH AMENDMENT

> *"The enumeration in the Constitution, of certain rights, shall not be construed to deny or disparage others retained by the people."*

The Founding Fathers strongly believed that all rights belonged to the people of the United States. The **Ninth Amendment** was added to make sure that even if a right is not specifically stated in the Constitution, it is a right that still belongs to the people. The Ninth Amendment acts as a constitutional safety net. It makes clear that the Bill of Rights is not an exclusive list. In addition to those rights listed in the Bill of Rights, individuals may also have other rights. Just because a right is not specifically stated in the Constitution does not mean that this right does not exist. The U.S. Supreme Court has held, for example, that people enjoy a right to privacy based on the Ninth Amendment and parts of other amendments, such as the Fourth Amendment.

THE TENTH AMENDMENT

"The powers not delegated to the United States by the Constitution, nor prohibited by it to the States, are reserved to the States respectively, or to the people."

The authors of the U.S. Constitution were greatly concerned with the dangers of giving the federal government too much power. One of their objectives was to prevent the growth of central power that the British had once exercised over them as colonists. As you know, for this reason the delegates to the Constitutional Convention fashioned a government of limited, enumerated powers. At the same time, they gave Congress additional powers under the "Necessary and Proper" Clause — also known as the "Elastic" Clause.

To balance this grant of implied powers, the Bill of Rights included the **Tenth Amendment**. This amendment stated that the federal government has only those powers specifically granted to it by the U.S. Constitution. It essentially tells the federal government, "You can have this much power, but no more." All other powers are reserved (*saved for*) the states or the people. The purpose of the amendment is essentially to limit the power of the federal government.

The Tenth Amendment also stands as a reminder of the continuing importance of the state governments in our federal system of government. The amendment especially calmed the fears of many by ensuring that all powers not given to the federal government by the Constitution would be saved for the states and their citizens.

THE DECLARATION OF INDEPENDENCE AND THE BILL OF RIGHTS

Some of the rights in the Bill of Rights, like some provisions in the original Constitution, were responses to the grievances that were listed in the Declaration of Independence:

IMPACT OF COLONIAL GRIEVANCES ON THE CONSTITUTION	
Grievances listed in the Declaration of Independence	**Where each grievance was addressed in the Bill of Rights**
The King refused to give colonists permission to petition for a redress of their grievances.	The First Amendment guarantees citizens the right to petition the government for a redress of grievances.
The King quartered (*housed*) his troops in the colonists' homes without their permission.	The Third Amendment prohibits the government from quartering of soldiers in people's homes in peacetime.
The King deprived some colonists of the right to a trial by jury.	The Sixth Amendment guarantees a trial by jury to all persons accused of a crime.

ACTING AS AN AMATEUR HISTORIAN

1. Guarantees the freedoms of religion, speech, the press, and assembly.
2. Guarantees the right to keep and bear arms.
3. Prohibits the forcible quartering of soldiers in one's home.
4. Prohibits unreasonable searches and seizures.
5. Guarantees that no citizen can be deprived of life, liberty or property without **due process of law** (procedures according to established rules, such as a fair trial); also prohibits **double jeopardy** (being tried twice for the same crime) and **self-incrimination** (no person can be forced to give evidence against himself).
6. Guarantees those accused of a crime the right to a speedy trial by jury, to confront their accusers, and to be represented by a lawyer.
7. Guarantees a jury trial in many civil cases.
8. Prohibits excessive bail and cruel and unusual punishment.
9. States that the listing of some rights in the Constitution does not mean that people do not also enjoy other rights.
10. Reserves for the states and the people those powers not given to the federal government, forming a basis for the reserved powers.

Select two amendments listed in the chart above. Search the Internet or your library for an issue that deals with this amendment. The issue may be one that has been settled in a decision of the U.S. Supreme Court. For example, you might research this issue concerning the Second Amendment: do citizens have a right to carry weapons? Does this right include every type of weapon? Write a brief report describing the issue and how it is related to the amendment.

Amendment:	Amendment:
Issue: _____	Issue: _____
_____	_____
_____	_____
_____	_____
_____	_____
How was the issue resolved:	How was the issue resolved:
_____	_____
_____	_____
_____	_____
_____	_____
_____	_____

LEARNING WITH GRAPHIC ORGANIZERS

Complete the graphic organizer below by filling in each box indicating the protections found in the First Amendment of the Bill of Rights.

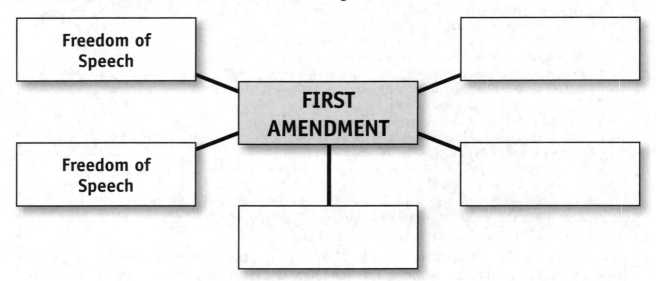

Freedom of Speech		
	FIRST AMENDMENT	
Freedom of Speech		

Complete the graphic organizer below by summarizing each of these amendments.

Seventh Amendment	Ninth Amendment	Tenth Amendment
<u>What does it say?</u>	<u>What does it say?</u>	<u>What does it say?</u>
<u>Why is it important?</u>	<u>Why is it important?</u>	<u>Why is it important?</u>

OTHER IMPORTANT AMENDMENTS

WHAT IS CITIZENSHIP?

What is a citizen? A **citizen** is a participating member of the community. It is no accident that the term "citizen" reminds us of the word "city." The idea of citizenship goes back to very ancient times. The first citizens were the free members of the city-states of Greece. They enjoyed rights of self-government but also had the obligation to help defend their city-state and pay taxes. Later, the Romans expanded the notion of **citizenship**. Rome expanded from a city-state to an empire, and the Romans wisely permitted members of conquered states to become full citizens of the Roman Empire.

Individuals being sworn in to become U.S. citizens.

You may be surprised to learn that the term "citizenship" was not defined in the original U.S. Constitution. It was not until 1868, with the passage of the Fourteenth Amendment, that the requirements for U.S. citizenship were finally added to the U.S. Constitution. Based on that amendment, there are actually two paths to American citizenship — by birth or naturalization.

The Bill of Rights applies to all people living in the United Sates, not just to those who enjoy the benefits of citizenship. These rights are enjoyed by visitors and permanent residents as well as by American citizens. However, there are some special rights that only U.S. citizens enjoy. These include the right to vote in elections and to participate in government by holding public office.

THE RESPONSIBILITIES OF CITIZENS

Earlier in this chapter, you learned about some of the rights of citizenship. In this section, you will learn about some of the responsibilities that go along with being a citizen.

Citizenship involves more than just being a member of a community. The survival of a democratic republic like the United States requires its citizens to participate actively in self-government. It is important for a democracy that its citizens remain involved in their communities. The responsibilities of citizenship include both things we must do and things we should do.

Serving on a jury is one of the important responsibilities that are required of an American citizen.

Citizenship responsibilities include those obligations that a person must do when he or she becomes a citizen. If a citizen refuses to perform these legal obligations, he or she may face punishment with fines or even imprisonment:

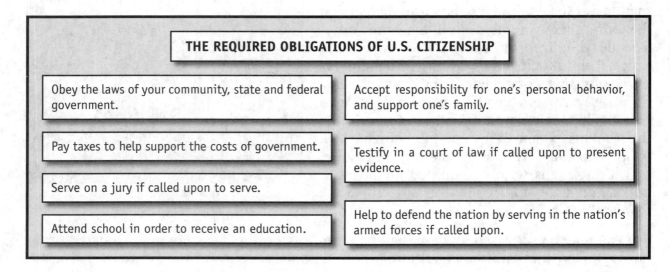

THE REQUIRED OBLIGATIONS OF U.S. CITIZENSHIP

Obey the laws of your community, state and federal government.	Accept responsibility for one's personal behavior, and support one's family.
Pay taxes to help support the costs of government.	Testify in a court of law if called upon to present evidence.
Serve on a jury if called upon to serve.	
Attend school in order to receive an education.	Help to defend the nation by serving in the nation's armed forces if called upon.

Most people look at the rights and obligations of U.S. citizenship as two different sides of the same coin. They are closely connected. You cannot exercise your rights of citizenship without also being aware of your obligations. For example, you have the **right** to a trial by jury if you are accused of a crime. But you also have an **obligation** to serve on a jury if you are summoned. If all citizens refused to meet their obligation for jury service, none of us could enjoy the right to a trial by jury.

Voting is considered an obligation of a citizen in a democracy.

In addition to the obligations of citizenship, there are also several additional **responsibilities** of good citizenship: things that a good citizen "should" do. These responsibilities generally require both time and effort, but our democracy relies on the active participation of its citizens. Citizens are not fined or imprisoned for failing to carry out these responsibilities. However, our democracy is based on its citizens voluntarily performing them some of the time. Meeting these responsibilities is a form of **civic virtue** — doing what is for the good of the community. As members of a democracy, Americans have a responsibility to preserve the benefits of our society for future generations. Preparing young people for their roles as citizens is another important responsibility shared by all adult citizens.

Here is a partial list of some of the things a citizen in a democracy should become involved in:

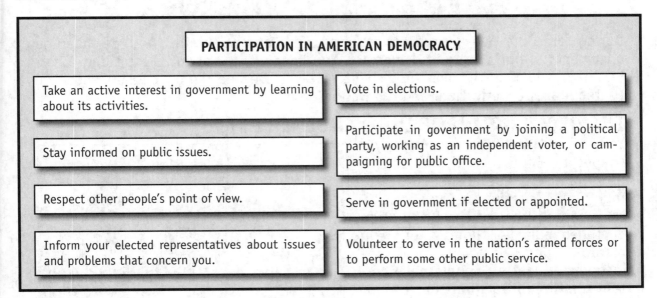

PARTICIPATION IN AMERICAN DEMOCRACY

Take an active interest in government by learning about its activities.	Vote in elections.
Stay informed on public issues.	Participate in government by joining a political party, working as an independent voter, or campaigning for public office.
Respect other people's point of view.	Serve in government if elected or appointed.
Inform your elected representatives about issues and problems that concern you.	Volunteer to serve in the nation's armed forces or to perform some other public service.

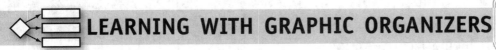

LEARNING WITH GRAPHIC ORGANIZERS

Complete the graphic organizer below by describing some of the most important rights and responsibilities of an American citizen.

UNITED STATES CITIZENSHIP

Rights of U.S. Citizens	Responsibilities of U.S. Citizens
1. _____ _____	1. _____ _____
2. _____ _____	2. _____ _____
3. _____ _____	3. _____ _____
4. _____ _____	4. _____ _____

CELEBRATING FREEDOM WEEK

During "Freedom Week," students in Texas study and celebrate the three founding documents of our system of democracy. You have learned about these three "Charters of Freedom" in the last three chapters — the Declaration of Independence, the United States Constitution, and the Bill of Rights.

THE DECLARATION OF INDEPENDENCE (1776)

You learned that this document was shaped by English traditions and by new traditions established by colonial representative assemblies. In the opening lines of the Declaration of Independence, Thomas Jefferson restated John Locke's political philosophy — that all people have certain **unalienable rights** that cannot rightfully be taken from them. Among these unalienable rights are life, liberty, and the pursuit of happiness.

A committee led by Thomas Jefferson meets to discuss the Declaration of Independence.

You should memorize the following lines and practice them with a classmate:

> *"We hold these truths to be self-evident, that all men are created equal, that they are endowed by their Creator with certain Unalienable Rights, that among these are Life, Liberty and the pursuit of Happiness. That to secure these rights, Governments are instituted among Men, deriving their just powers from the consent of the governed.*

Your teacher may want to quiz you on these words. You should also try to write down what the paragraph means in your own words. You can check back on pages 95–96 to review the meaning of this passage. You should recall that the rest of the Declaration went on to explain why the colonists felt they had the right to rebel and to establish their own country. The colonists listed their many grievances against the British king. For example, the king had dissolved representative houses repeatedly and kept standing armies in the colonies without the agreement of colonial legislatures.

THE U.S. CONSTITUTION (1787)

This document established the basic structure of our government. It established a government based on **popular sovereignty** — "We the People" — in which power rests with the people, who elect their representatives. The authors of the Constitution sought to create a national government strong enough to defend the nation's interests and to promote its general welfare. They gave the new national government many important powers and made federal law supreme over state law. To ensure that the new national government was not too strong, they divided its powers between the federal and state governments. Power was further divided at the national level through the separation of powers. The idea was to create an effective government, but one that would also respect the rights of its citizens.

THE BILL OF RIGHTS (1791)

In this chapter, you learned how the authors of the U.S. Constitution originally failed to include a bill of rights. In order to win support for ratification, Federalists agreed to add the Bill of Rights. These amendments further defined the unalienable rights promised by the Declaration of Independence. They included freedom of religion, free speech, freedom of the press, the right to petition and assemble, and the right to "due process" of law when accused of a crime.

At the time that the Bill of Rights was adopted, American society was still largely unequal. Women could not vote or hold office, and many African Americans were still bound in slavery and had no rights at all. The customs and rights of American Indian nations were likewise ignored. Only wealthy white men with property could vote or participate in the political process.

JUDGING THE PAST:
A FAILURE TO MEET IDEALS?

Why, then, should we celebrate these documents? It is important to realize that people living in earlier periods should be judged from the standards of their time, not ours. In 1791, the American experiment in democracy was still in its infancy. American democratic ideas had even spread to other lands, helping to bring about the French Revolution. But in most places, inequality and bigotry still flourished.

Over the following decades, the democratic ideals of these three documents gradually unfolded and reshaped America. Different groups — immigrants, slaves, women — each found support in Jefferson's stirring words. Eventually, the slaves were freed, women gained the right to vote, and minority groups were given the support they needed to participate in American society as equals. These changes were not achieved without struggle, but over the next two hundred years, freedom and equality gradually triumphed.

FREEDOM WEEK PROJECT

To celebrate Freedom Week, your teacher may ask you to complete a Freedom Week Project. This project may take one of many different forms:

★ Write a report or produce a PowerPoint presentation on how a particular group struggled to achieve equality in America.

★ Interview your parents, relatives, and neighbors to find out what adults in your community know about these three historic documents.

★ Conduct a "Freedom Week Fair," with booths devoted to each document. Invite students from other classes to visit your fair.

★ Develop a list of Internet websites for students to learn more about the Declaration of Independence, the U.S. Constitution, the Bill of Rights, the Civil Rights Movement, and the Women's Rights Movement. Briefly describe what each website is about.

CHAPTER STUDY CARDS

First Amendment (1791)

Protections of Individual Freedoms

★ Congress cannot make laws establishing a state religion.

★ Congress cannot stop you from practicing your religion.

★ Congress cannot make laws limiting your right to freedom of speech.

★ Congress cannot make laws limiting freedom of the press.

★ Congress cannot make laws prohibiting people from assembling.

★ People have a right to petition the government in order to correct wrongs.

Bill of Rights (1791)

Other amendments in the Bill of Rights.

★ **Protections of Individual Freedoms**
 • **Second Amend:** Gives citizens the right to bear arms.
 • **Third Amend:** No quartering of soldiers in people's homes.

★ **Protections of the Rights of the Accused**
 • **Fourth Amend:** No unreasonable searches.
 • **Fifth Amend:** SEE NEXT CARD.
 • **Sixth Amend:** Fair and impartial trial; right to a trial by jury; right to a lawyer.
 • **Eighth Amend:** No cruel or unusual punishments; no excessive bail.

The Fifth Amendment

★ **Eminent Domain.** A person's property cannot be taken by the government for public use without just compensation.

★ **Indictment.** A person cannot be put on trial without a formal accusation by a grand jury.

★ **Double Jeopardy.** No one can be tried twice for the same crime.

★ **Self-Incrimination.** A person cannot be forced to testify against himself or herself.

Responsibilities of U.S. Citizens

Responsibilities include those things a citizen "must" do.

★ Obey the laws.
★ Pay taxes to help support the government.
★ Serve on a jury if called upon to do so.
★ Attend school to receive an education.
★ Testify in court if called upon to give evidence.
★ Defend the nation by serving in the armed forces if called upon.

Name _____

CHAPTER 9: The Rights and Responsibilities of American Citizens   **161**

Responsibilities of U.S. Citizens

Responsibilities of citizenship include things a good citizen "should" do:

★ Take an interest in government by learning about its various activities.
★ Stay informed on key public issues.
★ Respect other people's point of view.
★ Inform your representatives about issues that are of concern to you.
★ Vote in local, state and national elections.
★ Participate in government by joining a political party or working in a campaign.
★ Serve in government if elected or appointed to a position.

Other Important Amendments

★ **Seventh Amendment.** This amendment guarantees the right to a jury trial in many civil disputes.
★ **Ninth Amendment.** This amendment says that just because the U.S. Constitution lists some rights, this does not mean that citizens do not also have other rights.
★ **Tenth Amendment.** This amendment states that all powers not specifically given to the federal government are reserved for the states or the people.

CHAPTER 9 CONCEPT MAP

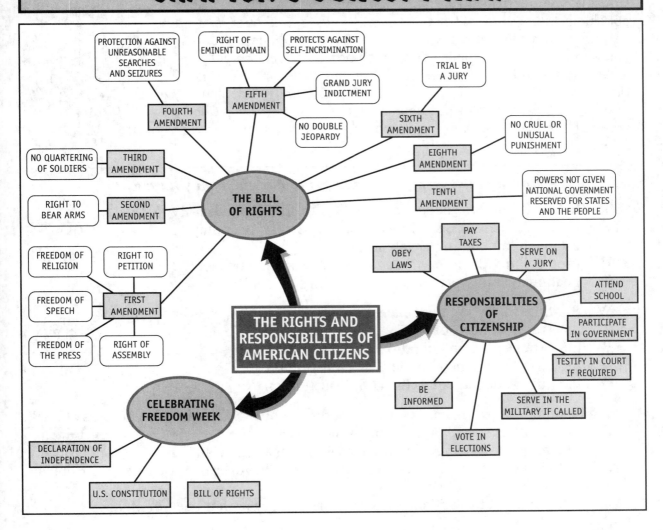

CHECKING YOUR UNDERSTANDING

1

… no warrants shall issue, but upon reasonable cause, supported by oath, describing the place to be searched and the persons or things to be seized." — *Fourth Amendment*	No person shall be held to answer for a capital … crime, unless on [an] indictment of a grand jury. — *Fifth Amendment*	… the accused shall be confronted with the witnesses against him; and have the assistance of counsel. — *Sixth Amendment*

Which statement best summarizes the main idea behind all three amendments?

A   Even persons accused of a crime enjoy certain basic rights.   `Citi 19(B)`
B   Criminal defendants must be fully prosecuted.
C   Criminal acts should lead to the loss of a person's liberty.
D   Accused persons are usually guilty of committing some crime.

EXAMINE **the question.** This question tests your ability to draw a conclusion from three different amendments. You should read each carefully. Then think about what they all have in common. RECALL **what you know.** You should realize that each of these amendments establishes rights and protections for individuals accused of a crime. These rights protect us from false accusations or unfair treatment by government officials. APPLY **what you know.** The best answer is **Choice A**. All three of these amendments deal with rights for someone accused of a crime.

Now try answering some additional questions on your own.

2   The Bill of Rights was added to the U.S. Constitution primarily to —
F   provide the President with power in times of emergency   `Citi 19(B)`
G   establish fair and impartial elections
H   protect individual liberties against government abuse
J   guarantee voting privileges to minorities

3   Which of the following guarantees our freedoms of the press and religion?
A   the Treaty of Paris of 1783
B   the Articles of Confederation   `Citi 19(B)`
C   the First Amendment to the U.S. Constitution
D   the Fifth Amendment to the U.S. Constitution

4   Which of the following has been an important application of the "due process of law"?
F   Freedoms of speech and the press have been limited.   `Citi 19(B)`
G   The reciting of prayers in public schools has been prohibited.
H   Individuals accused of committing crimes have been protected from abusive behavior by the police.
J   The power of the Supreme Court in criminal cases has been limited.

5 The adoption of the Bill of Rights (1791) addressed Anti-Federalist criticism of the new Constitution by —

    A allowing the national government to coin money   `Govt 17(A)`

    B establishing a process for impeaching federal officials

    C providing for an indirect method of electing the president

    D protecting citizens from abuses of power by the national government

6 Which action would be protected by the First Amendment?

    A A family refuses to permit soldiers to be housed in its home.   `Govt 21(B)`

    B A reporter publishes an article critical of city officials.

    C A man on trial refuses to testify against himself.

    D A woman asks to see a lawyer before answering questions from the police.

7 King George III had quartered British soldiers in the homes of colonists. This abuse of royal power was listed as a grievance in the Declaration of Independence. Which document prohibited similar conduct?

    F the Declaration of Independence   `Govt 15(C)`

    G the Articles of Confederation

    H the original Constitution of 1787

    J the Bill of Rights

8 Sandra is taken to the police station where she is placed in a room alone, unable to see or talk to anyone. After five hours, she signs a confession and is released. Which of her rights has been violated?

    A freedom of speech   `Citi 19(B)`

    B prohibition against "double jeopardy"

    C ban on "cruel and unusual" punishments

    D right to the assistance of legal counsel

9 According to the Sixth Amendment, a person accused of a crime in the United States "shall enjoy the right to a speedy and public trial, by an impartial jury." This best shows the influence of the —

    F Magna Carta   `Citi 19(B)`

    G Articles of Confederation

    H Declaration of Independence

    J The *Federalist Papers*

10 Which statement describes a limitation on government action established by the Bill of Rights?

    A The Supreme Court can declare acts of Congress unconstitutional.   `Citi 19(B)`

    B Congress controls interstate commerce.

    C The President shares control over foreign policy with Congress.

    D Government officials cannot enter your home without your permission or a court order.

11 In order to win ratification of the U.S. Constitution, Federalists like Alexander Hamilton and James Madison promised to —

F add a later bill of rights   `Citi 21(A)`

G establish an electoral college

H admit new states to the Union on equal footing with established states

J give the Senate the power to ratify treaties

12

> It is the right of the subjects to petition the king, and all commitments [imprisonments] and prosecutions for such petitioning are illegal. That excessive bail ought not to be required, nor excessive fines imposed; no cruel and unusual punishments inflicted.
>
> — *The English Bill of Rights, 1689*

Which historical document later gave similar guarantees to Americans?

A Declaration of Independence   `Citi 19(B)`

B Articles of Confederation

C The *Federalist Papers*

D Bill of Rights

13 The "due process" clause in the Fifth Amendment and the right to an attorney in the Sixth Amendment were both designed to —

F protect freedom of expression   `Citi 19(B)`

G assure that laws are properly enacted

H ensure fair treatment for those accused of crimes

J provide for judicial review of laws

14 An issue first raised in the Declaration of Independence that was addressed in the Bill of Rights was that there needs to be —

A a federal system of government   `Govt 15(C)`

B limitations on governmental power

C a strong chief executive

D a system of checks and balances

15 The responsibilities of a U.S. citizen include all of the following **EXCEPT**:

F serving on a jury   `Citi 19(C)`

G serving in the military

H voting

J marrying

16 What has been the impact of the First Amendment's separation of church and state on the American way of life?

A It has brought about an end to religious differences.   `Cult 25(C)`

B It has helped to promote religious freedom.

C It has increased American interest in religion.

D It has fostered inequality between religious groups.

17

> The powers not delegated to the United States by the Constitution, nor prohibited by it to the States, are reserved to the States respectively, or to the people.
>
> — *United States Constitution, 10th Amendment*

This amendment in the Bill of Rights was intended to —
F   give the people the right to vote on important issues
G   reduce the rights of citizens
H   limit the powers of the federal government
J   assure federal control over the states

`Citi 19(B)`

18

> … Now, one of the most essential branches of English liberty is the freedom of one's house. A man's house is his castle; and whilst he is quiet, he is as well guarded as a prince in his castle….
>
> — *James Otis, Against the Writs of Assistance, 1761*

Which provision in the Bill of Rights shares this same belief?
A   right to a fair trial
B   protection against unreasonable searches and seizures
C   guarantee against double jeopardy
D   prohibition of cruel and unusual punishment

`Citi 19(B)`

19

> He has…. quarter[ed] large bodies of armed troops among us.

This excerpt from the Declaration of Independence listed a specific grievance that led the writers of the Bill of Rights to include the following:
A   "A well regulated militia, being necessary to the security of a free state, the right of the people to keep and bear arms, shall not be infringed."
B   "No Soldier shall, in time of peace be quartered in any house, without the consent of the owner, nor in time of war, but in a manner to be prescribed by law."
C   "The powers not delegated to the United States by the Constitution, nor prohibited by it to the states, are reserved to the states, or to the people."
D   "Excessive bail shall not be required, nor excessive fines imposed, nor cruel and unusual punishments inflicted."

`Govt 15(C)`

20 In the United States, evidence that is obtained illegally cannot be used in a court of law. This rule is based on an individual's constitutional right to

F face one's accusers in an open and public court

G be protected against double jeopardy

H a speedy and public trial by an impartial jury

J protection against unreasonable searches and seizures

> Citi 19(B)

21 What right does a U.S. citizen enjoy that a permanent resident living in the United States does not?

A the right to an attorney if accused of a crime

B freedom of religion

C the right to vote in a Presidential election

D the right to assemble

> Citi 19(D)

22 What is the primary focus of the First Amendment of the U.S. Constitution?

F rights of self-expression

G rights of the accused

H property rights

J states' rights

> Citi 19(B)

23

> Finally, the equal right of every citizen to the free exercise of his Religion according to the dictates of conscience is held by the same tenure with all our other rights. If we recur [go] to its origin, it is equally the gift of nature….
>
> — *James Madison, 1785*

The belief expressed in this statement was put into law by the —

A signing of the Mayflower Compact

B creation of the Articles of Confederation

C establishment of a federal system of government

D addition of the First Amendment to the United States Constitution

> Cult 25(C)

24

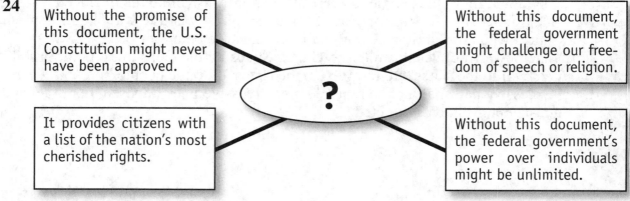

Without the promise of this document, the U.S. Constitution might never have been approved.

Without this document, the federal government might challenge our freedom of speech or religion.

It provides citizens with a list of the nation's most cherished rights.

Without this document, the federal government's power over individuals might be unlimited.

Which document best completes this graphic?

F Treaty of Paris

G Declaration of Independence

H Articles of Confederation

J Bill of Rights

> Citi 19(B)

25

> Congress shall make no law respecting an establishment of religion, or prohibiting the free exercise thereof; or abridging the freedom of speech, or of the press; or the right of the people peaceably to assemble, and to petition the Government for a redress of grievances.
>
> — *First Amendment, United States Constitution*

What is one impact of this amendment on American society?

A   Congress cannot pass a law creating a national religion.   `Cult 25(C)`
B   Religious groups cannot hire former members of Congress.
C   Members of the press cannot hold public office.
D   The Supreme Court cannot limit free speech during wartime.

26

| Fourth Amendment | Fifth Amendment | Sixth Amendment | Eighth Amendment |

What do these four amendments to the United States Constitution have in common?

F   They expand the powers of the presidency.   `Citi 19(B)`
G   They set immigration restrictions.
H   They strength the authority of state governments.
J   They protect the rights of people accused of a crime

27

> The powers not delegated to the United States by the Constitution, nor prohibited by it to the States, are reserved to the States respectively, or to the people.
>
> — *Tenth Amendment, United States Constitution*

The purpose of this provision was to

A   protect states' rights   `Citi 19(B)`
B   create a process for allowing amendments
C   grant the central government power over the states
D   limit the power of the executive branch

---

28   Which statement best describes a limitation placed on the federal government?

F   The Supreme Court can declare acts of Congress unconstitutional.   `Citi 19(B)`
G   Only Congress has the power to control interstate commerce.
H   The President shares control of foreign policy with the legislature.
J   The Federal Bureau of Investigation (FBI) cannot enter your home without permission or a court order.

Name _____

THE EARLY REPUBLIC, 1789–1828

TEKS COVERED IN CHAPTER 10

- **History 1A** Identify the major eras and events in U.S. history through 1877, including the early republic....
- **History 1B** Explain the significance of the following dates: 1803, Louisiana Purchase....
- **History 5A** Describe major domestic problems faced by the leaders of the new republic including maintaining national security, creating a stable economic system, and setting up the court system.
- **History 5B** Summarize arguments regarding protective tariffs, taxation, and banking system.
- **History 5C** Explain the origin and development of American political parties.
- **History 5D** Explain the causes, important events, and effects of the War of 1812.
- **History 5E** Identify the foreign policies of Presidents Washington through Monroe and explain the impact of Washington's Farewell Address and the Monroe Doctrine.
- **History 6B** Analyze the westward growth of the nation, including the Louisiana Purchase....
- **History 7A** Analyze the impact of tariff policies on sections of the U.S. before the Civil War.
- **Geography 10A** Locate places and regions directly related to major eras and turning points in the United States during the ... 18th and 19th centuries.
- **Geography 11A** Analyze how physical characteristics of the environment influenced population distribution, settlement patterns, and economic activities in the United States during the 18th and 19th centuries.
- **Geography 11B** Describe the positive and negative consequences of human modification of the physical environment of the United States.
- **Economics 12A** Identify economic differences among different regions of the U.S.
- **Economics 13A** Analyze the economic effects of the War of 1812.
- **Economics 13B** Identify the economic factors that brought about rapid industrialization and urbanization.
- **Government 18A** Identify the origin of judicial review.
- **Government 18B** Summarize the issues, decisions, and significance of landmark Supreme Court cases, including *Marbury v. Madison, McCulloch v. Maryland,* and *Gibbons v. Ogden.*
- **Citizenship 21A** Identify different points of view of political parties and interest groups on important historical issues.
- **Citizenship 22A** Analyze the leadership qualities of elected and appointed leaders of the United States such as George Washington [and] John Marshall....
- **Science, Technology, and Society 27A** Explain the effects of technological and scientific innovations such as the steamboat, the cotton gin, ... and interchangeable parts.
- **Science, Technology, and Society 27C** Analyze how technological innovations brought about economic growth such as the development of the factory system....

— IMPORTANT IDEAS —

A. Americans and their leaders faced many challenges in the years after the ratification of the U.S. Constitution, when the new republic was established.

B. **George Washington** became the nation's first President in 1789. He established the first **Cabinet**. The first Congress passed the Bill of Rights and the **Judiciary Act of 1789**, completing the nation's federal court system.

C. To create a stable economic system, **Alexander Hamilton**, the Secretary of the Treasury, set out an economic plan in which the federal government would both assume the debts of the national and state governments and create a national bank, a whiskey tax, and a protective tariff to help American manufacturers. All of **Hamilton's Financial Plan** was accepted except for the tariff.

D. Western farmers rebelled against the new whiskey tax. The "**Whiskey Rebellion**" collapsed when Washington and Hamilton made a show of force.

E. Jefferson and Madison disagreed with Hamilton's Plan, giving rise to the first American political parties — the **Federalists** and the **Democratic-Republicans**.

F. Americans were also divided in their support of the **French Revolution**. Jefferson and Madison supported it, while Adams and Hamilton feared mob rule in America. Washington kept the nation neutral when war broke out between France and Britain. In his **Farewell Address**, Washington warned against entangling alliances, believing the nation should avoid ties to Europe.

G. Jefferson was elected in the "**Revolution of 1800**." This was a peaceful transition of power from the Federalists. In 1803, Jefferson approved the **Louisiana Purchase**, doubling the nation's size and giving America control of the Mississippi River. Jefferson continued Washington's policy of neutrality with Europe.

H. Chief Justice **John Marshall** issued a series of landmark Supreme Court decisions which helped strengthen the national government, established the role of the Supreme Court, and unified the nation. In *Marbury v. Madison*, Marshall established the principle of **judicial review** — that the Supreme Court can rule whether a law is constitutional. In *McCulloch v. Maryland*, he established the supremacy of federal law and the ability of Congress to exercise powers needed to carry out its duties. In *Gibbons v. Ogden*, he expanded the scope of Congress' power to regulate commerce between the states.

I. Americans finally became involved in a conflict with Britain in the **War of 1812**. Britain's impressment of U.S. sailors and U.S. ambitions in Canada were the main causes. The war proved the nation could defend itself.

J. The Federalist Party collapsed after the war, giving rise to the "**Era of Good Feelings**." During these years, Americans felt renewed national pride. **The Missouri Compromise** (1820) preserved unity, and the **Monroe Doctrine** (1823) asserted American influence in the Western Hemisphere.

K. During these years, Americans also saw the spread of steamboat travel, increasing numbers of factories, and construction of canals, such as the Erie Canal.

In this chapter, you will learn about life in the new nation, from the Presidency of George Washington to that of James Monroe. Our earliest Presidents established many new traditions that have survived until today. America also greatly expanded in size in these years and preserved its independence in the War of 1812.

KEY TERMS AND PEOPLE IN THIS CHAPTER

- George Washington
- Cabinet
- Alexander Hamilton
- Hamilton's Financial Plan
- Political Parties
- Democratic-Republicans
- Federalists
- Protective Tariff
- French Revolution
- Proclamation of Neutrality

- Whiskey Rebellion
- Farewell Address
- Factories
- Industrial Revolution
- National Road
- Thomas Jefferson
- John Adams
- Louisiana Purchase
- Lewis and Clark
- *Marbury v. Madison*

- John Marshall
- War of 1812
- Lowell System
- "Era of Good Feelings"
- *McCulloch v. Maryland*
- *Gibbons v. Ogden*
- Erie Canal
- Robert Fulton
- Missouri Compromise
- Monroe Doctrine

ESSENTIAL QUESTIONS

- What challenges faced the new nation under the Constitution?
- How did the first American political parties emerge?
- How did the Supreme Court establish its decisive role in American life?
- How did American social and economic life change?
- How did the United States conduct its relations with other nations?

THE PRESIDENCY OF GEORGE WASHINGTON: 1789-1797

In 1789, **George Washington** was inaugurated as the nation's first President. As President, Washington guided the new government as it applied the ideas expressed in the Constitution to create a functioning federal republic. Upon taking office, Washington faced several major challenges. He had to define the authority of the central government, create a stable economic system, build a military, maintain national security, conduct foreign relations, and enter into treaties with several Indian tribes. In this section, we will look more closely at both Washington's domestic and foreign policies.

Domestic policy refers to government policies dealing with conditions within the nation.
Foreign policy concerns relations with other countries.

WASHINGTON'S DOMESTIC POLICY

DEFINING OUR NEW CENTRAL GOVERNMENT

The Constitution allowed the President to appoint officials in charge of executive departments. The chief officials that Washington appointed began meeting together with him in what came to be known as the **Cabinet**. Over the years, additional Cabinet departments were created. The Cabinet was one of the important precedents established by Washington. A **precedent** is an action taken for the first time, which is followed by others afterwards.

*President Washington (far right)
meets with his Cabinet.*

CREATING A STABLE ECONOMY

The most pressing problems facing Washington's government were economic. As a result of the American Revolution, the national government owed $54 million. The states owed another $24 million, and the paper money issued by the Continental Congress and the Articles of Confederation was worthless. The job of solving these economic problems fell to **Alexander Hamilton**, our nation's first Secretary of the Treasury. Hamilton drew up a four-part plan for getting the nation on a sound financial basis:

HAMILTON'S ECONOMIC PLAN

Repay the Debt.	**National Bank.**	**Whiskey Tax.**	**Protective Tariff.**
Hamilton believed the national government should pay off the debts of both the states and the previous national government in order to establish the nation's credit.	Hamilton proposed creation of a national bank as a place to deposit taxes, to provide a sound currency, and to make loans to the national government.	Hamilton proposed a tax on whiskey to raise money from western farmers.	Hamilton asked Congress to pass a high **tariff** — a tax on imported foreign goods which would protect American industries from foreign competition.

THE RISE OF POLITICAL PARTIES

Hamilton's program was strongly opposed by **Thomas Jefferson**, Washington's Secretary of State. Jefferson, Madison and their followers believed Hamilton's plan would just benefit wealthy Americans since speculators had bought up much of the debt. They also felt that the Constitution did not give the federal government the right to create a national bank. This disagreement gave rise to America's first **political parties** — associations that try to elect their members to government offices so that they will pass laws favorable to their ideas.

Alexander Hamilton

Hamilton's followers became known as the **Federalists**. Jefferson's supporters called themselves the **Democratic-Republicans**. Their disagreements were heightened by the outbreak of a revolution in France, where commoners rebelled against the king and nobles.

	Federalists	**Democratic-Republicans**
Main Party Leaders	Alexander Hamilton and John Adams	Thomas Jefferson and James Madison
Constitutional Views	Loose constructionists: the national government should take all steps needed to govern the nation	Strict constructionists: the national government should only have powers expressly listed in the Constitution
Views on Government	Favored a strong federal government	Favored states' rights
Views on Foreign Policy	Pro-British: Federalists feared the French Revolution as an example of mob rule	Pro-French: Jefferson was sympathetic to the French Revolution
Main Supporters	Merchants and manufacturers	Farmers and skilled craftsmen
Who Should Vote	Only those meeting property qualifications	Vote should be open to all adult males

DEFEAT OF THE PROTECTIVE TARIFF

All of Hamilton's program was approved although tariff rates on manufactured goods were not made as high as he suggested. Southern states opposed high tariff rates because tariffs would make it harder for Southerners to sell their crops to Britain and to buy British goods.

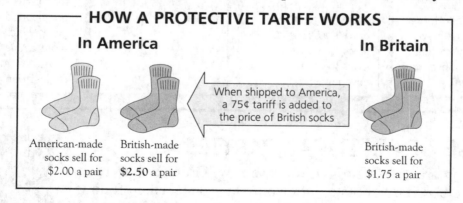

— HOW A PROTECTIVE TARIFF WORKS —

In America **In Britain**

When shipped to America, a 75¢ tariff is added to the price of British socks

American-made socks sell for **$2.00** a pair

British-made socks sell for **$2.50** a pair

British-made socks sell for **$1.75** a pair

THE WHISKEY REBELLION OF 1794

Farmers living west of the Appalachian Mountains often converted their excess grain into whiskey, which was easier to carry over the mountains than bushels of grain. The new federal whiskey tax caused great hostility among them. Farmers in Western Pennsylvania refused to pay the tax and threatened tax collectors.

Washington called up the militia to put down the rebellion. Washington, with Alexander Hamilton by his side, was ready to use force, but the rebels fled before any fighting took place.

APPLYING WHAT YOU HAVE LEARNED

★ Imagine you are a representative in Congress in 1794. Write a speech either for or against Hamilton's financial plan.

★ How were Shays' Rebellion and the Whiskey Rebellion handled differently? Explain your answer.

WASHINGTON'S FOREIGN POLICY

During Washington's Presidency, the revolution in France became increasingly violent. The revolutionaries overthrew and executed Louis XVI, the French King. War between France and Britain then broke out in 1793. Jefferson's supporters continued to favor the French revolutionaries, while Alexander Hamilton, John Adams, and other Federalists favored the British.

PROCLAMATION OF NEUTRALITY (1793)

The United States had won its independence largely through the military and financial support of France. Some French leaders thought it was time for the Americans to return the favor and that the Franco-American alliance of 1778 was still in effect.

Hamilton and his supporters were able to persuade Washington that France's war was totally European in nature. Washington finally became convinced that there was nothing to be gained if the United States involved itself in this European conflict. Compared to European powers, the United States was weak militarily. To avoid being drawn into the Anglo-French conflict, Washington adopted a policy of **neutrality** — the United States would avoid taking sides in any European conflict or becoming involved in any foreign war.

ACTING AS AN AMATEUR HISTORIAN

U.S. History   Search

1776

Washington believed America should not become entangled in the conflicts of foreign nations. His **Proclamation of Neutrality** stated this nation's position:

> "It appears that a state of war exists between Austria, Prussia, Sardinia, Great Britain, and the Netherlands on the one part, and France on the other. The duty and interest of the United States require that they should adopt a conduct friendly and impartial toward the [warring] powers. I have thought fit to declare the position of the United States to observe a conduct towards those powers respectfully; and warn our citizens to avoid all acts which may in any manner tend to [go against] this position."

★ In your own words, describe Washington's Proclamation of Neutrality.

★ Do you think Washington chose a wise policy? Explain your answer.

The French Ambassador, **Citizen Genêt**, nevertheless tried to recruit U.S. ships and volunteers to help the French. Many French felt the Americans owed them help. Washington sent a complaint to Genêt, who quickly backed down. Meanwhile, **John Jay** negotiated a treaty with Britain to promote trade. **Thomas Pinckney** negotiated another treaty with Spain, settling America's borders. The new treaty gave U.S. citizens the right to ship goods along the Mississippi River, all the way down to the port of New Orleans.

WASHINGTON'S FAREWELL ADDRESS

After two terms in office, Washington declined a third term. He especially disliked the new party rivalry. In 1796, Washington delivered his **Farewell Address**. Although known as his most famous "speech," it was actually delivered in the form of a letter to the public published in the form of an "address" or speech.

Washington wrote his Farewell Address with the help of Alexander Hamilton.

Washington used his Farewell Address to give his countrymen his advice as a "departing friend" on what he saw as the greatest threats to the nation's survival. Washington addressed relations between the North and South and the importance of moral virtue. He warned against the rise of political parties and the challenges of foreign policy.

ACTING AS AN AMATEUR HISTORIAN

In his Farewell Address, Washington warned of possible dangers ahead:

> "The great rule of conduct for us in regard to foreign nations is in extending our commercial relations, to have with them as little political connection as possible. It is our true policy to steer clear of permanent alliances with any portion of the foreign world.
>
> As an important source of strength and security, cherish public credit. One method of preserving it is to use it as sparingly as possible; avoid the accumulation of debt, not only by shunning occasions of expense, but by vigorous exertions to discharge debts, which unavoidable wars may have occasioned, not ungenerously throwing upon [future generations] the burden, which we ourselves ought to bear."

★ What are some of the dangers that Washington cautioned the nation against?

★ Which of these dangers does our nation still face today?

Washington believed two terms were the most any President should serve. For the next 130 years, Presidents followed this precedent by not seeking more than two terms.

LEARNING WITH GRAPHIC ORGANIZERS

Complete the following chart on the highlights of the Presidency of George Washington.

Hamilton's Financial Plan	Emergence of Political Parties	Proclamation of Neutrality

PRESIDENCY OF GEORGE WASHINGTON

Pinckney Treaty with Spain	Whiskey Rebellion	Washington's Farewell Address

PORTRAIT OF THE NATION IN 1800

By 1800, the United States consisted of 16 states with a combined population of just over five million people. Almost one million of these were enslaved African Americans. American culture was a unique mixture of British, Irish, European, Native American, and African traditions, under American conditions.

Agriculture. America was still an **agrarian** (*agricultural*) society. Crops were the basis of the nation's wealth. Some crops, like cotton and tobacco in the South, were grown for export. Farmers in the West grew wheat or raised livestock for Americans to eat.

Rural vs. Urban Centers. In 1800, the vast majority of Americans lived in the countryside. Most Americans were **self-sufficient** in what has been referred to as the "**Age of Homespun.**" They lived on a farm in the countryside, grew their own food, and made their own clothes, shelter and furniture. Only one in 25 Americans was a city dweller. Larger cities were located along the Atlantic coast, from Boston to Baltimore. Philadelphia was the nation's largest city, with 69,000 inhabitants.

Corner of Broadway and Chambers Street, NYC, c. 1825

Social Differences. Great differences existed among Americans based on class, race and gender. Wealthy planters and merchants enjoyed travel and luxuries. However, most Americans were farmers or workers with lives of toil. Women had few rights. Enslaved African-American slaves had almost no rights at all.

Rise of Industry. A new industrial society was only just starting to emerge in the Northeast. Eli Whitney introduced the use of standardized **interchangeable parts**. In the 1790s, **Samuel Slater** defied British law by building a machine that could spin cotton fibers into thread. Slater's spinning mill in Rhode Island was followed by a gradual increase in the use of machines and a shift from working at home or in small shops to working in **factories**.

Samuel Slater's cotton mill, near Pawtucket, Rhode Island.

Techniques of mass production were pioneered by the American inventor **Eli Whitney**. Whitney won a contract to produce 10,000 muskets. The key to his winning this bid was his new process for manufacturing interchangeable firing-mechanism parts. The inspiration came from techniques that Whitney had developed in the manufacture of his cotton gin.

Whitney's plan was for machines to produce standardized parts which could be used with other parts to assemble a whole product without a laborer filing and fitting each part together. This interchangeability allowed easy assembly of new devices and easier repair of existing devices, while minimizing the time and skill needed for a person to assembly or repair a product. Use of interchangeable parts in the manufacture of muskets (*guns*) was a major contribution to the development of America industry.

The shift of manufacturing to factories, known as the **Industrial Revolution**, would soon lead to the rise of new industries and rapidly growing cities.

Transportation. America's vast and untamed landscape made travel difficult. Cities were connected by roads that were little more than dirt trails. A few had log or plank roads. Most short travel was done by walking. For longer trips, people rode on horse-drawn wagons. Travel on roads was slow: a trip from Boston to New York took three days by stage coach. Western settlers sought roads to aid settlement and for the transfer of goods. They wished for a way to make it easier to market their goods and to buy essential supplies in return. In 1806, Congress set aside funds to build the first federally funded road,

Construction of the National Road begins.

the **National Road**. Travel by water was easier and cheaper than travel overland. Goods were often carried along streams and rivers to ports along the coast. People took ferries to cross rivers and took boats to travel down rivers, across lakes, or along coastlines.

Communication. Communications were slow. There were no telephones, telegraphs, televisions, or computers. People communicated primarily by letter. Letters had to be carried over dusty, unpaved roads or by packet boat. Mail was often mangled or even lost. News about events traveled slowly. Most people received their information from local newspapers. Most were published weekly or monthly, and were shared by many readers.

Regional Differences. The three main regions from colonial times — New England, the Middle Atlantic Colonies, and the South — were replaced by three sections: the **North** (Northeast), the **South** and the emerging **West** (today, the Midwest). Differences in climate and physical geography led to economic specialization, The North was the first section to build factories and railroads, and became a center of manufacturing, shipping,

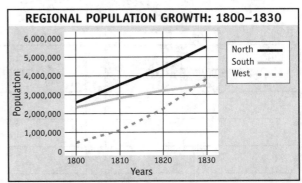

REGIONAL POPULATION GROWTH: 1800–1830

large towns and cities, and small farms. The West was a region of family farms that served as the nation's "bread basket." The South became dominated by plantations, cash crops and slavery, with smaller family farms further inland.

The nation's population was growing at an enormous rate. The land available for settlement increased by almost the size of Europe — from 4.4 million to 7.8 million square kilometers.

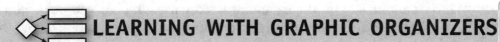 **LEARNING WITH GRAPHIC ORGANIZERS**

The early 1800s were a time of change in the history of the new young nation, Complete the following graphic organizer describing the state of affairs taking place in the nation.

Population of the Nation	Economy of the Nation	Rural vs. Urban Centers
_____	_____	_____
_____	_____	_____
_____	_____	_____
_____	_____	_____
_____	_____	_____
_____	_____	_____
_____	_____	_____

THE UNITED STATES IN THE EARLY 1800s

Transportation	Communications	Emergence of Regional Differences
_____	_____	_____
_____	_____	_____
_____	_____	_____
_____	_____	_____
_____	_____	_____
_____	_____	_____

THE PRESIDENCY OF THOMAS JEFFERSON: 1801-1809

The second President of the United States, **John Adams**, was a Federalist who continued many of Washington's policies. Adams was hostile to France and promoted laws restricting foreigners and the press. In 1800, John Adams lost the Presidential election to Thomas Jefferson.

Jefferson sought to show that he was one of the people. The capital had just been moved from Philadelphia to Washington, D.C. Jefferson walked alone from his boardinghouse to the Capitol to take the oath of office. His inauguration marked the first transition of the executive branch from one party to another. Sometimes known as the "**Revolution of 1800**," this change occurred without violence.

JEFFERSON'S VIEWS ON GOVERNMENT

Jefferson saw his election as a turning point. He believed the best government was one that governed least. Jefferson opposed special privileges for the wealthy and had strong sympathies for the common farmer. As President, he set about reducing the size of the army, ending naval expansion, and lowering government costs.

Thomas Jefferson

ACTING AS AN AMATEUR HISTORIAN

In his First Inaugural Address (1801), Jefferson spoke of what he thought was necessary to make America a prosperous nation. Here is what he said:

U.S. History   *Search*

1776

"With all these blessings, what more is necessary to make us a happy and prosperous people? Still one thing more, fellow citizens — a wise and frugal government, which shall restrain men from injuring one another, which shall leave them otherwise free to regulate their own pursuits of industry and improvement, and shall not take from the mouth of labor the bread it had earned. This is the sum of good government."

★ What did Jefferson see as "good government"?

★ Is what Jefferson said 200 years ago still relevant to our nation today?

THE LOUISIANA PURCHASE (1803)

Jefferson had always dreamed of extending the United States westward. When France took the Louisiana Territory back from Spain, Jefferson sent envoys to France to negotiate the right to send goods down the Mississippi River to New Orleans. In 1803, Napoleon Bonaparte, the new ruler of France, offered to sell all of the **Louisiana Territory**.

Although Jefferson was uncertain whether the Constitution allowed the federal government to buy new territory, he went ahead with the purchase. The Louisiana Purchase doubled the size of the nation. It gave Americans control of the Mississippi River. In 1804, Jefferson sent **Meriwether Lewis** and **William Clark** to explore this vast region. Their expedition laid the groundwork for the future westward expansion of the United States.

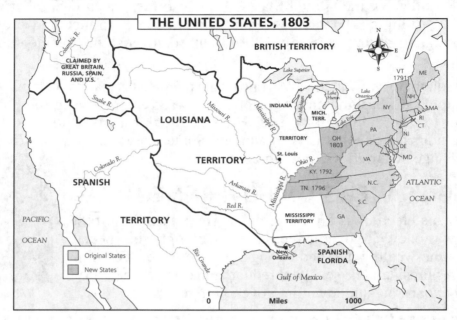

MARBURY v. MADISON (1803)

Marshall became Chief Justice of the Supreme Court in 1801.

Just before President John Adams left office, he appointed **John Marshall** as Chief Justice of the U.S. Supreme Court. The Supreme Court was often viewed as the weakest of the three branches, but Marshall made the Supreme Court a new center of government power. The Marshall Court established the principle of judicial review in *Marbury v. Madison*.

Background: President Adams, just before leaving office, appointed Marbury as a justice of the peace. The new Secretary of State, James Madison, refused to deliver his commission (*official papers*) making him a justice of the peace. Marbury asked the Supreme Court to require Madison to deliver his commission. The first Congress had passed the **Judiciary Act of 1789** to create the lower federal courts. Marbury argued this act also gave the Supreme Court the power to force Madison to deliver the commission.

Decision/Significance: The Court ruled that the part of the Judiciary Act that gave the Supreme Court the power to order delivery of the Commission went against the Constitution. The Court declared that this part of the act was null and void. This case established **judicial review** — the right of the Supreme Court to declare a law unconstitutional. This greatly strengthened the power of the judiciary by making it the final authority in interpreting the Constitution.

ACTING AS AN AMATEUR HISTORIAN

Marbury v. Madison was the first significant decision handed down by the U.S. Supreme Court after John Marshall was sworn in as its Chief Justice in 1801:

> "It is emphatically the province and duty of the judicial department to say what the law is. Those who apply the rule to particular cases, must of necessity [explain] and interpret that rule. If two laws conflict with each other, the courts must decide on the operation of each...."

★ What was Marshall's decision? Do you agree with his decision?

★ Why was the court ruling in *Marbury v. Madison* of such importance?

THE EMBARGO ACT OF 1807

War continued to rage between Britain and France. British ships started stopping U.S. ships to search for deserters from the British navy. Sometimes they took Americans to serve on British ships. This practice of **impressment** (*forced military service*) greatly humiliated Americans and put pressure on President Jefferson to take action.

An American sailor is seized (impressed) by British seamen.

To avoid war, Jefferson pushed the **Embargo Act** through Congress. Under the act, American ships were prohibited from trading with European nations. In the last days of Jefferson's Presidency, Congress replaced the Embargo Act with the **Non-Intercourse Act** (1809). This act lifted the embargo on U.S. shipping except for ships bound for British or French ports.

APPLYING WHAT YOU HAVE LEARNED

★ Research important people and events from this period and devise skits to show how various *precedents* were set in the new nation: consider the Cabinet, the Pinckney Treaty, the Louisiana Purchase, and *Marbury v. Madison*.

★ Did Thomas Jefferson live up to his ideals as President? Explain your answer.

★ Using the Internet or your local library for information, create your own map showing the route Lewis and Clark took to the Pacific.

LEARNING WITH GRAPHIC ORGANIZERS

The United States experienced important changes under President Thomas Jefferson. Fill in the following chart by describing some of the terms and events associated with Jefferson's Presidency.

"Revolution of 1800"

_____
_____
_____
_____
_____
_____
_____

Views on Government

_____
_____
_____
_____
_____
_____
_____

Louisiana Purchase (1803)

_____
_____
_____
_____
_____
_____

Louis and Clark Expedition

_____
_____
_____
_____
_____
_____
_____

Embargo Act of 1807

_____
_____
_____

PRESERVING THE NATION'S INDEPENDENCE: THE WAR OF 1812

After Jefferson served two terms as President, he followed the precedent set by Washington and stepped down from the Presidency. His good friend and fellow Democratic-Republican, **James Madison**, became the nation's fourth President in 1809. Three years later, Americans were drawn into another war with Great Britain in 1812. This war is known as the **War of 1812**, or the "Second War for Independence."

CAUSES OF THE CONFLICT

Ever since 1793, France and Britain had been continuously at war against each other with only one short break. Americans continued to trade with Europe, but tried to keep out of the war between these two nations. However, British ships continued to stop American ships and to seize (or *impress*) U.S. sailors. Some British troops in Canada also encouraged Native American Indians to attack American settlements. At the same time, several young Congressmen thought the time was ripe to seize Canada from the British, who were fighting Napoleon in Europe. In 1812, President Madison asked Congress to declare war on Britain.

MAIN EVENTS OF THE WAR

American forces tried to invade Canada, but they were unsuccessful. In retaliation, British troops temporarily occupied Washington, D.C. and burned down the White House. Madison's wife, Dolley Madison, acted quickly to remove paintings and other valuables from the White House before the British arrived.

Much of the fighting during the War of 1812 took place on the Great Lakes and in upstate New York. In 1813, British troops further retaliated for the attack on Canada by burning the American settlement at Buffalo. Meanwhile, American and British ships clashed in the **Battle of Lake Erie**.

In December 1814, a peace treaty was finally signed between Britain and the United States. The treaty was actually silent about those issues that had

Oliver Perry at the Battle of Lake Erie

caused the war. All it stated was that captured prisoners, ships and lands were to be returned. The British made no promises to stop searching American vessels, but with an end to the war between France and Britain, they had little need to do so. Americans felt they had proved they could protect their independence. Communications from Europe were so slow that the bloodiest battle of the war was actually fought after the treaty was signed. General Andrew Jackson defeated the British at the Battle of New Orleans in January 1815.

One legacy of the war was **Francis Scott Key's** "The Star Spangled Banner." Key wrote this poem while imprisoned in Baltimore on a British ship. It later became our national anthem.

IMPACT OF THE WAR OF 1812

The United States emerged with worldwide respect for resisting Great Britain. European rulers realized they could not interfere with American trade. The morale of American citizens increased greatly. They had fought one of the greatest military powers in the world and managed to survive. The Great Lakes were no longer disputed, but became the shared property of Canada and the United States. The War of 1812 also spurred the economic growth of the United States. The Northeast saw a major spur in manufacturing. A British blockade had created a shortage of cotton cloth in the United States during the war, and Northeastern manufacturers met the demand. People bought American manufactures because they could not get British ones.

To encourage manufacturing, the government placed tariffs on imported goods, making American products more competitive with imported goods. This also encouraged the creation of the **Lowell System** in Massachusetts. This system placed all stages of manufacturing under one roof, replacing the earlier domestic system, where people worked at home.

APPLYING WHAT YOU HAVE LEARNED

★ Make your own diagram showing the causes of the War of 1812 on one side and the effects of the war on the other side.

★ Research how the War of 1812 led to economic changes in the nation and present your results in a PowerPoint presentation to the class.

★ Would you agree that the War of 1812 should be called the "Second War for Independence"? Explain your answer.

THE "ERA OF GOOD FEELINGS"

The happy end of the War of 1812 led to the "**Era of Good Feelings**," a period in which all Americans belonged to the same political party — the **Democratic-Republicans**. This was partly due to the collapse of the Federalist Party, the old party of Alexander Hamilton and John Adams. The Federalists, largely based in New England, had opposed the war because it had cut off trade with Europe, hurting New England shipping. Some New England Federalists even passed resolutions calling for New England to secede (*leave*) from the Union. At the same time, many of the most important Federalist ideas had already been adopted. By the end of the war, the Federalist Party had become so unpopular that the party had dissolved.

The "Era of Good Feelings" was a time in which American **nationalism**, or pride in the nation, surged. Americans had preserved their independence from Great Britain and had learned to cooperate in a common effort.

CLAY'S "AMERICAN SYSTEM"

In these years, Americans cooperated to improve their transportation routes by building roads and canals. **Henry Clay**, a spokesman for moderate policies, sought to resolve differences between the North and South while representing the nationalist outlook of the West. Clay proposed his "**American System**" to Congress.

Henry Clay (1777–1852)

His system consisted of a high tariff (*tax on imports*) to protect American manufactured goods from competition with cheaper British products. Clay then proposed that the revenues collected from the tariff should be used to pay for internal improvements, such as new roads and canals, in the West. In this way, Clay hoped his American System would bind the industrial East and the agrarian West together. Despite Clay's good intentions, the American System never went into effect. The national system of internal improvements was never adequately funded by Congress; the failure to provide funds was due in part to sectional jealousies and a belief that such spending was never provided for in the Constitution.

THE ERIE CANAL

In the early 1800s, it was easier and cheaper to ship goods by water than by land. In 1816, the Governor of New York proposed a 360-mile canal connecting Lake Erie to the Hudson River. Farmers could then ship goods from the Great Lakes to New York City entirely by water. After a long and heated debate, state lawmakers voted to build the canal.

The **Erie Canal** was the most ambitious project ever constructed up to that time. A path 50 feet wide had to be cut through forests, swamps, and hills. Then a ditch 40 feet wide and 4 feet deep had to be dug. The canal was an important modification of the physical environment. Without the heavy equipment we have today, thousands of workers were needed to cut trees, rip out tree stumps, blast through rock, and dig the canal. One out of every four workers was Irish. At the peak of construction, more than four thousand workers were laboring on the canal. Canal workers earned about $10 a month in 1832.

ERIE, OSWEGO and CHAMPLAIN CANALS

CANADA	Lake Champlain

LAKE ONTARIO

CHAMPLAIN CANAL

Lake George

Black R.

OSWEGO CANAL

Lake Oneida

Lake Sacandaga

Niagara R.

ERIE CANAL

ERIE CANAL

ERIE CANAL

Mohawk R.

Hudson R.

Buffalo

Finger Lakes

Genesee R.

LAKE ERIE

Albany

In order to pass through the mountains and come down gradually to the level of elevation (*height*) of the Hudson River, the engineers of the canal designed a series of locks. These locks were spaces that could be closed off. They acted like giant bathtubs in which boats could be raised and lowered with the water.

After seven years, the **Erie Canal** was completed in 1825. Barges were pulled slowly through the canal by mules. Cities along its route grew and prospered. Western farmers could now send goods from the Great Lakes along the canal and down the Hudson River. New York City grew to become the nation's largest city.

A towpath on one side used mules to pull barges along the canal.

APPLYING WHAT YOU HAVE LEARNED

Look for resources in your school library or on the Internet about the Erie Canal and compare its impact with a trail or roadway in your local area.

THE BEGINNING OF THE TRANSPORTATION REVOLUTION

America's transportation system went through other important changes in these years. Other states copied New York by building their own canals. As more people moved west, private companies opened special roads called **turnpikes**. The **steamboat**, invented by **Robert Fulton** in 1807, revolutionized water transportation. Fulton used a steam engine to drive a large wheel with paddles. Steam power was more dependable than wind and could even be used to move boats upstream against the current.

During its first test, *The Clermont* failed. However, after a few adjustments to its engine, the boat was on its way. Fulton's boat was able to make a 150-mile trip from New York City to Albany traveling against the current of the Hudson River in only 32 hours. Soon, steamboats were traveling up and down the Mississippi and other rivers, carrying both people and goods.

Robert Fulton's The Clermont.

GIBBONS v. OGDEN (1824)

During this period, the Supreme Court encouraged the growth of a national market by its decision in the case of *Gibbons v. Ogden*.

Background. Ogden had been granted a monopoly by New York State to operate a steamboat between New York and New Jersey. Gibbons was granted a similar license by the federal government. Ogden sued to stop Gibbons from competing with him. Gibbons appealed to the Supreme Court.

Decision / Significance. Marshall ruled that Congress could regulate ferry boats crossing the Hudson River between New York and New Jersey as part of its power under the Constitution to control "interstate commerce" (*trade between states*). Only the federal government, according to the U.S. Constitution, could regulate interstate commerce, including activities affecting interstate commerce. This established the federal government's right to regulate anything that involves commerce between the states. It set the stage for future expansion of Congressional power over other activities once thought to be under the control of the states.

THE PURCHASE OF FLORIDA (1819)

The border between Spanish colonial territory and the United States was a source of heated debate with Spain. Plagued by many problems, Spain feared losing Florida without compensation. Spanish leaders therefore chose to negotiate a settlement. The United States agreed to purchase Florida in 1819 for $5 million. It also agreed to recognize Spanish sovereignty over Texas.

McCULLOCH v. MARYLAND (1819)

Another key decision by Chief Justice John Marshall was *McCulloch v. Maryland*. This case also tested the relationship between state and federal law.

Background. In 1818, the Maryland legislature imposed a tax on the Maryland branch of the Second National Bank. The National Bank was unpopular since it competed with state banks. Maryland legislators hoped that state taxes on the federal bank would shut down the Maryland branch. James McCulloch, the federal bank's cashier, did not pay the taxes the Maryland law required, and Maryland sued for payment. After the state of Maryland won the dispute in its own courts, the case was appealed to the U.S. Supreme Court.

Decision / Significance. The case presented two key issues: (1) Does Congress have the power to create a bank, even though that power is not specifically mentioned in the Constitution? (2) Does Maryland have the power to tax an institution of the federal government? Marshall ruled that Congress could indeed charter a national bank, since this would help Congress carry out its other powers. Marshall said that the "necessary and proper" clause (*elastic clause*) in the Constitution gives Congress all those powers needed to carry out its powers listed in the Constitution. He also said that since the federal government had the right to establish the bank, Maryland had no right to interfere by taxing it.

ACTING AS AN AMATEUR HISTORIAN

McCulloch v. Maryland marked the first time the Supreme Court ruled on federal and state laws in conflict. In this case, Chief Justice John Marshall handed down one of his most important decisions regarding the extent of federal power:

> "Let the end be legitimate, let it be within the scope of the Constitution, and all means which are appropriate, which are plainly adapted to that end, which are not prohibited, but consistent with the letter and spirit of the Constitution, are constitutional..... The power to tax involves the power to destroy; that the power to destroy may defeat and render useless the power to create...."

★ Summarize Chief Justice Marshall's decision in your own words.

★ Do you agree with Chief Justice Marshall's decision? Explain your answer.

★ How did Marshall show leadership in the three cases you just studied?

LEARNING WITH GRAPHIC ORGANIZERS

Complete the graphic organizer below. For each Supreme Court decision describe it and evaluate its impact.

Marbury v. Madison	*McCulloch v. Maryland*	*Gibbons v. Ogden*
Description: _____	Description: _____	Description: _____
Impact: _____	Impact: _____	Impact: _____

THE MISSOURI COMPROMISE OF 1820

The American Revolution and the Constitutional Convention had failed to resolve the issue of slavery in America. George Washington had freed his own slaves on his death, but Thomas Jefferson, the author of the Declaration of Independence, had not. Many early American leaders had imagined that slavery would just gradually die out. However, the invention of the **cotton gin** by Eli Whitney in 1793 made it easier for unskilled slaves

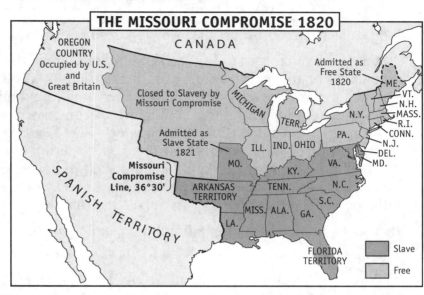

to remove seeds from the type of cotton that grew in the South. This invention led to the spread of slavery in the South. The factories of England and the Northern United States kept up the demand for raw cotton. With the purchase of the Louisiana Territory, the issue of slavery again came into sharp focus. Should the territories of the Louisiana Purchase enter the Union as free or slave states? The problem had to be faced when Missouri applied for admission as a slave state.

Henry Clay engineered a compromise in which slavery was forbidden in the Louisiana Territory north of the "Missouri Compromise Line" (*36°30′*), except in Missouri. One free state (*Maine*) and one slave state (*Missouri*) were admitted to the Union at the same time to keep the balance between free and slave states in the Senate.

THE MONROE DOCTRINE

James Monroe fought in the American Revolution, helped negotiate the Lousiana Purchase, and served as Secretary of State under President Madison. In 1817, Monroe became President. In 1823 in his annual message to Congress, Monroe issued a bold statement on foreign policy. He repeated the nation's longstanding commitment to neutrality and offered a warning to Europe. The American and French Revolutions had inspired people in Latin America to be free. During the Napoleonic Wars, Spain had been cut off from its colonies. The Spanish colonists grew accustomed to self-government. When Spain's king was restored, he tried to reassert control. Colonists in Latin America then declared their independence. Later, it was feared that France would help Spain reconquer her colonies.

Monroe announced that the United States would oppose any attempts by European powers to establish new colonies or to restore Spanish rule in countries in the Western Hemisphere that had achieved their independence.

ACTING AS AN AMATEUR HISTORIAN

Monroe reacted to European threats by issuing the **Monroe Doctrine**:

> "Our policy in regard to Europe is not to interfere in the internal concerns of any of its powers; to cultivate friendly relations with it, and to preserve the just claims of every power, submitting to injuries from none. But this continent's circumstances are different. It is impossible that the [European] powers should extend their political system to any portion of [this] continent without endangering our peace and happiness;… It is impossible that we should behold such [involvement] with indifference. It is still the true policy of the United States to leave the parties to themselves, in the hope that other powers will pursue the same course."

What was President Monroe telling Spain and other European powers?

The Monroe Doctrine told Europeans to keep their hands off the Western Hemisphere. Besides warning Spain and France, Monroe was also addressing Russia, whose advance down the Alaskan coast threatened U.S. claims to the Oregon Territory in the West. In this way, the United States established its own "sphere of influence" in North America.

APPLYING WHAT YOU HAVE LEARNED

★ In a group, debate if President Monroe acted fairly in issuing his "Doctrine."

★ Create a political cartoon for an event that took place during the "Era of Good Feelings." Your artwork is less important than the point you trying to make.

★ Using the Internet or your school library, research the life of James Monroe before becoming President. Assess his contributions as one of the early leaders of the United States.

THE "ERA OF GOOD FEELINGS" ENDS

The "Era of Good Feelings" came to an end with the disputed Presidential election of 1824. You will learn more about this election in the next chapter.

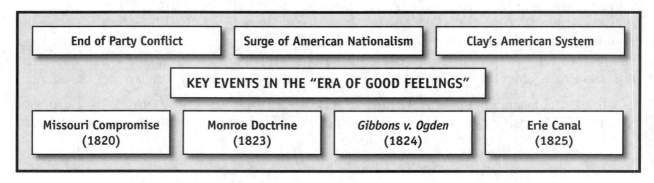

End of Party Conflict	Surge of American Nationalism	Clay's American System

KEY EVENTS IN THE "ERA OF GOOD FEELINGS"

Missouri Compromise (1820)	Monroe Doctrine (1823)	*Gibbons v. Ogden* (1824)	Erie Canal (1825)

LEARNING WITH GRAPHIC ORGANIZERS

Complete the graphic organizer below. For each event listed, describe it and evaluate its impact on the United States.

War of 1812	Monroe Doctrine	"Era of Good Feelings"
Description: _____	Description: _____	Description: _____
Impact: _____	Impact: _____	Impact: _____

CHAPTER 10 CONCEPT MAP

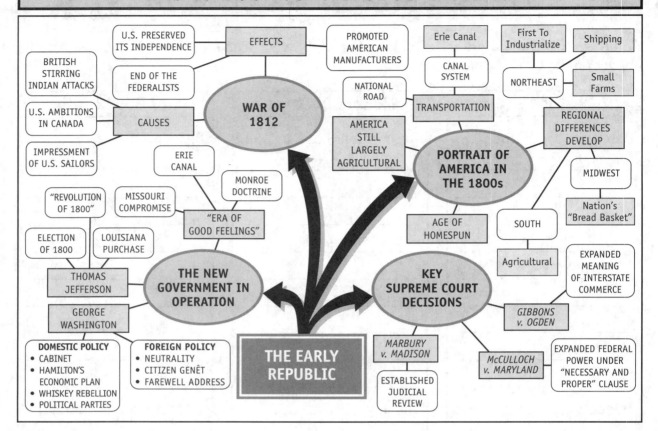

CHAPTER STUDY CARDS

The New Nation (1789–1815)

★ **Washington's Presidency.**
  • Established precedents: Cabinet, two terms
  • **Hamilton's Economic Program.**
  • Formation of political parties.
★ **Jefferson's Presidency.**
  • **Election of 1800.** "Revolution of 1800."
  • **Louisiana Purchase (1803).**
  • *Marbury v. Madison* (1803).
★ War of 1812. War fought against Britain.
  • **Causes of the War.**
    - Impressment of sailors by the British.
  • **Effects of the War.**
    - U.S. preserved its independence from Britain.

"The Era of Good Feelings," 1815–1824

★ **"Era of Good Feelings."** Time in which American nationalism surged.
  • Party unity and national pride.
★ **Purchase of Florida (1819).**
★ **Henry Clay's "American System."**
★ **Missouri Compromise (1820).**
  • Compromise on slavery in new territory.
★ **Monroe Doctrine (1823).** Closed the Western Hemisphere to any further European colonization.
★ *Gibbons v. Ogden* **(1824).** Extends Congressional power over interstate trade.
★ **Erie Canal Built.** Completed in 1825.

CHECKING YOUR UNDERSTANDING

1

> In every political society, [parties] are unavoidable. A difference of interests, real or supposed, is the most natural and fruitful source of these.
>
> — *James Madison (1792)*

> [Political parties] serve to distract the public and [weaken the government]. Parties [stir up] the community with ill-founded jealousies and false alarms.
>
> — *George Washington (1796)*

What were James Madison and George Washington disagreeing about in these statements?

A the necessity of political parties   **Citi 21(A)**

B the rise of sectional rivalry

C the right of Americans to donate funds to political parties

D fear that political parties will use intimidation to elect their candidates

---

EXAMINE **the question.** This question tests your ability to recognize two different points of view. RECALL **what you know.** Both passages deal with the emergence of political parties. **Choice B** is wrong, since they are not about sectionalism. **Choices C** and **D** are also wrong. The documents say nothing about donations or the use of intimidation. The best answer is **Choice A**. Madison saw the emergence of political parties as unavoidable, while Washington feared that political parties would distract and weaken the government.

Now try answering some additional questions on your own.

2 Alexander Hamilton's economic plan was designed to —

F help build the national economy   **Hist 5(B)**

G encourage British imports

H prevent Congressional control of interstate commerce

J strengthen the powers of state governments

3 Why did President George Washington caution Americans against forming alliances with foreign nations in his Farewell Address?

A He feared trade with Latin America would be harmed.   **Hist 5(E)**

B He was troubled that France might establish colonies in the Americas.

C He worried that the nation might later be dragged into a foreign war.

D He sought to protect America's Western frontier.

4   **DIFFERENCE BETWEEN POLITICAL PARTIES**

Federalists	Democratic-Republicans
Sought a strong national government	Sought stronger state governments
Favored manufacturers and merchants	Favored self-sufficient farmers
Loose construction of the Constitution	Strict construction of the Constitution
Supported a national bank	Opposed a national bank

What conclusion can best be drawn from the information in this chart?
F   Political parties usually agree on most issues.   Hist 5(C)
G   The Federalists opposed most tariffs.
H   The Democratic-Republicans favored a strong national bank.
J   Political parties often have differing visions of the nation's future.

5

> I know too that it is a maxim [principle] with us, and I think it a wise one, not to entangle ourselves with the affairs of Europe....
>
> — *Thomas Jefferson, 1787*

Which document echoes the advice given by Thomas Jefferson in this statement?
A   Mayflower Compact   C   Articles of Confederation   Hist 5(E)
B   Declaration of Independence   D   Washington's Farewell Address

6   Which statement is true of the Louisiana Purchase in 1803?
F   It extended the nation's boundary to the Pacific Ocean.   Hist 1(B)
G   It removed the Spanish from North America.
H   It doubled the size of the United States.
J   It banned the expansion of slavery in the western territories.

7   Which would be a primary source of information about the War of 1812?
A   a battle plan from 1813 for the attack on Fort McHenry   Hist 5(D)
B   a recent novel about the Battle of New Orleans
C   a movie on the life of President James Madison
D   a military history of the war written in 1905

8   The Embargo Acts and the War of 1812 were similar in that both events dealt with a conflict involving the —
F   British kidnapping of American sailors   Hist 5(E)
G   emergence of manufacturing in the Northeast
H   launch of a protective tariff on British imports
J   decisions of the U.S. Supreme Court

9 Eli Whitney and Samuel Slater were important to the spread of the Industrial Revolution to the United States because they — STS 27(A)

   A created new methods of production   **C** increased steel production

   B devised new forms of transportation   **D** built steam-powered machines

10 What conclusion can be drawn from the information in the graph?

   F The U.S. government encouraged foreign trade between 1800 and 1812.

   G American trade was affected by events taking place in Europe.

   H Trade increased sharply with the passage of the Embargo Acts

   J American trading ships were attacked by France and Great Britain.

Hist 5(E)

Source: *Historical Statistics of the United States*

11 A major reason President Thomas Jefferson supported the purchase of the Louisiana Territory in 1803 was that it —

   A gave the United States ownership of Florida   Hist 6(B)

   B allowed the United States to gain control of California

   C gave the United States control of the Mississippi River

   D removed the Spanish from North America

12 Washington's Proclamation of Neutrality (1793), Jefferson's Embargo Act (1807), and the Monroe Doctrine (1823) were all efforts to —

   F avoid political conflicts with European nations   Hist 5(E)

   G directly support European revolutions

   H aid Great Britain in its war against France

   J promote military alliances

13 The decision in *Marbury v. Madison* (1803) was important because it —

   A upheld the constitutionality of the National Bank   Govt 18(B)

   B restricted Congress's power to use the "elastic clause"

   C permitted the federal government to regulate interstate commerce

   D established the Supreme Court's power to judge the constitutionality of laws

14 Which areas were added to the United States by the Louisiana Purchase?

   F territory from the Atlantic Ocean to the Appalachians   Hist 6(B)

   G territory from the Appalachians to the Mississippi River

   H territory from the Rocky Mountains to the Pacific Ocean

   J territory from the Mississippi River to the Rocky Mountains

15

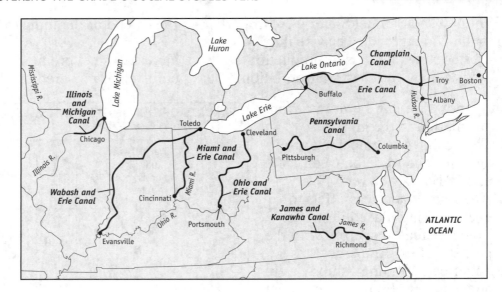

Which was a consequence of the modifications to the physical landscape of the United States shown on the map?

A   They provided new routes to ship Southern cotton to England.   `Geog 11(B)`

B   They introduced water supplies to irrigate Western farm lands.

C   They made it easier to ship goods by water rather than by land.

D   They provided new sources of waterpower to run factories and mills.

16

> It is our true policy to steer clear of permanent alliances with any portion of the foreign world; so far as we are now at liberty to do it; for let me not be understood as capable of patronizing infidelity to existing engagements. I hold the maxim [principle] no less applicable to public than to private affairs, that honesty is always the best policy. I repeat it, therefore, let those engagements be observed in their genuine sense. But, in my opinion, it is unnecessary and would be unwise to extend them....
>
> — *President George Washington, Farewell Address, 1796*

Using this passage, President Washington was offering this advice because he believed —

F   the destiny of the United States was to rule other countries   `Hist 5(E)`

G   the United States should seek alliances with other nations

H   alliances could draw the United States into foreign wars

J   the United States should break its agreements with France

17   Why did Jefferson and Madison oppose Hamilton's Financial Plan?

A   They feared the plan favored the rich.   `Hist 5(C)`

B   They wanted to see a strong federal government.

C   Hamilton was from New York.

D   They wanted to help Southern manufacturers.

18 The decision in *Gibbons v. Ogden* (1824) basically addressed which of the following issues?

F   the issue of congressional privileges

G   the regulation of interstate commerce

H   the right of states to tax a federal property

J   the Supreme Court's right to declare Congressional acts unconstitutional

`Govt 18(B)`

19 One similarity in the foreign policies of Presidents George Washington, Thomas Jefferson, and James Monroe was that they —

A   favored France over England

B   sought colonies in other parts of the world

C   came to the defense of Latin American nations

D   sought to avoid involvement in European political struggles

`Hist 5(E)`

20 Which power did the U.S. Supreme Court establish in *Marbury v. Madison*?

F   judicial review

G   hearing appeals from lower federal courts

H   deciding cases involving two or more states

J   judicial independence through lifetime tenure

`Govt 18(A)`

21 President George Washington pursued a foreign policy of neutrality during his administration because he believed that —

A   treaties were prohibited by the Constitution

B   the United States should not expand by force

C   the nation should develop its own interests in the Western Hemisphere

D   alliances should be established with both France and England

`Hist 5(E)`

22 Under John Marshall's leadership the Supreme Court issued decisions that —

F   declared racial segregation laws unconstitutional

G   gave states the power to tax the Bank of the United States

H   increased the ability of Congress to limit the powers of the President

J   emphasized the supremacy of federal laws over state laws

`Citi 22(A)`

23 During the early 1800s, major improvements to a nationwide system of trade were advanced with the —

A   construction of canals

B   use of gasoline-powered boats on rivers

C   completion of the transcontinental railroad

D   construction of an interstate highway system

`Geog 11(B)`

24 Which was an important leadership quality of President George Washington?

F   strong support for the emerging party system

G   a willingness to listen to different points of view

H   a failure to make his own decisions

J   eagerness to engage in conflict with European powers

`Citi 22(A)`

Name _____

CHAPTER 11

THE AGE OF JACKSON

TEKS COVERED IN CHAPTER 11

- **History 1A** Identify the major eras and events in U.S. history through 1877, including the Age of Jackson, [and] reform movements....
- **History 5F** Explain the impact of the election of Andrew Jackson, including expanded suffrage.
- **History 5G** Analyze the reasons for the removal and resettlement of Cherokee Indians during the Jacksonian era, including the Indian Removal Act, *Worcester v. Georgia*, and the Trail of Tears.
- **History 7A** Analyze the impact of tariff policies on sections of the United States before the Civil War.
- **History 7D** Identify the provisions and compare the effects of congressional conflicts and compromises prior to the Civil War, including the role of John Quincy Adams.
- **Economics 13B** Identify the economic factors that brought about rapid industrialization and urbanization.
- **Economics 14A** Explain why a free enterprise system of economics developed in the new nation, including minimal government regulation, taxation, and property rights.
- **Economics 14B** Describe the characteristics and the benefits of the U.S. free enterprise system through 1877.
- **Government 17B** Explain constitutional issues arising over the issue of states' rights, including the Nullification Crisis....
- **Citizenship 21A** Identify different points of view of political parties and interest groups on important historical issues.
- **Citizenship 22B** Describe the contributions of significant political, social, and military leaders of the United States such as ... Elizabeth Cady Stanton.
- **Citizenship 24B** Evaluate the impact of reform movements, including educational reform, temperance, the women's rights movement, prison reform, abolition, the labor reform movement, and care of the disabled.
- **Culture 25B** Describe religious influences on social movements, including the impact of the Second Great Awakening.
- **Culture 26A** Identify examples of American art, music, and literature that reflect society in different eras such as the Hudson River School artists, the "Battle Hymn of the Republic," and transcendental literature.
- **Culture 26C** Analyze the relationship between the arts and continuity and change in the American way of life.
- **Science, Technology, and Society 27A** Explain the effects of technological and scientific innovations such as the steamboat, the cotton gin, the telegraph, and interchangeable parts.
- **Science, Technology, and Society 27B** Analyze how technological innovations changed the way goods were manufactured and distributed, nationally and internationally.
- **Science, Technology, and Society 28A** Compare the effects of scientific discoveries and technological innovations that have influenced daily life in different periods in U.S. history.
- **Science, Technology, and Society 28B** Identify examples of how industrialization changed life in the United States.

— IMPORTANT IDEAS —

A. **Andrew Jackson**, a popular military hero, accused John Quincy Adams and Henry Clay of stealing the election of 1824 by a "**corrupt bargain**."

B. Jackson was elected President in 1828. He saw himself as the representative of the "**common man**" and invited the public to attend his inauguration.

C. In these years, state governments ended property requirements for voting, allowing all adult white males to vote. Political parties adopted new tactics to reach more voters: popular rallies, parades, and nominating conventions.

D. Jackson favored the "**spoils systems**"— replacing government officials with his own supporters. This policy gave more citizens a role in government and prevented the creation of a permanent class of government officials.

E. Jackson proposed the **Indian Removal Act** in 1830. The act required the Indians to adopt Western ways or move West. The Cherokees refused to do so and appealed their case to the Supreme Court. **John Marshall** ruled in their favor. In *Worcester v. Georgia*, the Court again ruled in favor of the Cherokees. This could not prevent Jackson from removing the Cherokees. The delay in their move led to thousands of Cherokee deaths along the "**Trail of Tears**."

F. Southerners opposed the **Tariff of Abominations** and the **Tariff of 1832**. **John C. Calhoun** wrote that a state had the right to **nullify** within its borders a federal law it believed was unconstitutional. In 1832, South Carolina threatened to **secede** but backed down when President Jackson threatened to use force.

G. Jackson opposed the **Second National Bank**, which he felt favored the rich in the North. He withdrew government funds and refused to renew its charter.

H. The American **free enterprise system** is based on respect for private property, minimal government interference in the economy, and the free interaction of producers and consumers. Prices are set by the interaction of consumer demand and the available supply from producers.

I. The **Industrial Revolution** started in the 1760s in Britain and spread to the United States. It began in the textile industry, but soon transferred to other industries. Work shifted from homes to factories, where workers could be supervised and where water and steam power could be used to run machines.

J. The **Age of Jackson** was a period of reform. Protestant preachers traveled the countryside and preached for days at camp meetings in the **Second Great Awakening**. **Abolitionists** sought to end slavery. **Dorothea Dix** campaigned to improve conditions in mental hospitals. Other reformers belonged to the **Temperance Movement**, which sought to ban the drinking of alcohol.

K. During this period, women met at the **Seneca Falls Convention** (1848) where they demanded equality with men, including the right to vote.

L. This period was also a golden age of literature and art, with such prominent writers as **Ralph Waldo Emerson**, **Nathaniel Hawthorne**, **Herman Melville**, and **Edgar Alan Poe**, and the painters of the **Hudson River School**, including **Thomas Cole**.

In this chapter, you will learn about Andrew Jackson and America's first "Age of Reform." Many historians view Jackson's Presidency as a turning point in the progress of American democracy. It was the "Era of the Common Man," marked by a growth in the involvement of the average citizen in public life. It was also a time when Native American Indians were forced westward, and the threat of secession was avoided.

KEY TERMS AND PEOPLE IN THIS CHAPTER

- Andrew Jackson
- Henry Clay
- Battle of New Orleans
- Age of "Common Man"
- "Spoils System"
- "Jacksonian Democracy"
- Indian Removal Act
- *Worcester v. Georgia*
- "Trail of Tears"

- Nullification Crisis
- John C. Calhoun
- Nullify
- Compromise Tariff
- Industrial Revolution
- Mass Produced
- Eli Whitney
- Interchangeable Parts
- Horace Mann

- "Second Great Awakening"
- Abolitionists
- Seneca Falls Convention
- Elizabeth C. Stanton
- Susan B. Anthony
- Dorothea Dix
- Temperance Movement
- Hudson River School
- Transcendentalism

ESSENTIAL QUESTIONS

- What was "Jacksonian Democracy"?
- How did Jackson's policies affect the political, economic, and social life of the nation?
- How did social and economic life change as the United States began to move from an agrarian to an industrial society?

THE PRESIDENCY OF ANDREW JACKSON: 1829-1837

In 1824, General **Andrew Jackson**, the hero of the War of 1812, won the popular vote, but fell short of enough of votes in the Electoral College to win the election. The contest was decided in the House of Representatives, which selected **John Quincy Adams** (*son of President John Adams*) as President. When Adams later appointed Speaker of the House **Henry Clay** as his Secretary of State, Jackson accused Adams and Clay of making a "corrupt bargain." The Democratic-Republicans split between the supporters of Jackson, who called themselves "**Democrats**," and his opponents, who called themselves "**Whigs**."

General Andrew Jackson

THE AGE OF JACKSON

A native of Tennessee, Andrew Jackson was not born to wealth. He defeated British forces at the **Battle of New Orleans** in 1815. Later, he spent several years fighting Native American Indians in Georgia and Florida. After his defeat in the **election of 1824**, Jackson and his supporters spent the next four years campaigning for the Presidency. They introduced new campaign tactics, like popular rallies, parades, and nominating conventions.

The Age of the "Common Man." Jackson was finally elected President in 1828. His supporters were the "common people" — laborers, farmers, and frontiersmen. Jackson saw himself as the spokesman of the "common man" — the average American.

The Inauguration. Jackson invited the public to visit the White House for his inauguration. A crowd of 20,000 people, many in muddy boots, passed through the building. Some broke glassware and china dishes in their struggle to get refreshments.

The Expansion of Democracy. Jackson's two terms in office saw an expansion of American democracy. This was a time in which state governments were changing their requirements for voting. When the republic was founded, most states required white adult males to own some property in order to vote. Now, these property qualification were lifted.

Large crowds of people trampled through the White House after Jackson's inauguration.

DEMOCRATIC CHANGES UNDER JACKSON

Voting Rights.	**Choosing a President.**	**Campaign Methods.**
In the 1820s, states eliminated the requirement that voters own property, so that most white males over 21 could vote.	Selection of Presidential candidates by party leaders was replaced by nominating conventions, where popularly elected members of each political party chose their candidates.	With increased numbers of voters, new campaign methods emerged. Candidates held dinners, rallies, and public meetings. Jackson invited ordinary people to his inauguration.

The "Spoils System." Jackson believed the President should act as the voice of the common people. To make government more responsive to popular needs, Jackson favored the "**spoils system**." Supporters who helped in his election campaign were appointed to government posts in place of existing officials.

Jackson believed in changing office-holders to give average citizens more experience in government. He felt circulating government posts was less likely to lead to government corruption and abuse than reliance on permanent government officials after their election. Other Presidents had replaced some government officials, but Jackson did so on a much larger scale than before.

"JACKSONIAN DEMOCRACY"

Historians often refer to the end of property qualifications, the "spoils system," and new forms of campaigning as "**Jacksonian Democracy**." Politics became an activity of ordinary citizens. Jackson was a Westerner, a man born outside the upper classes of society. Jackson believed that the nation had been corrupted by special interests. He despised the wealthy, privileged bankers, investors and merchants of the Northeast. His wife's death, which he blamed on the attacks of his opponents, added to his bitterness.

JACKSON AND NATIVE AMERICAN INDIANS

Before becoming President, Jackson had served on the frontier, fighting the Creeks and the Seminoles. Jackson believed that Native American tribes might ally with foreign invaders and therefore posed a danger to the nation. In 1817, he negotiated the removal of Eastern Cherokees in exchange for lands further west. He further believed that Indian removal was the only way for Indians to preserve their traditions and maintain a separate identity. One of Jackson's first acts as President was to propose the **Indian Removal Act (1830)** to remove tribes still east of the Mississippi River. Under this proposal, the Cherokees, Creeks, Choctaws, Chickasaws, and Seminoles would trade their lands for new lands west of the Mississippi. In addition, the federal government would provide them with money, rifles, and provisions for one year. Most of the tribes signed new treaties with the federal government.

THE CIVILIZED CHEROKEE NATION

The Cherokees lived in North Carolina, Tennessee, Georgia, and South Carolina. President Washington had announced a policy to "civilize" the Native Americans. A tribe would be "civilized" if its members learned to read and write, became Christian, learned to farm, and adopted a democratic government. Once a tribe was considered civilized, it was to be protected by the federal government. The Cherokees took up Washington's challenge. One of their leaders, Sequoyah, impressed by the ability of settlers to communicate over distances, developed an 86-character alphabet that represented syllables in spoken Cherokee. The Cherokees adopted a written Constitution with an elected government and published their own newspaper.

Sequoyah (1770–1840)

Based on their accomplishments, the Cherokees rejected Jackson's proposal. When the State of Georgia tried to remove them, the Cherokees took their case to the U.S. Supreme Court. In *Cherokee Nation v. Georgia*, they claimed they were an "independent" nation, protected by treaty. John Marshall held that the tribe was a "dependent" nation subject to federal, not state, law. The Cherokees won their case, but Jackson was determined to remove them anyway. He concluded a treaty with some Cherokee tribe members, giving them two years to relocate to Oklahoma.

Worcester v. Georgia. Meanwhile, Georgia passed a law in 1830, stating that any white person living among Indians without a license from the governor would be sent to prison. State legislators feared white missionaries were encouraging Indians to resist removal. Samuel Worcester, a missionary, was arrested and sentenced to prison for four years for living among the Cherokees. Worcester sued to obtain his freedom. His case came before the U.S. Supreme Court in 1832.

ACTING AS AN AMATEUR HISTORIAN

U.S. History   Search

1776

In ***Worcester v. Georgia***, John Marshall freed Worcester and declared:

> "The Cherokee Nation is a distinct community, occupying its own territory, with boundaries accurately described, in which the laws of Georgia can have no force, and the citizens of Georgia have no right to enter without the [permission] of the Cherokees themselves. The whole [relationship] between the United States and this nation is, by our Constitution and laws, [placed] in the government of the United States. The act of Georgia under which the plaintiff was prosecuted is void…. The acts of Georgia are [against] the Constitution, laws, and treaties of the United States."

Based on this excerpt, why did the U.S. Supreme Court free Worcester?

Cherokee leaders delayed moving. Ironically, because of this legal delay, the Cherokees were now forced to move in late fall and winter, when the weather had turned bitterly cold.

In 1837, federal troops were called in to escort 16,000 Cherokees to their new home in Indian Territory. One-fourth of them died from exposure, starvation, and fevers, during the march along the 800-mile journey, known as the **"Trail of Tears."**

The "Trail of Tears" journey of the Cherokee.

THE "TRAIL OF TEARS"

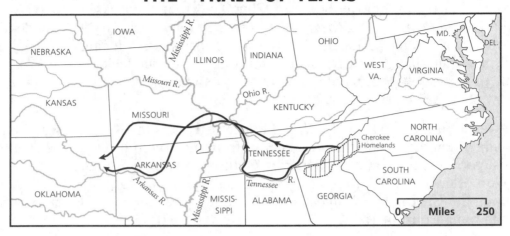

THE NULLIFICATION CRISIS

During Jackson's Presidency, the nation faced a crisis arising out of the tariff issue and states' rights. You will recall that Northern manufacturers favored a high tariff to protect their industries from foreign competition. Southern states, which sold cotton and other crops to England, opposed a high tariff on imports.

The Tariff of Abominations. In the spring of 1828, Jackson's supporters demanded changes in the tariff rates proposed by President John Quincy Adams. To embarrass Adams, some members of Congress increased duties on raw materials, while lowering the tariff on manufactured textiles — displeasing both the South and Northeast. They thought the bill would be rejected, but it actually passed.

The **Tariff of 1828**, became known as the **Tariff of Abominations**. A leading spokesmen against the tariff was Vice President **John C. Calhoun** (1782–1850). He secretly published *The Exposition and Protest*, an essay pronouncing the tariff unconstitutional. Calhoun argued that each state had the right to **nullify** (*cancel*) an unconstitutional federal law in its own territory. Calhoun saw the Union as a "compact" of states.

The Webster-Hayne Debate. Calhoun's ideas surfaced again in 1830. When a Senator proposed that sales of public lands in the West be halted, Senator Hayne of South Carolina advanced Calhoun's nullification theory. Senator **Daniel Webster** denounced this theory, telling the Senate that the Union was not a compact of states, but the work of the American people. Webster saw the American people as the creators of the federal Union.

Daniel Webster speaks to the Senate.

Webster also pointed out that the Constitution assigned the task of determining a law's constitutionality to the Supreme Court, not to the states. He ended his speech with the stirring words: "Liberty and Union, now and forever, one and inseparable."

Several months later, the nation learned President Jackson's views when he confronted his Vice President, John C. Calhoun, with a toast to "Our federal Union — it must be preserved." Calhoun replied with a toast to "the Union — next to our liberty, most dear."

South Carolina Threatens Secession. In 1832, a new tariff lowered duties by ten percent. **John Quincy Adams**, who returned to the House of Representatives in 1830, helped steer the new tariff through Congress. South Carolina, believing the tariff was still too high, put Calhoun's **nullification theory** into practice. A state convention passed a law, the **Ordinance of Nullification**, voiding the tariff, banning the collection of its duties in South Carolina, and threatening to secede from the Union if the federal government tried to enforce it.

President Jackson immediately spoke out against nullification, calling it nothing more than treason. He acted quickly by dispatching U.S. naval ships to Charleston harbor and ordered that federal fortifications there be strengthened. To bolster Jackson, Congress responded with the **Force Bill**, giving the President the power to use military force against South Carolina. Jackson also issued a warning in his "Proclamation to the People of South Carolina," which called resistance to federal law a form of treason.

Henry Clay finally proposed a compromise through a reduction in tariffs over the next ten years. Faced with the use of federal troops, South Carolina withdrew its nullification law and averted a national crisis. Jackson showed that, despite his support for states' rights, he would use force to preserve the Union.

JACKSON DECLARES WAR ON THE BANK

President Washington had introduced a National Bank as part of Hamilton's financial plan. A Second National Bank had been chartered in 1816. Jackson greatly disliked the National Bank. He thought it gave an unfair monopoly to wealthy moneyed interests in the Northeast.

Although the Bank was found to be constitutional by the Supreme Court in *McCulloch v. Maryland*, Jackson set out to eliminate it. When Jackson was re-elected President in 1832, he ordered the removal of all federal deposits from the National Bank. This massive withdrawal of funds had the effect of crippling the National Bank. Jackson ordered these funds to be placed in state banks, which he felt were more agreeable to lending money to farmers. When it came up for renewal, Jackson refused to renew the National Bank's charter. Although many Americans admired Jackson, others thought he was far too dictatorial in the way he handled the bank and other matters.

This cartoon shows how many felt Jackson acted as a monarch.

ACTING AS AN AMATEUR HISTORIAN ———

★ Look up information on the Internet about the journey of the Cherokees along the Trail of Tears. Then write a journal entry as if you were a Cherokee boy or girl, describing what you might have experienced on the journey.

★ Use primary sources from your school library or the Internet to examine different points of view on Jackson's policies. Make a political cartoon to illustrate one of these viewpoints.

★ To understand past events, it is important to be able to identify different points of view. Write a page comparing the four points of view shown below concerning the removal of the Native American Indians to the West. Two of these sources are from Jackson's day and two give more recent points of view.

Jackson Addresses Congress	Cherokee Refuse to Leave
I suggest for your consideration setting apart an ample district west of the Mississippi and outside the limits of any state, to be guaranteed to the Indian tribes as long as they shall occupy it. But they should be distinctly informed that if they remain within the limits of the Eastern states they must be subject to our laws. — *Jackson's Message to Congress* *December 7, 1829*	We wish to remain on the land of our fathers. We have a perfect right to remain without interruption. Shall we be compelled by a civilized people, with whom we have lived in peace for the last forty years, and for whom we have willingly bled in war, to say good-bye to our homes, our streams, and our beautiful forests? No. We are still firm. — *Memorial of the Cherokee Nation* *August 21, 1830*

A Modern Historian	A Recent Editorial
The idea of Indian removal goes back several decades and originated with Thomas Jefferson. Jackson favored it for several reasons: to protect the American people and provide for greater security for the U.S., and to prevent the wiping out of Indian life and culture that would occur if the tribes were to remain in the eastern states. — *Robert Remini* *The Jacksonian Era, 1989*	Jackson not only menaced the Indians, but disregarded a treaty which demanded the return of Creek territory. Jackson stubbornly refused to acknowledge Creek ownership of any land. During his Presidency, he failed to recognize tribes as civilized sovereign nations. Jackson stands as a symbol of the injustices that occurred during white expansion. — *Editorial, The American Indian Nation,* *June, 1987*

LEARNING WITH GRAPHIC ORGANIZERS

Complete the graphic organizer below by describing some of the events associated with Jackson's Presidency and their importance.

Election of 1828

Event: _____

_____

_____

_____

Importance: _____

_____

_____

_____

_____

"Jacksonian Democracy"

Event: _____

_____

_____

_____

Importance: _____

_____

_____

_____

_____

Indian Removal Act

Event: _____

_____

_____

_____

Importance: _____

_____

_____

_____

_____

KEY EVENTS DURING THE JACKSON PRESIDENCY

"Trail of Tears"

Event: _____

_____

_____

_____

Importance: _____

_____

_____

_____

_____

Nullification Crisis

Event: _____

_____

_____

_____

Importance: _____

_____

_____

_____

_____

War on the Bank

Event: _____

_____

_____

_____

Importance: _____

_____

_____

_____

_____

RISE OF THE FREE ENTERPRISE SYSTEM

In this section, you will learn how the American economy developed. Every society must answer three basic economic questions to determine how to use its limited resources:

1 What should be produced?

2 How should it be produced?

3 Who gets what is produced?

In the United States, Americans have a free enterprise system to answer these three basic economic questions. In a **free enterprise system**, individuals are free to produce and sell whatever they wish; they are also free to buy and use whatever they can afford. The three basic economic questions are answered by the free interplay between **producers** (*those who make and sell goods and services*) and **consumers** (*those who buy and use goods and services*).

In the **free enterprise system**, individuals enjoy the freedom of making their own economic decisions. People have the right to own property and to use their property as they see fit. Some individuals invest their money in businesses to produce and sell goods and services. They hope to make a **profit** (*extra money after all expenses are paid*).

Under a free enterprise system, several producers often make the same goods or offer the same services. This gives consumers a choice. This forces producers to attract consumers to their product by providing higher quality items at reduced prices. Less efficient producers will go out of business because they cannot compete successfully. In a free enterprise system, government involvement is limited to setting rules and acting as a referee to settle disputes. Government also collects taxes needed for defense and other essential public services. However, government interference is less in a free enterprise system than under other economic systems.

The roots of the free enterprise system can be traced to Great Britain. Although Britain practiced mercantilism, the British still enjoyed the freest economy in Europe. Americans inherited the free enterprise system from them. In America, there was even less government involvement and more land and natural resources available than in Britain.

THE START OF THE INDUSTRIAL REVOLUTION

The Industrial Revolution first began in Great Britain. It gradually spread to other parts of Europe, the United States, and later, the rest of the world.

THE INDUSTRIAL REVOLUTION BRINGS CHANGE

Before the Industrial Revolution, weavers and craftsmen worked at home, spinning wool, cotton and linen by hand into finished cloth. This was known as the **domestic system**. The Industrial Revolution began in Great Britain in the 1760s. Britain already enjoyed many advantages, including a powerful middle class, a colonial empire to supply it with raw materials, plentiful coal to run its machines, and a prosperous agriculture in which fewer people were needed to work on farms.

NEW INVENTIONS PROPEL CHANGE

Two important British inventions helped trigger the Industrial Revolution. The **spinning jenny** (1764) allowed several threads to be spun at once, permitting many threads to be made quickly and inexpensively. James Watt's improved **steam engine** (1769) made steam power available for mechanical purposes. Steam power could be used to drive many machines at once. The steam engine led in turn to the construction of large factories, the invention of the steamboat, and the development of railroad trains.

THE SHIFT FROM HOME TO FACTORY

You have already learned that in the 1790s, **Samuel Slater** had begun producing cotton thread by machine in a factory in New England. In Massachusetts, **Francis Cabot Lowell** (1775–1817), a successful merchant, and other investors built new factories during the War of 1812. In factories, workers could be supervised and could use machines driven by water or steam power, resulting in increased production. As the production of textiles and other goods increased, their prices fell.

A young female Lowell factory worker.

With lower prices, consumer demand rose for textiles. People could now afford factory-made clothes. Producers were able to produce for mass markets at home and internationally, not just for a few local customers. As demand grew, more and more factories were built, employing ever larger machines and greater numbers of workers. These changes set in motion the chain reaction known as the Industrial Revolution:

| Rise of the factory system | **+** | Use of steam power | **+** | Mass production of goods | **=** | Industrial Revolution |

MASS PRODUCTION AND INTERCHANGEABLE PARTS

Using machinery and steam power, factories produced thousands of yards of cloth each day. Soon, factories also began producing others types of goods. Factory goods were **mass produced** — the manufacture of goods in large quantities using standardized designs, so that all the goods produced are the same. As you learned in the last chapter, Eli Whitney made an important contribution in the standardizing of parts, making them interchangeable from one item to another. This made manufacturing easier and less costly.

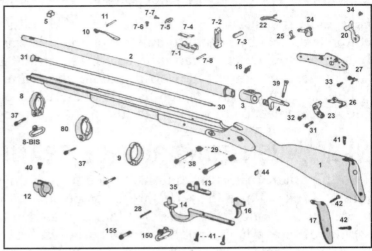

Whitney made parts interchangeable, revolutionizing manufacturing.

As the Industrial Revolution spread, more and more goods were made in factories. People began buying more manufactured goods, rather than relying on making almost everything for themselves.

The Development of Railroads. In England and America, inventors applied the steam engine to a wheeled wagon moving along a track, creating the first railroad locomotive. The railroad revolutionized land transportation. By 1840, **railroad** lines criss-crossed parts of America. The most important of these was the **New York Central**, which ran parallel to the Erie Canal. The railroad expanded land transportation just as the Erie Canal had expanded water transport.

The Telegraph. The spread of railroads was accompanied by the invention of the **telegraph** (*a device for sending and stopping electrical impulses*), which provided a faster way to communicate. The telegraph, which received its first practical demonstration in 1844, made instant communication with the entire nation a reality. Thanks to the telegraph, daily newspapers could now publish next-day accounts of speeches, elections, and battles.

ECONOMY AND SOCIETY BY THE 1830s

American society was still largely rural in the 1830s. Most Americans lived on farms or in small rural villages. Very few Americans lived in cities. Most farmers still grew crops to meet their own needs, although the market for cash crops was growing in importance.

Patterns of work and family life were nonetheless beginning to be affected by the rise of industry. The Industrial Revolution changed the American economy and affected the way people lived. These changes occurred at different places in the United States at different times.

THE NATURE OF WORK

The mass production of goods in factories required new work habits. Pre-industrial craftsmen had worked at home and performed a variety of tasks. They could divide their time between tasks as they wished. Factory work was tedious and monotonous: workers, including children, often performed the same simple task for 12 hours each day. Factory work was also highly disciplined: workers had to arrive at the factory on time and pay close attention to their work throughout the day. In 1820, there were only 350,000 factory workers in the United States; by 1860, there were already two million.

THE WORKING CONDITIONS OF WOMEN AND CHILDREN

During these years, women were an important part of the workforce. Farm women had to work in the fields as well as cook, clean, make clothes, and care for their children. Other women worked outside the home as servants, laundresses, cooks, or factory workers. With the rise of industry, even more women found work outside the home. For example, the Lowell factories in New England employed young single women as workers.

Children were expected to respect and obey their parents. Often they worked on the farm, in addition to helping with household chores. With the rise of industry, some children worked long hours in mines and factories. Industrial society also required more educated leaders and managers. People became more aware of childhood as a distinct stage of life, with its own special needs.

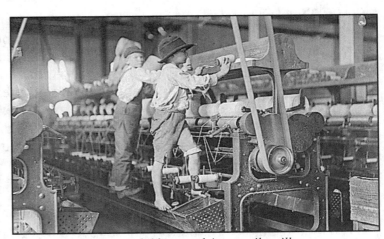
Young children work in a textile mill.

AMERICA'S FIRST AGE OF REFORM

The period from the 1820s to the Civil War witnessed the growth of several new reform movements. The spread of "Jacksonian Democracy," as well as the new challenges of industrialization, helped stimulate these movements.

RELIGIOUS REVIVAL: THE "SECOND GREAT AWAKENING"

There was a revival of strong religious feelings, sometimes called the "**Second Great Awakening**." Methodists, Baptists and other Protestant groups held outdoor religious services and won new converts.

The new Protestant Evangelicals emphasized the ability of each person to achieve salvation. They deliberately borrowed the tactics of mass politics — setting up mass meetings, giving out handbills, advertising in newspapers, and printing religious pamphlets. Roving preachers set up "circuit routes" throughout rural areas, where they set up camps.

New Protestant groups, like the Mormons in upstate New York, also appeared. Members of these groups saw social reform as part of God's plan. This new religious movement centered on reform and repairing moral injustices. The "Second Great Awakening," being as moralistic as it was, played an important role in stirring reform movements to end slavery, reform prisons, and ban alcoholic beverages.

ACTING AS AN AMATEUR HISTORIAN

In the decades after independence Evangelical Protestantism quickly spread throughout the nation. Preachers encouraged religious emotions at meetings. Methodist preacher Peter Cartwright (1785–1872), in his autobiography *The Backwoods Preacher*, described a typical revival:

> "They would erect a shed, sufficiently large to protect 5,000 people from wind and rain, and cover it with boards or shingles; seat the shed, and here they would [come] together from 40 to 50 miles around. Ten, twenty, and sometimes thirty ministers, of different denominations, would preach night and day, four or five days together; and I have known these camp-meetings to last three or four weeks. Great good resulted from them. I have seen more than a 100 sinners fall like dead men under one powerful sermon, and I have heard more than 500 Christians all shouting the high praises of God; and I will venture to assert that many happy thousands were awakened and converted to God at these meetings."

★ Describe in your own words what happened at one of these meetings.

★ Why did Cartwright believe these revivals did "great good"?

ABOLITIONISTS

One of the first targets of reform, greatly encouraged by Protestant Evangelicals, was slavery. Reformers known as **abolitionists** sought to end slavery. You will learn more about the abolitionists in the next chapter.

PRISON REFORM

When Andrew Jackson became President, America's prisons generally did not try to reform their prisoners. Most city and county jails punished criminals by simply placing drunks, thieves and murderers together in one large room. Debtors were also sometimes thrown into prison. Prisons were often dirty and unhealthy; some prisons required their inmates to keep a strict silence; guards beat prisoners; and food was of poor quality. Reformers campaigned for better prison conditions in the 1830s and 1840s, based on the view that criminals could be rehabilitated.

Eliza Farnham was the warden of a women's prison in New York State in the 1840s. She believed in treating prisoners fairly. She allowed prisoners to talk, opened a prison library, and established a school inside the prison to teach prisoners to read and write.

IMPROVED TREATMENT FOR MENTAL ILLNESS

Dorothea Dix

In the 1800s, most people lacked the knowledge needed to care for those with mental illness. Many mentally ill patients were locked in unheated rooms, chained to their beds and beaten into obedience. Some were even sent to jail. **Dorothea Dix** (1802–1887) led the fight for better treatment of the mentally ill. Dix was distressed to learn that they were often housed with criminals or abused. Her report to the state legislature of Massachusetts revealed these shocking conditions. Dix toured other states to report on their treatment of the mentally ill. Dix also campaigned for general prison reform. Some states established separate buildings to house those with mental disorders. These patients were permitted to work outdoors and to enjoy recreation. Further improvements in treatment were delayed until mental illness was better understood in the next century.

TEMPERANCE MOVEMENT

Excessive drinking was considered a serious social issue.

Many Americans worried that drinking alcoholic beverages ruined people's health, disrupted family life, led to unemployment, and promoted "ungodly" behavior. Some Protestant preachers denounced drinking alcohol as a sin. In 1826, the American Temperance Society was founded. Its chief objective changed from moderation to total abstinence from alcoholic drinks. In 1851, Maine became the first state to ban the drinking of alcohol.

EDUCATION:
THE COMMON SCHOOL MOVEMENT

Before the Industrial Revolution, most American children received little formal schooling. Wealthy children were taught reading, writing, arithmetic, foreign languages, and prayers by a private tutor. Reformers like **Horace Mann** of Massachusetts fought to provide free public elementary school to every child. He and other reformers insisted that elementary school should be both free and compulsory. These reformers wanted American children of all social classes to mix together in the same common schools. Mann also introduced the first schools to train teachers.

WOMEN'S RIGHTS MOVEMENT

In the middle 1800s, men held most positions of authority in American society. Women were generally excluded from public life and left in charge of the home and children. Men held final authority, both in household decisions and in public life. Women were denied equality of citizenship: they lacked the right to vote or to hold public office.

Legally. Women were denied full equality of citizenship. They lacked the right to vote, to serve on juries, and to hold public office.

Socially. Women were expected to care for their home and children. They received little schooling. In fact, almost no colleges were willing to accept women.

HOW WOMEN WERE TREATED IN THE 1800s

Economically. Once a woman married, her husband usually took control of her income and property. Women were paid less than men for the same work. Higher paying jobs were not open to women.

Some women began to see this lack of equality and opportunity as a serious problem that also needed reform. Women reformers began to organize themselves in the struggle for equality. **Elizabeth Cady Stanton**, **Lucretia Mott** and other reformers organized the **Seneca Falls Convention** in New York in 1848. This convention passed the *Declaration of Sentiments*. It called on men not to withhold a woman's rights, take her property, or refuse her the right to vote.

ACTING AS AN AMATEUR HISTORIAN

The following passage is from the *Declaration of Sentiments*:

U.S. History   Search

1776

> "We hold these truths to be self-evident: ***that all men and women*** are created equal; that they are endowed by their Creator with certain inalienable rights; that among these are life, liberty, and the pursuit of happiness; that to secure these rights governments are instituted, deriving their just powers from the consent of the governed. Whenever any form of Government becomes destructive of these ends...."

How was this similar to and different from the Declaration of Independence?

The Seneca Falls Convention was treated with scorn by the press and many religious leaders. Despite this, the *Declaration of Sentiments* was a major turning point. It launched the movement to change women's role in American life. The focus of the Women's Rights Movement quickly turned to securing **suffrage** (*the right to vote*). The fact that women did not have the right to vote was seen as a recognition of their inferior status in society. Women reformers saw this denial as a violation of basic democratic principles.

LEARNING WITH GRAPHIC ORGANIZERS

Complete the graphic organizer below. For each reform movement, indicate its goal, characteristics, and important leaders.

Temperance Movement
Goals: _____ _____ _____
Characteristics: _____ _____ _____
Leaders: _____ _____ _____ _____

Education Reform
Goals: _____ _____ _____
Characteristics: _____ _____ _____
Leaders: _____ _____ _____ _____

Prison Reform
Goals: _____ _____ _____
Characteristics: _____ _____ _____
Leaders: _____ _____ _____ _____

THE AGE OF REFORM

Treating Mental Illness
Goals: _____ _____ _____
Characteristics: _____ _____ _____
Leaders: _____ _____ _____ _____

Women's Rights
Goals: _____ _____ _____
Characteristics: _____ _____ _____
Leaders: _____ _____ _____ _____

LITERATURE AND ART

The emerging national spirit made this period a "Golden Age" of literature and art.

AMERICAN LITERATURE

A famous writer, Ralph Waldo Emerson, set the tone for this period with his **Transcendentalist** philosophy. Emerson felt he could experience the divine in the beauty of nature and in his own inner spirit. "I am part or particle of God," he wrote, "I am the lover of uncontained and immortal beauty." Emerson believed in the goodness of the individual. His views had a great influence on other writers at the time. It was in these years that such masterpieces as Nathaniel Hawthorne's *The Scarlet Letter* and *The House of Seven Gables*, Herman Melville's *Moby-Dick*, Henry David Thoreau's *Walden*, and Walt Whitman's *Leaves of Grass* were published. **Washington Irving**, the author of stories about old New York such as *Rip Van Winkle* and *The Headless Horseman*, was the first American writer to achieve fame in Europe. Irving was followed by **James Fenimore Cooper**, author of the adventure story *The Last of the Mohicans*. **Nathaniel Hawthorne** wrote about Puritan New England, while **Herman Melville's** novel about whaling, *Moby-Dick*, is considered by many to be the greatest American novel ever written. The whaling ship was seen as a metaphor for the United States and the problems created by slavery. **Edgar Allan Poe** perfected the art of writing suspenseful short stories.

AMERICAN ART

A group of New York City-based landscape painters, known as the **Hudson River School**, flourished in these same years. The school was founded in 1825 by **Thomas Cole** (1801–1848), an English immigrant. Inspired by the natural beauty of New York's Hudson River Valley and the Adirondack and Catskill Mountains, the artists of the Hudson River School achieved fame by painting romantic landscapes.

A painting by Thomas Cole, a noted Hudson River School artist.

Rather than using nature as a mere backdrop for history paintings or portraits, nature took center stage in their canvases. Their scenes show the power and beauty of America's wilderness. Human figures were almost dwarfed into insignificance by the majesty and grand proportions of nature. Their art interpreted themes of discovery and exploration, and played a key role in helping to change Americans' view of nature. Their landscapes promoted a more sympathetic view of nature and may have even encouraged further Western expansion. Other artists of the Hudson River School included **Frederick Edwin Church** (1826–1900), **Albert Bierstadt** (1830–1902), **Thomas Moran** (1837–1926), and **Asher Durand** (1796–1886).

American artist **John James Audubon** drew birds, mammals, plants, and other subjects from nature. From 1820 to 1838, he drew hundreds of species of birds, giving special attention to the relationship between animals and their habitats.

His *Birds of America*, containing life-sized portraits of 1,065 individual birds, is the most important work on birds ever published. Audubon's works in pastel show what American wildlife and woodlands were like before the spread of human settlement. Audubon was also

James Audubon (1785–1851)

responsible for the discovery of many new species of North American birds and mammals.

  LEARNING WITH GRAPHIC ORGANIZERS

Complete the graphic organizer below by describing some of the leading individuals in the arts in America during this period.

Washington Irving	Herman Melville	Edgar Allan Poe

LITERATURE AND ART IN AMERICA

Hudson River School	Ralph Waldo Emerson and Transcendentalism

CHAPTER 11 CONCEPT MAP

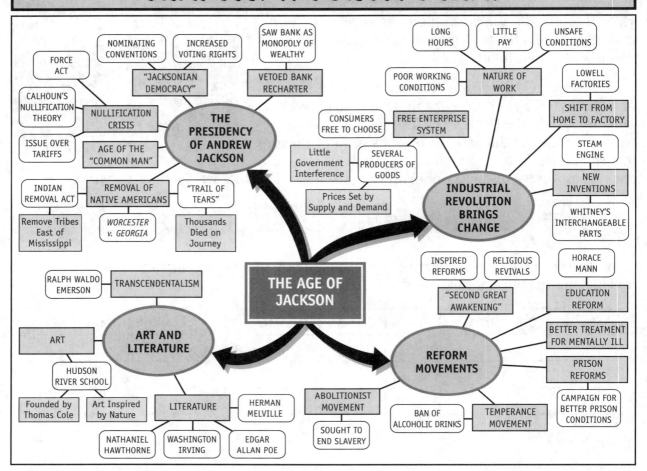

CHAPTER STUDY CARDS

Presidency of Jackson

★ **Election of 1828.** Jackson emerges as victor.

★ **Age of the "Common Man."**
  • Jackson believed he symbolized the common man in America.

★ **"Jacksonian Democracy."**
  • States ended property qualifications for voting.
  • Nominating conventions.
  • "Spoils System."
  • New campaign methods: dinners, rallies, public meetings.

Presidency of Jackson (Continued)

★ **Indian Removal Act (1830).** Government given power to relocate Native Americans from east to west of the Mississippi River.
  • Removal of Cherokees.
  • Cherokees take case to Supreme Court.
  • *Cherokee Nation v. Georgia*.
  • *Worcester v. Georgia*. (see next page)
  • **"Trail of Tears."** Thousands died from cold, starvation and disease along the 800-mile journey.

★ **Bank.** Jackson disliked moneyed interests and declared "war" on the National Bank.

CHAPTER STUDY CARDS

Worcester v. Georgia (1832)

★ **Issue:** Georgia claimed jurisdiction over the Cherokees. They claimed Cherokee lands were within their jurisdiction. The Cherokees claimed they were independent.

★ **Supreme Court.** Established Indian tribes standing as "domestic dependent nations."

★ Court ruled states couldn't pass laws regulating Indians on lands within state borders.

★ Despite winning the case, the Cherokees lost in reality. Six years after decision, they were forced to move to lands in the west.

Jackson and the Nullification Crisis

Issue: Does a state have the power to nullify (*cancel*) a federal law within its borders?

Tariff Crisis (1832–1833)

★ **Tariff of Abominations (1828).**
★ **Calhoun's Exposition and Protest (1828).**
★ **Webster-Hayne Debate, 1830.**
★ **Tariff of 1832.**
  • South Carolina threatened to secede.
  • President Jackson threatened force.
  • South Carolina backs down.
★ **Compromise Tariff of 1833.**

Economy and American Society

★ **Free Enterprise System.**
  • Individuals free to produce and sell whatever they wish.
  • People go into business to make a profit.
  • Prices are set by supply and demand.
★ **Industrial Revolution.** Began in England.
  • Factory work replaces home production.
  • Mass Production in factories.
  • Use of steam engine in factories.
★ **Traditional Role of Women and Children.**
  • Women and children had few rights.

The Age of Reform

★ **Religious Revival.**
  • "Second Great Awakening."
★ **Abolitionist Movement.**
  • Sought to abolish slavery.
★ **Prison Reform.**
★ **Treatment of Mentally Ill.**
★ **Temperance Movement.**
★ **Women's Rights Movement.**
  • Seneca Falls Convention (1848).
  • Issued the *Declaration of Sentiments*.
  • Elizabeth Cady Stanton, Lucretia Mott.

CHECKING YOUR UNDERSTANDING

1

> The Cherokees are nearly all prisoners. They have been dragged from their homes and encamped at the forts and military places, all over the nation…. The propert[ies] of many [have] been taken and sold before their eyes for almost nothing.

This quotation from an eyewitness on the "Trail of Tears" describes events resulting from the —

A   Intolerable Acts
B   Lewis and Clark Expedition
C   Quartering Act
D   Indian Removal Act

Hist 5(G)

EXAMINE **the question.** This question tests your understanding of a statement that describes abuses committed against the Cherokees. RECALL **what you know.** You should remember that the Indian Removal Act gave the federal government the power to relocate Native Americans to lands in the West. APPLY **what you know. Choices A, B, and C** are wrong, since none of these deal with abuses to the Cherokees. All three of these choices involve acts from an earlier time period. The best answer is **Choice D.**

Now try answering some additional questions on your own.

2   What was President Jackson's response to the nullification crisis?

   F   He admitted that the Union was a "compact" of states.   `Govt 17(B)`

   G   He conceded South Carolina's right to secede.

   H   He offered to raise tariffs to keep South Carolina in the Union.

   J   He threatened to use force against South Carolina if it did not repeal its nullification policies.

3   During Andrew Jackson's Presidency, the "spoils system" resulted in —

   A   federal laws being nullified by the states   `Hist 5(F)`

   B   the expansion of the right to vote to all free males

   C   an end to political corruption in the federal government

   D   rewarding supporters of elected officials with government jobs

4   Which is a characteristic of the free enterprise system?

   F   Most private property is held in common.   `Econ 14(A)`

   G   Government officials make most economic decisions.

   H   There is a general agreement on all tax policies.

   J   Individuals enjoy freedom to produce and buy most goods and services.

5   In the 1840s, Seneca Falls, New York, became the scene of an important convention for —

   A   women's rights   `Citi 24(B)`

   B   labor union organization

   C   temperance reform

   D   prison reforms

6   Which set of events is in the correct chronological order?   `Hist 5(G)`

   F   Seneca Falls Convention → Indian Removal Act → "Trail of Tears" → "First Great Awakening"

   G   War of 1812 → "Trail of Tears" → Seneca Falls Convention → Indian Removal Act

   H   Election of Andrew Jackson → Indian Removal Act → *Worcester v. Georgia* → "Trail of Tears"

   J   Boston Massacre → Indian Removal Act → "Trail of Tears" → Election of Andrew Jackson

Name _____

7 Prior to 1850, what was the primary reason that the North developed an economy increasingly based on manufacturing while the South continued to rely more on an agricultural-based economy?

   A Protective tariffs applied only to Northern seaports.   `Geog 10(C)`

   B Slavery in the North promoted rapid economic growth.

   C Manufacturers failed to make a profit in the South.

   D Geographic conditions supported different types of economic activity.

8 Which was an important effect of the "Second Great Awakening"?

   F Andrew Jackson was elected President.   `Citi 25(B)`

   G President Jackson refused to renew the National Bank.

   H Protestant Evangelicals sought to end slavery and achieve other reforms.

   J Congress supported the First Amendment separating Church and state.

9 Which political leader created a crisis by arguing that South Carolina and other states had the right to "nullify" federal laws they believed were unconstitutional?

   A John Quincy Adams   **C** John C. Calhoun   `Govt 17(B)`

   B Henry Clay   **D** Daniel Webster

10

> We have been obliged to preach woman's rights, because instead of listening to what we had to say on temperance, many have questioned the right of a woman to speak on any subject. In all courts and legislatures, all business waits until that point [is] settled. Now, it is not settled in the mass of minds that woman has any rights on this footstool, and much less a right to stand on an even pedestal with man, look at him as an equal, and rebuke the sins of her day and generation. Let it be understood, that we are a woman's rights society; we believe it is a woman's duty to speak whenever she feels the [urge] to do so....
>
> — *First Annual Meeting of the Woman's State Temperance Society, Rochester, New York, 1853*

According to this document, which constitutional right was denied to women?

   F freedom of the press   **H** freedom of speech   `Citi 24(B)`

   G the right to bear arms   **J** freedom of religion

11 In the early 1800s, urbanization was mainly the result of the —

   A shortage of land for new farms   `Econ 13(B)`

   B federally funded national roads

   C impact of industrialization

   D migration of Native American Indians

12 Which statement expresses a belief of Ralph Waldo Emerson and the Transcendentalists?

   F We can find our true selves in nature.   `Cult 26(A)`

   G We must strive to obtain wealth.

   H We will be rewarded in the afterlife.

   J We must remain in the same social class.

13

Election of 1824	
John Quincy Adams	113,122
Andrew Jackson	151,271
Henry Clay	47,531
William Crawford	40,856

Election of 1828	
John Quincy Adams	500,897
Andrew Jackson	642,533

Source: *U.S. Historical Statistics of the U.S.*

Based on the information in the chart, what factor best explains the large increase in voters between the election of 1824 and 1828?

A   Former slaves were emancipated and allowed to vote.   Hist 5(F)
B   An amendment was enacted ending voting fees.
C   Women were given the right to vote.
D   Many states had put an end to property qualifications.

14   Why did President Jackson support the introduction of a "spoils system"?
F   It would end vetoing bills he disliked   Hist 5(F)
G   It would have to be enforced by Supreme Court decisions
H   It would remove Native American Indians from their traditional lands.
J   It would open up jobs in government to average citizens.

15   The *Declaration of Sentiments*, adopted at the Seneca Falls Convention in 1848, was significant because it —
A   promoted the idea of equal rights for women   Citi 24(B)
B   demanded the immediate abolition of slavery
C   called for the prohibition of alcoholic beverages
D   asked government to restrict harmful business practices

16   Which best describes the contribution to the reform movement   Citi 24(B)
made by Dorothea Dix?
F   She encouraged the opening of free public elementary schools for all children.
G   She ended the sale of alcoholic beverages in her state.
H   She investigated the treatment of the mentally ill and improved their conditions.
J   Her books described the conditions of enslaved African Americans in the South.

17   An increase in the number of factories in the early-1800s in the United States contributed to —
A   an increase in the urban population   STS 28(B)
B   an increase in dependence on foreign laborers
C   a decrease in the amount of water and air pollution
D   a decrease in dependence on steam power

18

Year	Inventor	Invention
1798	Eli Whitney	System of interchangeable parts for guns
1807	Robert Fulton	First commercially successful steamboat
1829	Joseph Henry	Electromagnet, used in telegraphs & relays
1830	Peter Cooper	First U.S. steam locomotive
1835	Samuel Colt	First repeating revolver
1844	Samuel F.B. Morse	First telegraph
1846	Richard M. Hoe	Rotary printing press
1846	Elias Howe	First sewing machine

Based on the information in the chart, what conclusion can be drawn about how inventions changed life in the United States?

F Most inventions were made to increase factory production.   [STS 27(C)]

G The greatest changes occurred in the way people communicated.

H American inventors lacked the creativity shown by British inventors.

J American inventions affected a wide range of products and industries.

19

The Declaration of Independence (1776)	The Seneca Falls *Declaration of Sentiments* (1848)
We hold these truths to be self-evident, that all men are created equal, that they are endowed by their Creator with certain unalienable rights, that among these are life, liberty and the pursuit of happiness — That to secure these rights, governments are instituted among men, deriving their just powers from the consent of the governed, —That whenever any form of government becomes destructive of these ends, it is the right of the people to alter or to abolish it….	We hold these truths to be self-evident; that all men and women are created equal; that they are endowed by their Creator with certain inalienable rights; that among these are life, liberty and the pursuit of happiness; that to secure these rights governments are instituted, deriving their just powers from the consent of the governed. Whenever any form of government becomes destructive of these ends, it is the right of those who suffer from it to refuse allegiance to it,….

In what way did the ideas of the *Declaration of Sentiments* differ from the ideas found in the Declaration of Independence?

A The *Declaration of Sentiments* was written by Thomas Jefferson.   [Citi 24(B)]

B The Declaration of Independence granted voting rights to men and women.

C The Declaration of Independence supported the idea of nullification.

D The *Declaration of Sentiments* included the equality of men and women.

20 What was one of the South's objections to the higher tariffs enacted by Congress?

F They would allow them access to cheap foreign imports.   Hist 7(A)

G They would prevent domestic manufacturing from growing.

H They would redistribute wealth among American social classes.

J They would made it more difficult to export crops.

21 The use of interchangeable parts in the manufacture of goods advanced the growth of the manufacturing industry because it —

A allowed the continuation of the domestic system   STS 27(A)

B permitted large quantities of goods to be mass produced at lower cost

C made it possible for unskilled workers to operate machines

D brought an end to the common abuse of factory workers

22

Improvements in roads		Construction of canals
	?	
Invention of the steamboat		Development of the railroad

Which title belongs in the center of this diagram?

F Technological Innovations in Manufacturing   STS 27(B)

G Noteworthy European Scientific Inventions

H Effects of the Factory System

J Changes in Transportation

23 Which is the best description of the works of the Hudson River School?

A They excelled in portrait paintings.   Cult 26(A)

B They glorified the majesty of nature.

C They introduced abstract painting.

D Their paintings showed meetings during the "Second Great Awakening."

24 During the early 1800s, major improvements to the nation's system of trade were made with all of the following except the —

F construction of canals   STS 27(B)

G use of steamboats on rivers

H completion of a Transcontinental Railroad

J construction of toll roads

25 Which Supreme Court case best completes the partial outline below?

> **I.** _____
>   A. Heard under Chief Justice John Marshall
>   B. Concerned the relationship between the Cherokee people and a state
>   C. The Court ordered that Indian nations were subject to federal, not state law.

A *Marbury v. Madison*   **C** *Gibbons v. Ogden*   Hist 5(G)

B *McCulloch v. Maryland*   **D** *Worcester v. Georgia*

Name _____

CHAPTER 12

MANIFEST DESTINY AND THE RISE OF SECTIONALISM

- **History 1A** Identify the major eras and events in U.S. history through 1877, including ... westward expansion [and] sectionalism.
- **History 6B** Analyze the westward growth of the nation, including ... Manifest Destiny.
- **History 6C** Explain the causes and effects of the U.S.-Mexican War and their impact on the United States.
- **History 7B** Compare the effects of political, economic, and social factors on slaves and free blacks.
- **History 7C** Analyze the impact of slavery on different sections of the United States.
- **History 7D** Identify the provisions and compare the effects of congressional conflicts and compromises prior to the Civil War, including the role of John Quincy Adams.
- **Geography 10A** Locate places and regions directly related to major eras and turning points in the United States during the 19th century.
- **Economics 12A** Identify economic differences among different regions of the United States.
- **Economics 12B** Explain reasons for the development of the plantation system, the transatlantic slave trade, and the spread of slavery.
- **Economics 12DC** Analyze the causes and effects of economic differences among different regions of the United States at selected times.
- **Government 17B** Explain constitutional issues arising over the issue of states' rights ... including the Civil War.
- **Government 18C** Evaluate the impact of selected landmark Supreme Court decisions, including *Dred Scott v. Sandford*, on life in the United States.
- **Citizenship 20C** Analyze reasons for and the impact of selected examples of civil disobedience in U.S. history such as Henry David Thoreau's refusal to pay a tax.
- **Citizenship 21A** Identify different points of view of political parties and interest groups on important historical issues.
- **Citizenship 21C** Summarize historical events in which compromise resulted in a resolution such as the Missouri Compromise, the Compromise of 1850, and Kansas-Nebraska Act.
- **Citizenship 22B** Describe the contributions of significant political, social, and military leaders of the United States such as Frederick Douglass.
- **Culture 23A** Identify racial, ethnic, and religious groups that settled in the United States and explain their reasons for immigration.
- **Culture 23D** Analyze the contributions of people of various racial, ethnic, and religious groups to our national identity.
- **Culture 24A** Describe and evaluate the historical development of the abolitionist movement.
- **Science, Technology, and Society 27A** Explain the effects of technological and scientific innovations such as the steamboat, the cotton gin, the telegraph, and interchangeable parts.
- **Science, Technology, and Society 27B** Analyze how technological innovations changed the way goods were manufactured and distributed, nationally and internationally.

CONTINUED

- **Science, Technology, and Society 27C** Analyze how technological innovations brought about economic growth such as the development of the factory system....
- **Science, Technology, and Society 28B** Identify examples of how industrialization changed life in the United States.

In this chapter, you will learn how the United States expanded its borders to the Pacific coast. You will also learn how Americans became increasingly divided by sectional differences in the two decades before the Civil War.

KEY TERMS AND PEOPLE IN THIS CHAPTER

- "Manifest Destiny"
- Westward Expansion
- Annexation of Texas
- James Polk
- U.S.-Mexican War
- Mexican Cession
- Gadsden Purchase
- Immigration
- Eli Whitney
- Nat Turner Rebellion

- Free Blacks
- Sectionalism
- Abolitionists
- John Quincy Adams
- Harriet Beecher Stowe
- *Uncle Tom's Cabin*
- Frederick Douglass
- Henry David Thoreau
- Civil Disobedience
- Transcendentalism

- Underground Railroad
- John C. Calhoun
- States' Rights
- Underground Railroad
- *Dred Scott v. Sandford*
- Kansas-Nebraska Act
- Popular Sovereignty
- Republican Party
- Lincoln-Douglas Debates
- John Brown's Raid

ESSENTIAL QUESTIONS

- What role did "Manifest Destiny" play in westward expansion?
- Was the U.S.-Mexican War justified?
- What were the effects of territorial expansion on our nation?
- Could the divisions created by sectionalism have been avoided?
- How might the attempt at political compromises have been altered to lessen the threat of Civil War?
- Can Chief Justice Taney be blamed for the onset of the Civil War?

— IMPORTANT IDEAS —

A. The United States expanded westward to the Pacific Ocean by acquiring a series of new territories. These territories included the **Louisiana Purchase**, the purchase of **Florida**, the **annexation of Texas**, the acquisition of part of the **Oregon Territory**, the **Mexican Cession**, and the **Gadsden Purchase**.

B. Americans came to believe it was their fate, or "**Manifest Destiny**," to occupy North America from the Atlantic to the Pacific Ocean. Manifest Destiny had political, economic, and social roots. Americans felt they needed these territories to be secure against foreign powers and that these lands would bring new wealth. Finally, Americans believed God had ordained them to occupy the West.

C. By the mid-nineteenth century, the nation consisted of three different regions or "sections." Many Americans felt greater loyalty to their section than to the country as a whole. This strong regional loyalty was known as **sectionalism**.

D. The **North** was the most industrialized. Factory workers produced manufactured goods. Farmers raised livestock to supply food to towns and cities. Railroads connected natural resources with factories and consumers.

E. The **West** became the "**bread basket**" of the country, growing wheat and other crops. Cities developed on the banks of the Great Lakes and along major rivers.

F. The **South** was transformed by the invention of the **cotton gin** and the growing demand for cotton by English and Northern factories. Plantation owners grew, harvested, and shipped cotton with large forces of slaves.

G. Immigrants contributed to both economic and demographic growth in this period. **Irish immigrants** came to escape the famine in Ireland. **German immigrants** came to escape political repression. Many Irish settled in cities in the Northeast, while Germans often settled in Ohio, Michigan and Wisconsin.

H. Northern states abolished slavery. Some Southern slaves were freed by their owners and became **free blacks**. Most moved to the North.

I. **Abolitionists** wanted to abolish slavery. **William Lloyd Garrison, Frederick Douglass**, and **Harriet Tubman** were leading abolitionists. Harriet Beecher Stowe's *Uncle Tom's Cabin* revealed the brutality and violence of slave life.

J. Some slaves escaped slavery in the South on the **Underground Railroad**.

K. **Henry David Thoreau** developed the strategy of **civil disobedience**, refusing to obey laws a citizen believed to be unjust. Slavery apologists, like **John C. Calhoun**, argued that slavery was justified by the Bible.

L. The struggle over slavery focused on the issue of its extension into new territories. Southerners feared the North would take control of Congress and abolish slavery. Under the **Compromise of 1850**, California was admitted as a free state, and the **Fugitive Slave Law** was greatly strengthened.

M. The system of compromise started to breakdown when the **Kansas-Nebraska Act** let settlers decide if they wanted slavery, adding violence to the issue.

N. The **Republican Party** was founded against the further spread of slavery.

O. The *Dred Scott* decision, holding that African Americans had no right to citizenship, and that Congress could not limit slave owners' control of their property, ended the possibility of further compromise of the issue.

AMERICA EXPANDS WESTWARD

When the United States signed the peace treaty with Great Britain in 1783, its borders were the Mississippi River to the west, Canada to the north, and Florida to the south. In addition to the original thirteen colonies, the new United States then acquired recognition of its control of the Northwest Territory.

You have already learned about the **Northwest Ordinance** in 1787. This act established principles and procedures for the admission of new states. Over the next decades, the new republic rapidly expanded its territory across the continent.

LOUISIANA PURCHASE, 1803

In 1803, France offered to sell its land from west of the Mississippi River to the Rocky Mountains. The **Louisiana Purchase** doubled the size of the United States and gave it control of the key port of New Orleans, where the Mississippi River empties into the Gulf of Mexico.

THE PURCHASE OF FLORIDA, 1819

Spain was losing its hold on its colonial empire in South America. Its colonies had already risen in revolt. In this weakened state, Spain sought to sell Florida. Americans negotiated the purchase of Florida from Spain in 1819 for $5 million.

"MANIFEST DESTINY"

Many Americans came to believe that it was America's "**Manifest Destiny**," or fate, to extend the borders of the nation to the shores of the Pacific. This belief was in keeping with the belief that Americans were a "chosen people" with a divine mission to spread democracy, Christianity and Western culture. Occupying the entire breadth of North America from the Atlantic to the Pacific would also strengthen the nation's security and provide new economic opportunities.

THE POLITICAL, ECONOMIC, AND SOCIAL ROOTS OF "MANIFEST DESTINY"

Expanding Democracy. Americans believed they had a God-given mission to extend their system of democracy. Americans hoped to establish a democratic republic that reached to the Pacific, which would serve as an example to the world.

Pioneering Spirit. The pioneer spirit was seen as the perfect expression of American individualism. Americans admired the rugged pioneers who advanced into Texas, Oregon, California and the Southwest.

Security. Occupying the middle of the continent from coast to coast would discourage threats from rival powers like England, Spain, or Russia.

Romanticizing the West. Many Americans romanticized the West — in paintings, popular prints, and literature — as an ideal of nature.

Future Prosperity. Many Americans believed their future prosperity depended on the land and wealth to be gained from westward expansion. The success of farmers in Texas and the discovery of gold in California encouraged this belief.

OREGON TERRITORY (1846)

In 1818, Great Britain and the United States had agreed to joint control of the Oregon Territory, which reached as far north as the latitude 54° 40'. In the 1840s, large numbers of pioneers began moving along the **Oregon Trail** to the fertile Willamette Valley in Oregon. Thousands caught "Oregon Fever." Groups crossed the 2,000-mile trail in covered wagons. After crossing the Rocky Mountains, most of

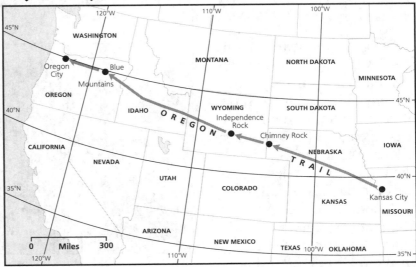

these pioneers moved to Oregon, but some moved southwest to California — then still a part of Mexico. The trail was often treacherous — over deserts, rivers, and mountains — and more than 20,000 people died along the route.

THE MORMONS IN UTAH

The **Mormons** were founded in upstate New York in 1830 by Joseph Smith, at the time of the "Second Great Awakening." They moved from New York to Ohio, Missouri, and Illinois, but were driven out of these states because of their unique religious beliefs, which included marrying several wives. In 1847, their leader, **Brigham Young**, led them westward by covered wagon to the Great Salt Lake in Utah, a seemingly desolate and barren region in the Great Basin, which

The move West by followers of Joseph Smith.

could be cultivated only through irrigation. Here they found comfort in their isolation. By the time of Young's death in 1877, 125,000 Mormons lived in Utah.

THE ANNEXATION OF TEXAS (1845)

In the 1820s, a group of Americans reached an agreement with the government of Mexico to settle in the region of Mexico known as "Texas." As the number of Anglo-American settlers increased, the Mexican government feared losing control of the area. In 1830, the Mexican government announced a law prohibiting additional settlers from immigrating to Texas from the United States.

These restrictions failed to stop the flow of American immigrants. Most settlers simply ignored the Mexican law. By 1834, there were more than 30,000 Americans in Texas, compared to less than 8,000 Mexican-born citizens.

Anglo-Americans living in Texas still objected to the ban on further immigration. They held a series of conventions demanding its repeal. When Mexican troops attempted to seize a cannon at Gonzales, fighting erupted. Texas volunteers took control of San Antonio. Mexican general and dictator **Santa Anna** marched a large army to Texas and slaughtered Texans at the Alamo and Goliad early in 1836.

Texans defend the Alamo against the forces of General Santa Anna.

Meanwhile, Anglo-American Texans declared their independence from Mexico. News of the massacres at the Alamo and Goliad inspired their actions.

Texas Wins Independence. Led by **Sam Houston**, the Texan rebels captured Santa Anna at the **Battle of San Jacinto**. To regain his freedom, Santa Anna signed a treaty recognizing Texas as an independent republic. Texas almost immediately asked to be annexed by the United States. The U.S. Congress, however, was divided over whether to admit a new slave state to the Union. They also feared such action would lead to war with Mexico. President Martin Van Buren opposed annexation of a new slave state. Congress therefore declined the request, and Texas became an independent republic. Houston's victory at the Battle of San Jacinto earned him the Presidency of the new Republic of Texas.

The Election of James Polk. In the election campaign of 1844, candidate **James K. Polk** promised to annex Texas and to obtain the Oregon Territory to its northernmost point. Unlike his opponent Henry Clay, Polk seized on the popular desire for westward expansion and captured the election. Once in office, President Polk compromised with the British over Oregon. He extended the existing eastern line between Canada and the United States westward across the Oregon Territory.

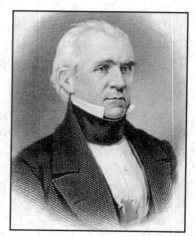

In 1845, Congress then voted to annex Texas. Even those divided on the issue of slavery could see the possibility of admitting new Northern states to preserve the existing balance of slave and free states. They feared letting Texas remain independent would block American westward expansion.

James Polk
(1795–1849)

A joint Congressional resolution stated that if any new states were to be created out of the lands of Texas, those north of the "Missouri Compromise Line" should enter as free states, while those south of the line should choose whether or not to permit slavery. Many Americans feared that the annexation of Texas, with its boundaries in dispute, was likely to lead to war with Mexico. Northern critics suspected that the whole project was being carried out in the interests of slavery.

U.S.-MEXICAN WAR (1846–1848)

Shortly after Texas was annexed, a dispute broke out between the United States and Mexico over the southern border of Texas. Was the border to be the Rio Grande or the Nueces River? President Polk ordered troops into the contested area.

Hoping to use the incident to extend America's borders, Polk declared war on Mexico. Americans living in California also rebelled and declared their independence. U.S. troops landed in Mexico and marched to Mexico City. Mexico was defeated and forced to give up California, Nevada, Utah, Arizona, and parts of Colorado and New Mexico. In the **Treaty of Guadalupe Hidalgo**, the United States agreed to pay Mexico $15 million for these areas, known as the **Mexican Cession**.

In the Mexican-American War, more than 1,700 Americans were killed.

GADSDEN PURCHASE (1853)

In 1853, the United States completed its expansion in the Southwest with the **Gadsden Purchase**. This small slice of territory was purchased from Mexico for $10 million. President Franklin Pierce was anxious to insure U.S. possession of the area. As the railroad age progressed, business-oriented Southerners saw that a railroad linking the South with the Pacific Coast would greatly expand trade opportunities. The area was seen as the most practicable route for a southern

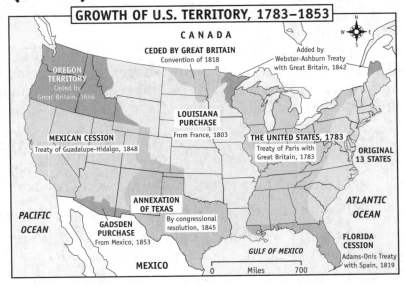

GROWTH OF U.S. TERRITORY, 1783–1853

CANADA

CEDED BY GREAT BRITAIN
Convention of 1818

Added by Webster-Ashburn Treaty with Great Britain, 1842

OREGON TERRITORY
Ceded by Great Britain, 1846

LOUISIANA PURCHASE
From France, 1803

MEXICAN CESSION
Treaty of Guadalupe-Hidalgo, 1848

THE UNITED STATES, 1783
Treaty of Paris with Great Britain, 1783

ORIGINAL 13 STATES

ANNEXATION OF TEXAS
By congressional resolution, 1845

PACIFIC OCEAN

GADSDEN PURCHASE
From Mexico, 1853

ATLANTIC OCEAN

FLORIDA CESSION
Adams-Onis Treaty with Spain, 1819

MEXICO

GULF OF MEXICO

0   Miles   700

railroad to the Pacific. James Gadsden, U.S. minister to Mexico, was responsible for negotiating the deal.

THE CALIFORNIA GOLD RUSH

In 1848, just as peace with Mexico was being signed, gold was discovered in California in the foothills of the Sierra Nevada. Word of the discovery quickly spread, and thousands of "Forty-Niners" arrived in California the following year. By 1850, San Francisco had grown to a population of 100,000. Those who participated in the Gold Rush came from many backgrounds, but few were women. Saloons sprang up in mining towns and San Francisco, while the prices of household goods soared. The Gold Rush lasted only a few years before mining companies took over, but California's population had greatly increased, and California became a new destination for settlers moving westward.

Prospectors panning for gold.

WESTWARD EXPANSION POSES A NEW CHALLENGE

America's expansion westward created a troubling political issue — should these newly acquired territories permit or prohibit slavery? Closely associated with this was another important issue: representation in Congress. Southern states wanted to be sure that the number of slave states in Congress remained roughly equal to

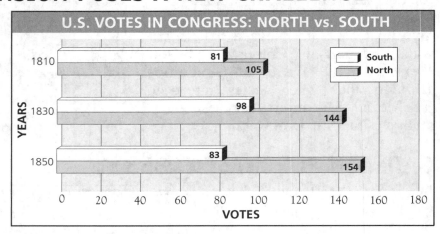

U.S. VOTES IN CONGRESS: NORTH vs. SOUTH

South
North

1810 — 81, 105
1830 — 98, 144
1850 — 83, 154

YEARS

VOTES: 0, 20, 40, 60, 80, 100, 120, 140, 160, 180

that of the free states. Southerners feared that if a new state were admitted to the Union from these western territories as a free state, it would upset the existing balance between free and slave states in Congress.

APPLYING WHAT YOU HAVE LEARNED

★ Make your own map showing the westward expansion of the United States.

★ How did the issue of slavery delay the annexation of Texas?

★ What do you think would have happened to the rest of North America if the United States had not expanded westwards?

★ What consideration did the governments of the United States and Mexico give to the rights of Native American Indians on these lands?

Name _____

 LEARNING WITH GRAPHIC ORGANIZERS

Complete the graphic organizer below by describing how the United States obtained each of these territories to extend its frontiers to the Pacific Ocean.

Louisiana Purchase	Purchase of Florida	Annexation of Texas

EXPANSION OF THE UNITED STATES TO THE PACIFIC

Oregon Territory	Mexican Cession	Gadsden Purchase

SECTIONAL DIFFERENCES GROW

America's westward expansion, population growth, and advances in technology led to important developments in patterns of settlement. The number of large American towns and cities increased. The diversity of people within these larger communities also grew. Finally, industrialization heightened existing regional differences. The three main regions were known at the time as "**sections**":

THE NORTH

The North (*now the Northeast of the United States*) was the first of these areas to industrialize. It became a center for manufacturing, shipping and small farms.

Economic Changes. With industrialization, processes of production were divided up and reorganized. Skilled craftsmen were replaced by unskilled workers who worked in large workshops or factories. Gradually, the number of workers in Northern factories increased.

Large textile mills like this became common throughout Northern cities.

Social Changes. Northern cities mushroomed in size. Wealth became concentrated in the hands of the richest families. Inequalities between the rich and poor increased. The size of the middle classes also expanded. There were many new opportunities for merchants, bankers, managers, foremen, sales clerks, and professionals. Even life in the countryside was transformed. Instead of mainly growing foods for themselves, Northern farmers began growing hay and raising sheep, cattle, and pigs to sell wool, milk, and meat. When their source of income declined, young people from farm families moved to the cities. By 1860, half the population of the North made its living in occupations other than farming. People began buying ready-made clothes, cast-iron stoves, coal, and kerosene lamps. Middle-class families could afford central heating, indoor plumbing, and wall-to-wall carpeting.

The Plight of the Factory Workers. Workers and the laboring poor were the chief victims of the new industrial society.

Workers often faced unemployment when factories reduced production. Working families could often not make ends meet on the wages of one family member. Women and children also had to work to meet the necessities of life.

Women and children workers were common in Northern factories.

Many women and children worked in factories. In 1840, the federal government agreed to the ten-hour workday on public projects. A few states also passed ten-hour workday laws.

THE WEST

The Appalachians had once posed an obstacle to the opening of lands further west, but the availability of cheap land and construction of the National Road and canals opened the region to settlers. Pioneers carried their possessions in Conestoga wagons. After the construction of the Erie Canal, farmers could send their produce up the Mississippi River to the Great Lakes, over the Erie Canal and down the Hudson River to New York City. The Midwest, with its flat land and fertile soil, became the main producer of grains like wheat and corn. Farmers began using machines like the mechanical plow, reaper, and thrasher. The West replaced the North as the nation's **"Bread Basket"** — growing corn and wheat, and milling flour.

Settlers moving west with a Conestoga wagon.

By the mid-1800s, the number of settlers moving to the West (*now the Midwest*) had increased rapidly. The desire for land and new opportunities continued to fuel westward expansion. The region's fertile soil attracted many farmers. Removal of the Native Americans to lands west of the Mississippi greatly accelerated westward settlement. All along major rivers, towns like Pittsburgh, Louisville, St. Louis, and Memphis sprang up. Ohio soon had more residents than Massachusetts.

Settlers to the West set about clearing the land and preparing it to grow crops.

The attraction of the West was more than just farmland for settlers — the lure of timber, gold, silver and grazing lands was an important motive for many to endure the hardships of the region. White settlers poured across the Mississippi to establish ranches, dig mines, and farm the land. Some free blacks also came West, convinced that economic prosperity could be found there.

APPLYING WHAT YOU HAVE LEARNED

★ What role did geography play in helping to make the North and West different?

★ What role did technological advances play in helping to shape each of these regions?

IMMIGRANTS SETTLE IN THE NORTH AND WEST

During these decades, the population of the North and West was also swelled by immigration — especially from Ireland and Germany.

Irish Immigration. In 1845, a new disease struck the potato crop in Ireland. Large numbers of people in Ireland lived on potatoes and had no food. During this period, over a million Irish people starved to death. The **Irish Potato Famine** led to a massive increase in Irish immigration to the United States. Even after the famine ended, large numbers of Irish continued to come to America. By 1870, one out of every five people in New York City had been born in Ireland.

Irish immigrants faced a series of hardships that began with their journey across the Atlantic. On overcrowded ships, diseases often spread quickly among passengers. Although most Irish immigrants worked on farms in Ireland, many moved into cramped and unsanitary apartments in cities like New York, Philadelphia and Boston. Since most of these immigrants lacked money, education and skills, they took jobs as laborers or servants. One of the most serious problems Irish immigrants faced was ethnic prejudice. Many Americans discriminated against them because of their Catholic religion. Employers often refused to hire Irish immigrants. To deal with these problems, Irish immigrants formed societies, published newspapers in their native language, started their own community libraries, and found support from the local Catholic Church.

German Immigration. Starting in the 1830s, a large number of Germans began leaving their homeland for America. Some Germans came for political reasons. A revolution for national unity and popular representation in Germany failed in 1848–1849, leading some Germans to flee. Even more German immigrants came in the following years for economic opportunities. Germany's population was growing rapidly, and there was not enough land or jobs to satisfy the needs of many German families.

With increased competition between railroads and steamships, the cost of travel to America became much cheaper. Many Germans packed their bags and took a chance in coming to America. Later, other family relatives came to join them. Between 1830 and 1880, more than one quarter of all immigrants to the United States were German. Some went to cities in the Northeast, like New York. Others settled in Midwestern states like Ohio, Michigan and Wisconsin.

German immigrants also faced many difficulties when they arrived. Most spoke only German. They had a hard time communicating in English. Many Germans moved to rural areas to become farmers. Those who settled in big cities often lived in overcrowded homes. Many were skilled craftsmen who brought their talents to America. Most of the immigrants worked hard so that they and their children could lead better lives.

THE SOUTH

At the time of the Constitutional Convention, it appeared that slavery in the United States would gradually die out. The prices of tobacco, rice, and indigo were falling, and planters in Virginia were introducing wheat, which did not require slave labor. Thomas Jefferson denounced slavery as despotism, although he did not free his own slaves.

Impact of the Cotton Gin. In 1792, however, the inventor **Eli Whitney** developed the **cotton gin** — a machine that combed through cotton and separated out the seeds. One machine could do the work of fifty workers separating the seeds by hand. As a result of this invention, cotton cultivation became profitable. Plantation owners began using more slaves, and the price of slaves more than doubled almost overnight. Over the next forty years, the plantation system and cultivation of "**King Cotton**" spread throughout the South. It was hard to satisfy the enormous demand for raw cotton from the factories of the Northeast and England.

Eli Whitney's Cotton Gin.

In Jacksonian times, the South actually had a variety of economies based on its geographic diversity. In the Piedmont and Appalachian regions of Virginia, North Carolina, Georgia, and Tennessee, families were mainly subsistence farmers, who may have grown a few cash crops. Few farmers had slaves. On the Atlantic Coastal Plain, however, plantation owners used slave labor to grow cotton, rice, and tobacco for export to Northern cities and European markets. Major Southern cities, like New Orleans and Charleston, served as ports for shipping Southern exports.

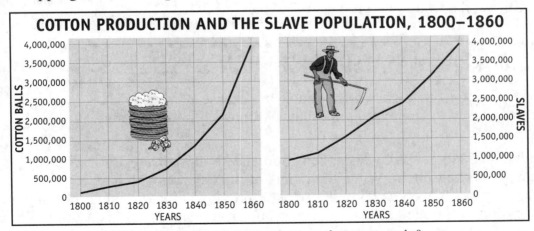

What relationship do you see between these two graphs?

An over-emphasis on the cultivation of cotton and other cash crops led some Southern states to ignore improvements in industry and transportation. Southern plantations often exhausted the soil, fell into debt, and failed to develop new technologies. Southern landowners invested their profits in land and slaves. The South fell behind the North in the number of railroads, factories, and schools. Southern cities generally remained small and lacked industry.

THE PECULIAR INSTITUTION: SOUTHERN SLAVERY

Throughout the South, most white families had no slaves. Slaves were generally owned by wealthy Southern landholders who grew cash crops, such as rice and sugar. Many slaves endured back-breaking work on plantations as field hands. Slaves were divided into gangs and assigned tasks like plowing and harvesting.

An African-American family under slavery.

The Life of the Slave. Living conditions for slaves were usually primitive. Enslaved workers generally lived in one-room cabins with their families and ate simple, unbalanced meals of cornmeal, pork, and molasses. Slaves lacked sanitary facilities or running water.

A few slaves, however, became skilled blacksmiths or carpenters and were hired out by their owners. Even then, their wages remained the property of their owners. Slaves were not allowed to marry legally but they were permitted to marry by custom and to have children — the main source of new slaves after the slave trade became illegal in 1808. Slaves were denied basic human rights: they could be beaten or be sold apart from their families at the whim of their owners.

Slaves were often auctioned off without regard to keeping families together.

ACTING AS AN AMATEUR HISTORIAN

In 1857, George Fitzhugh wrote a book in defense of slavery. It compared slaves to free Northern factory workers. The following excerpt is from his book.

U.S. History *Search*

1776

"When the laborer's day ends, he is burdened with the cares of family and household. When the labors of the day are over, a slave is free in mind as well as body. His master provides food, clothing, housing and everything else needed for the well-being of the slave and his family. Slaves in the South are the happiest, and freest people in the world. The children, the aged, and sick are not burdened by labor, and have all their necessities provided for them. Negro men and boys work, on average, not more than nine hours a day. The [free Northern] worker must work or starve. He is more a slave than the Negro because he works longer and harder for less than the slave."

How does Fitzhugh argue that slaves are better off than Northern workers?

Despite their horrible living and working conditions, many slaves held onto their rich African heritage through music, religion, and folklore. Many also resisted slavery by not cooperating, by escaping, committing sabotage or theft. In some cases, open rebellion was carried out. **Nat Turner's Rebellion** in 1831 caused a wave of fear among slave owners. The uprising terrorized white Southerners. As a result, Southern lawmakers passed stricter regulations, tightly controlling the activities of both enslaved and free blacks.

FREE AFRICAN AMERICANS

Benjamin Franklin and others organized an end to slavery in Pennsylvania, which became the first state to abolish it in 1780. Most other Northern states passed laws gradually eliminating slavery, while many Southern states then passed laws making it easier for slave owners to free individual slaves.

After the American Revolution, thousands of slaves were freed. In 1800, there were already 100,000 free African Americans in the United States, while by 1810, three-quarters of the African Americans in the North were free. On the eve of the Civil War, about ten percent of African Americans in the United States, about a half a million people, were free.

Some of them stayed in Southern cities where they became skilled craftsmen. A large number of free African Americans moved to the North, especially to port towns, where they worked in dockyards or opened shops in their own neighborhoods. Others became laborers or farm workers. Free African Americans opened their own churches, which became centers for education and community life. They also started mutual aid societies and schools. Even free African Americans lived in an atmosphere of fear and racial prejudice. Discrimination against free blacks increased when white workers began facing new competition from immigrant laborers. In the South, free blacks had few legal rights. Free African Americans also risked being falsely seized by slave-catchers as runaway slaves.

THE RISE OF SECTIONALISM

By the mid-1800s, each of these sections of the country had developed its own distinctive way of life. These differences led to **sectionalism** — the greater loyalty many Americans felt toward their own section than to the country as a whole. In particular, Southerners felt their way of life was being threatened by the North. Northerners feared the South wanted to spread slavery throughout the nation. The North's focus was on business and industry, as they concentrated on manufacturing, shipping, and trading goods. By contrast, the South's economy centered around plantations, cash crops, and steady agricultural growth.

APPLYING WHAT YOU HAVE LEARNED

★ Look on the Internet or in your local library to find examples of pictures or paintings of each section of the nation at this time.

★ Make a map showing sectional differences before 1860. Use boxes with labels to identify the political, economic, and social features of each section.

LEARNING WITH GRAPHIC ORGANIZERS

Complete the graphic organizer below by describing the development, growth, conditions, and lifestyle that emerged under slavery in the South.

Impact of the Cotton Gin	Why Slavery Grew in the South

SLAVERY IN THE SOUTH

Life of the Slave	The Free Blacks

ABOLITIONISTS AND STATES' RIGHTS

Abolitionists believed that slavery was morally wrong and wanted to end it. In the decades leading up to the Civil War, abolitionist leaders were men and women of high moral purpose and courage who sought to make the issue of slavery a focus of national politics. At first, most abolitionists were widely denounced. Mobs sometimes attacked them even in the North. Southerners burned antislavery pamphlets and excluded them from the mails. The U.S. Congress imposed the "gag rule" to avoid considering abolitionist petitions. **John Quincy Adams**, who had returned to Congress after his term as President, spent much of the final years of his political life fighting against this gag rule. He attempted to bring anti-slavery petitions before the House, and opposed the annexation of Texas and the Mexican-American War for promoting pro-slavery interests. Adams also successfully defended Africans who had rebelled on the Spanish slave ship Amistad, on the grounds that the United States had prohibited the slave trade and that all people have a natural right to be free.

In 1833, the British Empire abolished slavery. By 1838, more than 1,350 antislavery societies existed in the United States with almost 250,000 members. The book *Uncle Tom's Cabin* (1853) by **Harriet Beecher Stowe** depicted the evils of slavery and stirred the public conscience of the North.

William Lloyd Garrison and other abolitionists, including former slaves **Harriet Tubmann** and **Frederick Douglass**, published anti-slavery writings and delivered speeches throughout the North. They were also active in the "Underground Railroad," which helped many fugitive slaves to escape to Canada.

Frederick Douglass (1818–1895)

ACTING AS AN AMATEUR HISTORIAN

William Lloyd Garrison was a prominent abolitionist who started his own newspaper, *The Liberator*, in 1831. The passage below appeared in Vol. 1, No. 1:

> "I will be as harsh as truth, and as uncompromising as justice. On this subject [abolition of slavery] I do not wish to think, or speak, or write, with moderation. No! No! Tell a man whose house is on fire, to give a moderate alarm; tell the mother to gradually [pull] her baby from the fire into which it has fallen; — but urge me not to use moderation in this cause. I will not [hesitate] — I will not retreat a single inch — AND I WILL BE HEARD. The apathy of the people is enough to make every statue leap from its pedestal, and to hasten the resurrection of the dead...."

Describe one goal that Garrison was trying to achieve in *The Liberator*.

William Lloyd Garrison (1805–1879)

Thoreau's Civil Disobedience. A student of the American writer Ralph Waldo Emerson, **Henry David Thoreau** (1817–1862) moved to a simple home next to Walden Pond to live alone with nature. He was jailed for one night for failing to pay his taxes. He did this to protest against a government that enforced slavery and which he felt had wrongly gone to war with Mexico to extend slavery.

Henry David Thoreau (1817–1862).

In 1848, he delivered a lecture explaining his actions. He turned the lecture into an essay entitled "**On the Duty of Civil Disobedience**," in which he argued the moral necessity of resisting slavery. Thoreau believed it was the duty of citizens to disobey unjust government policies. Just speaking out against unjust acts would not bring about an end to them.

Thoreau argued that only backing up your words with action would yield results. Disobedience must occur through nonviolent acts of **civil disobedience** — such as refusing to pay taxes. Citizens should even be willing to go to jail. He declared, "Under a government which imprisons any unjustly, the true place for a just man is also a prison."

Thoreau and Transcendentalism. As you learned in the last chapter, Emerson was the founder of Transcendentalism. Emerson and Thoreau believed that people were born with an inner sense that enabled them to recognize moral truths. Using this inborn guide, or conscience, people can make their own moral decisions without relying on the judgments of others or of society. This inner moral sense was a part of us that **transcended**, or went beyond, our particular experiences.

Because the Transcendentalists trusted their inner moral guiding spirit, they were individualists. If the government adopted a law that offended their consciences, they would resist it, just as Thoreau did. Thoreau's writings encouraged others to resist unjust government laws. He greatly influenced such later defenders of human rights as Mohandas Gandhi and Dr. Martin Luther King, Jr. Both adopted Thoreau's concept of civil disobedience to successfully accomplish their goals.

ACTING AS AN AMATEUR HISTORIAN

This passage is from Thoreau's *On the Duty of Civil Disobedience*:

> "I think that we should be men first, and subjects afterward. It is not so desirable to cultivate a respect for the law, so much as for the right. How does it become a man to behave toward the American government today? I answer that he cannot without disgrace be associated with it. I cannot for an instant recognize that political organization as my government which is the slave's government also."

★ What is Thoreau saying in this paragraph?

★ What argument does Thoreau give to justify not paying his taxes?

The Underground Railroad. Some slaves escaped from the South with the help of the **Underground Railroad** — a vast network of people who helped fugitive slaves escape to the North or Canada (where slavery had been abolished). People allowed the escaping fugitives to rest in their barns, cellars, or houses. These safe places were called "stations." The fugitive slaves usually moved by foot at night, helped on their journey by a "conductor." They took advantage of the protection offered by nature, by hiding in swamps, bayous, forests, and waterways. They would

Escaping along the Underground Railroad.

generally travel 10 to 20 miles, until they reached the next station. There they would rest and eat, hiding in barns and other out-of-the-way places until they moved on to the next station. Some runaways sought refuge in cities such as Baltimore and New Orleans, where they tried to blend in with free blacks living there.

ACTING AS AN AMATEUR HISTORIAN

This passage by Frederick Douglass was taken from his book, *My Escape from Slavery*. Douglass was a gifted writer and speaker. In this passage, he describes his escape from slavery and how dehumanizing slavery was:

> "Though I was not a murderer fleeing from justice, I felt perhaps quite as miserable as such a criminal. The train was moving at a very high rate of speed for that [period] of railroad travel, but to my anxious mind it was moving far too slowly. Minutes were hours, and hours were days during this part of my flight. After Maryland, I was to pass through Delaware — another slave state, where slave-catchers awaited their prey, for it was not in the interior of the state, but on its borders, that these human hounds were most vigilant and active. The border lines between slavery and freedom were the dangerous ones for the fugitives...."

Why did Douglass fear when he came to a border crossing?

APPLYING WHAT YOU HAVE LEARNED

★ Investigate the abolitionist movement on the Internet and make a map showing some of the major stations of the Underground Railroad.

★ In your school library, public library, or on the Internet, read excerpts from Harriet Beecher Stowe's *Uncle Tom's Cabin*.

STATES' RIGHTS AND THE DEFENSE OF SLAVERY

The issue of slavery became closely tied to states' rights. Southerners argued that the federal government was failing to respect the arrangement in the Constitution that had bound the states together. They thought the federal government's growing powers were being used by the North and the West against the South to charge high tariffs and to challenge the preservation of slavery. Apologists for slavery pointed out it was written in the Bible. They argued Southern slaves were far better off than workers in the North toiling in factories. The slave-owner felt responsibility for the welfare and health of his slaves, while the factory-owner recognized no such duty towards his workers.

John C. Calhoun had stated in 1828 that a state had the right to **nullify** a federal law within its borders or even to **secede** from the Union if it wished. South Carolina threatened to secede in 1832 but was stopped by President Andrew Jackson's threat of force. The principle of **states' rights** and state sovereignty would eventually lead several Southern states to secede from the Union in 1860–1861.

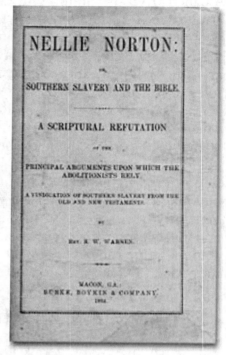

Southerners often justified slavery with passages from the Bible.

ACTING AS AN AMATEUR HISTORIAN

In 1837, Calhoun stood on the floor of the Senate and declared that slavery was a "positive good." He was firmly convinced that slavery was essential to the civilized South:

> "I hold that in the present state of civilization, where two races of different origin, and distinguished by color and other physical differences, as well as intellect, are brought together, the relation now existing in the slaveholding states between the two, is, instead of an evil, a positive good. There never has yet existed a wealthy and civilized society in which one portion of the community did not live on the labor of the other."

★ What is Senator Calhoun's argument in this passage?

★ How might you have responded to him if you had been a Senator in 1837?

John C. Calhoun
(1782–1850)

LEARNING WITH GRAPHIC ORGANIZERS

Complete the graphic organizer below describing the accomplishments of each abolitionist. Look on the Internet for more information:

Harriet Beecher Stowe
_____
_____
_____
_____
_____
_____
_____
_____
_____
_____

Harriet Tubman
_____
_____
_____
_____
_____
_____
_____
_____

William L. Garrison
_____
_____
_____
_____
_____
_____
_____
_____

ABOLITIONIST LEADERS

Henry David Thoreau
_____
_____
_____
_____
_____
_____
_____

Frederick Douglass
_____
_____
_____
_____
_____
_____
_____

FAILURE OF POLITICAL COMPROMISE

Different sectional interests and the debate over slavery were tearing the nation apart. To keep the Union together, Congressmen had agreed to a series of compromises. The **Missouri Compromise** (1820) and the **Compromise of 1850** temporarily kept the peace. However, in the late 1850s, these compromises broke down, making a conflict between the North and South almost inevitable.

The Missouri Compromise (1820). You have already learned how, during the "Era of Good Feelings," this compromise prohibited slavery in most of the Louisiana Purchase above the "Missouri Compromise Line." It set a pattern by admitting one free state and one slave state into the Union at the same time.

The Compromise of 1850. After the U.S.-Mexican War, the same issue came up as in 1820. Should the new lands of the Mexican Cession be slave or free states? The first territory to have enough inhabitants to seek admission was California. After bitter debate, Henry Clay came up with his last great compromise. This compromise admitted California as a free state. In exchange, Congress passed a tighter **Fugitive Slave Law**, letting Southern slave owners hunt down slaves who escaped to the North. The new Fugitive Slave Law was severely criticized in Stowe's *Uncle Tom's Cabin*, (1853). In the rest of the Mexican Cession, local residents were to decide for themselves whether or not to permit slavery.

Kansas-Nebraska Act. The period of compromise started to unravel in 1854. Senator Stephen Douglas of Illinois proposed to extend the new doctrine of **"popular sovereignty"** — people in a territory would decide for themselves whether that area should have slavery. In 1854, Congress passed a law allowing settlers in the territories of Kansas and Nebraska, part of the original Louisiana Territory, to decide for themselves whether or not to permit slavery. This overturned the Missouri Compromise, which had previously prohibited slavery there. Senator Stephen Douglas had proposed this bill to get Southern support for a railroad in the North. But the act led to bloodshed in Kansas between the supporters and opponents of slavery. Both sides sent supporters into the territory to win the vote.

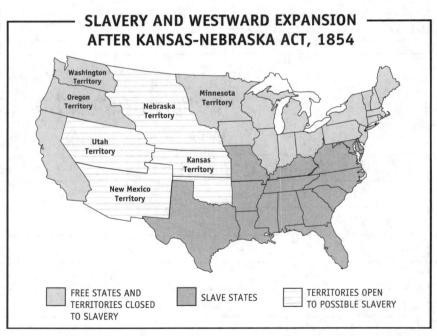

SLAVERY AND WESTWARD EXPANSION AFTER KANSAS-NEBRASKA ACT, 1854

Washington Territory
Oregon Territory
Minnesota Territory
Nebraska Territory
Utah Territory
Kansas Territory
New Mexico Territory

FREE STATES AND TERRITORIES CLOSED TO SLAVERY

SLAVE STATES

TERRITORIES OPEN TO POSSIBLE SLAVERY

Founding of the Republican Party (1854). Critics of the Kansas-Nebraska Act formed a new political party, the **Republican Party**. Republicans agreed to let slavery continue in the South, but they opposed any further extension of slavery into any of the new territories.

Dred Scott v. Sandford **(1857).** A Southern slave, Dred Scott, was taken by his owner to the North and then back into slavery in the South. Scott sued for his freedom. Having been on free soil, he argued that he could not be taken back into slavery.

Decision/Significance. In 1857, Chief Justice Roger Taney read the Supreme Court's decision. As a "descendant of African born slaves," Dred Scott was declared to be a non-citizen, and therefore was not entitled to bring a lawsuit before the court. Taney further asserted that Africans could never become U.S. citizens since, he claimed, Africans were not included when the Constitution was written. Taney then ruled that slaves were property, and that Congress had no right to take away a slaveholder's property. This meant that Congress could not lawfully prohibit slavery in new territories: since slavery was still legal, the Missouri Compromise of 1820 was unconstitutional. Chief Justice Taney's ruling meant that slavery could spread.

Dred Scott

ACTING AS AN AMATEUR HISTORIAN _____

In 1857, 80-year-old Chief Justice Taney was a Southern supporter of slavery who was intent on protecting Southerners from attacks by abolitionists. In delivering the Court's majority opinion in *Dred Scott v. Sandford*, he said:

> "[African Americans] had no rights which the white man was bound to respect; and that the negro might justly and lawfully be reduced to slavery for his benefit. He was bought and sold and treated as an ordinary article of merchandise, whenever profit could be made by it. [Referring to language in the Declaration of Independence] it is too clear for dispute, that the enslaved African race were not intended to be included, and formed no part of the people who framed and adopted this declaration...."

Most abolitionists were enraged at this decision, but Frederick Douglass found a bright side, believing that the decision would bring slavery to the attention of the nation and would be a step toward its ultimate destruction. Was Douglass justified in his optimism about the case?

Lincoln-Douglas Debates. The *Dred Scott* decision questioned the power of Congress to control the spread of slavery. In 1858, former U.S. Representative **Abraham Lincoln** challenged Senator Stephen Douglas, author of the Kansas-Nebraska Act, to a series of formal debates. Douglas had introduced the doctrine of popular sovereignty to the slavery question.

Under this doctrine, the population of a territory could decide for themselves whether or not to permit slavery. Lincoln told listeners that African Americans were human beings with the rights guaranteed by the Declaration of Independence. Lincoln condemned the *Dred Scott* decision and promised to oppose the further spread of slavery.

Lincoln-Douglas Debate at Charleston, Illinois.

Lincoln further explained that he favored popular sovereignty, but since African Americans were human beings, no person could claim a moral right to enslave them. Unlike the Supreme Court in the *Dred Scott* case, Lincoln felt that African Americans were entitled to the basic rights guaranteed in the Declaration of Independence: of life, liberty, and the pursuit of happiness. Lincoln went further in seeing slavery as a stain on American society, the world's first experiment in true self-government. The nation, he said, "cannot endure permanently, half slave and half free."

ACTING AS AN AMATEUR HISTORIAN

In 1858, delegates met in Illinois at the Republican State Convention. They chose Abraham Lincoln as their candidate for the U.S. Senate. Lincoln spoke to his Republican colleagues:

> "We are now into the fifth year, since a policy was initiated of putting an end to slavery agitation. In my opinion, it will not cease, until a crisis shall have been reached, and passed. 'A house divided against itself cannot stand.' I believe this government cannot endure, permanently half slave and half free. I do not expect the Union to be dissolved — I do not expect the house to fall — but I do expect it will cease to be divided. It will become all one thing or all the other. Either the opponents of slavery, will [end] the further spread of it…; or its advocates will push it forward, till it shall become lawful in all the States, North as well as South."

Based on this speech, how would you summarize Lincoln's views on slavery?

John Brown's Raid. In 1859, **John Brown**, a white abolitionist, launched a slave revolt at **Harpers Ferry**. He planned to spark slave uprisings in both Kansas and Virginia. Brown attacked a government arsenal and seized weapons to give to his supporters, but the rebellion failed to spread. The uprising was quickly crushed, and Brown was tried and executed. His attempted uprising sounded an alarm bell among Southerners who feared future slave revolts. Meanwhile, Brown was seen as a hero to many in the North. His name became a symbol for the anti-slavery movement. His act of violence also demonstrated to many that the slave question had brought the country to the verge of civil war.

APPLYING WHAT YOU HAVE LEARNED

★ Abraham Lincoln's "House Divided" speech spoke of the dangers of disunion because of slavery. Look up that section of the speech in the library or on the Internet. Describe in your own words why Lincoln felt slavery posed a danger.

★ Should John Brown be considered an American hero or a villain? Explain.

★ Turn your classroom into the U.S. Senate in the 1850s. Assign roles as Democratic or Republican Senators from the North, South, and West. Then see if you can negotiate a compromise on the issue of the extension of slavery in order to avoid the Civil War.

★ Make your own illustrated timeline of major events involving sectional rivalry from the Missouri Compromise of 1820 to John Brown's Raid of 1859.

LEARNING WITH GRAPHIC ORGANIZERS

In the next chapter, you will learn about the Civil War. Some of the developments you read about in this chapter relate to causes of that conflict. Complete the graphic organizer below by identifying each of the following causes of the Civil War.

Sectionalism	Issues of State's Rights	Abolitionist Movement
_____	_____	_____
_____	_____	_____
_____	_____	_____

Dred Scott Decision		Kansas-Nebraska Act
_____	**CAUSES OF THE CIVIL WAR**	_____
_____		_____
_____		_____

Issue of Slavery in the New Territories	Founding of the Republican Party	John Brown's Raid in Virginia
_____	_____	_____
_____	_____	_____
_____	_____	_____

CHAPTER 12 CONCEPT MAP

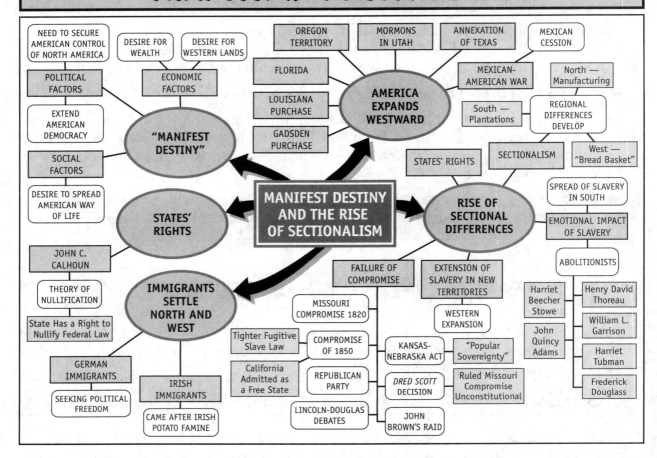

CHAPTER STUDY CARDS

America Expands Westward

- ★ **Louisiana Purchase (1803).** U.S. buys Louisiana Territory from France.
- ★ **Florida (1819).** Spain, faced with losing its colonial empire, sells Florida to the U.S.
- ★ **"Manifest Destiny."** Fate of Americans to expand their borders to the Pacific.
- ★ **Annexation of Texas (1845).** In 1845, the U.S. annexed Texas.
- ★ **Oregon Territory (1846).** U.S. treaty with Britain, settles the border of Oregon.
- ★ **U.S.-Mexican War (1846–1848).** U.S. gains Mexican Cession with California and Southwest United States.

Sectional Differences Grow

- ★ **Sectionalism.** The North, South, and West each developed its own unique way of life.
- ★ **North.**
  - Rise of factory system.
  - Became a center of industry.
- ★ **West.** Emerged as the nation's **"Bread Basket."**
- ★ **South.**
  - **"King Cotton"** and slavery dominated the South's economy.
  - Large plantations, based on slave labor.
  - Most Southerners were small farmers with no slaves.

The Abolitionist Movement

★ **Goals of the Abolitionist Movement.**
  • Saw slavery as morally wrong.
  • Sought to bring about an end to slavery.
★ **Leading Abolitionists.**
  • **Harriet Beecher Stowe:** Wrote *Uncle Tom's Cabin* about the evils of slavery.
  • **Harriet Tubman.**
  • **Frederick Douglass.**
  • **William Lloyd Garrison.** *The Liberator*
★ **Underground Railroad.** Slaves escaped to the North and many went on to Canada.

The Breakdown of Compromise

The major issue was the extension of slavery in the newly acquired territories of the West.
★ **Missouri Compromise (1820).**
★ **Compromise of 1850.** California entered as free state, **Fugitive Slave Law** bolstered.
★ **Kansas-Nebraska Act (1854).** Extended the idea of "**popular sovereignty**" to parts of the old Louisiana Territory, where slavery had been prohibited.
★ **Republican Party** formed in 1854 to oppose the extension of slavery.
★ *Dred Scott* **Decision (1857).** Supreme Court ruled that Congress cannot limit slaves; Missouri Compromise is unconstitutional.

CHECKING YOUR UNDERSTANDING

1 The climate and topography of the Southeastern United States had a major impact on the history of the United States before 1860 because the region —
  A developed as the largest domestic source of steel production   `Econ 12(B)`
  B became the center of commerce and manufacturing
  C was the area in which most immigrants chose to settle
  D grew agricultural products that encouraged the continuation of slavery

EXAMINE **the question.** This question deals with the impact of climate and topography of the South on U.S. history. RECALL **what you know.** You should recall that the climate and topography of the South was favorable to growing cotton, rice and tobacco that relied heavily on slave labor. APPLY **what you know. Choices A, B, and C** are all incorrect. These choices were more characteristic of the North and West than the South. **Choice D** is the best answer since the South grew agricultural products that encouraged the continuation of slavery.

Now try answering some additional questions on your own.

2 Which event was most influenced by the American belief in "Manifest Destiny"?
  F the start of the U.S.-Mexican War   `Hist 6(B)`
  G Cherokee march along "Trail of Tears"
  H defeat of Britain in the American Revolution
  J acquisition of the Florida

3 In which section of early 19th-century America did the emergence of the plantation system have a key economic effect?
  A New England   **C** the Mid-Atlantic states   `Econ 12(B)`
  B the South   **D** the West

4

(1) The Court is of the opinion that Dred Scott is not a citizen of Missouri within the meaning of the Constitution and is not entitled to sue in its courts....

(2) The right of property in a slave is expressly affirmed in the Constitution. And the government is pledged to protect this right in all future time if the slave escapes from his owner....

The courtroom scene during the Dred Scott trial.

(3) Upon these considerations, it is the opinion of the Court that the act of Congress which prohibited a citizen from holding and owning property of this kind [slaves] in the territory of the U.S. north of the line mentioned is not [permitted] by the Constitution and is therefore void.

Ruling of Justice Roger Taney, Dred Scott v. Sandford (1857)

Based on the excerpt, which conclusion can be drawn about Chief Justice Taney's decision in the *Dred Scott* case?

F   Scott was a citizen of the United States.   `Govt 18(C)`
G   By living in Missouri, Scott was no longer a slave.
H   Scott was considered as property that could not be taken from its owner.
J   The Missouri Compromise allowed Scott to bring a case to the Supreme Court.

---

5   What best explains why slavery had nearly disappeared in the North before the Civil War?

A   Slave rebellions had forced an end to slavery in the North.   `Hist 7(C)`
B   Slavery did not fit the economic interests of the North.
C   The Constitution required the end of slavery in the North.
D   Slave ownership was too expensive for Northern farmers.

6   In the 1850s, why did many escaped slaves flee to Canada?

F   They feared being drafted into the Northern army.   `Hist 7(B)`
G   More factory jobs were available in Canada.
H   The Fugitive Slave Act kept them at risk in the United States.
J   Northern abolitionists refused to help fugitive slaves.

7   What was the main goal of supporters of "Manifest Destiny" in the 1840s?

A   to convince Canada to become part of the United States   `Hist 6(B)`
B   to expand United States territory to the Pacific Ocean
C   to build a canal across Central America
D   to acquire naval bases in the Caribbean

8

WILLIAM LLOYD GARRISON   FREDERICK DOUGLASS

- Published the *Liberator*   **?**   - Published *The North Star*
- Printer/Baptist   - Writer/Orator
- Bostonian   - New Yorker

What term belongs in place of the question mark in the Venn diagram?

F Women's Rights Movement   Citi 24(A)
G Temperance Movement
H Abolitionist Movement
J Educational Reformers

9 Both the Missouri Compromise of 1820 and the Compromise of 1850 settled conflicts between the North and the South over —

A the admission of new states into the Union   Citi 21(C)
B presidential election results
C immigration to the United States
D the role of the Supreme Court in declaring acts unconstitutional

10 Which area on the map was annexed by the United States in 1845?

F Area 1   Hist 6(B)
G Area 2
H Area 3
J Area 4

11 Which area on the map was part of the Mexican Cession?

A Area 1   Hist 6(B)
B Area 2
C Area 3
D Area 4

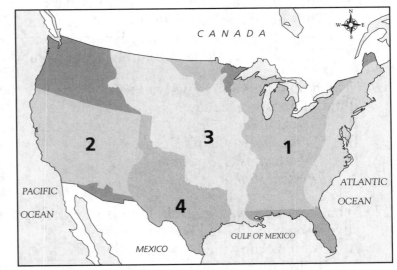

12 The *Dred Scott* decision had a major impact on life in the United States because it —

F limited the power of the Supreme Court to rule on cases of race   Govt 18(C)
G supported Congress' right to forbid slavery in the territories
H reopened the issue of slavery in the territories
J reaffirmed the President's right to serve more than two terms in office

13 Based on the graph, which conclusion is most accurate?

A   Most Southerners owned some slaves. `Econ 12(B)`

B   The majority of Southern families owned over 20 slaves.

C   No Southern families owned more than 100 slaves.

D   A majority of Southerners owned no slaves.

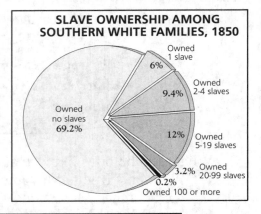

SLAVE OWNERSHIP AMONG
SOUTHERN WHITE FAMILIES, 1850

Owned 1 slave 6%
Owned 2-4 slaves 9.4%
Owned no slaves 69.2%
Owned 5-19 slaves 12%
Owned 20-99 slaves 3.2%
Owned 100 or more 0.2%

14 Abolitionists in the pre-Civil War period were most likely to support the —

F   removal of the Cherokee Indians from Georgia `Cult 24(A)`

G   passage of the Fugitive Slave Act

H   activities of the Underground Railroad

J   use of popular sovereignty in the territories

15 What did the Louisiana Purchase of 1803, the annexation of Texas in 1845, and the U.S.-Mexican War of 1846 have in common?

A   They all brought about a war with Spain. `Hist 6(B)`

B   They all increased the territory of the United States.

C   They all resulted in territory being taken from the United States.

D   They all involved land forcibly taken from Mexico.

16 Which literary work argued in favor of the moral necessity of fighting slavery, even if it meant resisting the law?

F   *Common Sense* `Citi 20(C)`

G   *On the Duty of Civil Disobedience*

H   *The Headless Horseman*

J   *Rip Van Winkle*

17 What was one way that abolitionists reacted to advertisements like the one on the right?

A   by supporting the Underground Railroad `Cult 24(A)`

B   by opposing the marriage of slaves

C   by banning freed slaves from Northern states

D   by proposing a stricter fugitive slave law

100 DOLLARS REWARD!

Ranaway from the subscriber on the 27th of July, my Black Woman, named **EMILY,** Seventeen years of age, well grown, black color, has a whining voice. She took with her one dark calico and one blue and white dress, a red corded gingham bonnet; a white striped shawl and slippers. I will pay the above reward if taken near the Ohio river on the Kentucky side, or THREE HUNDRED DOLLARS, if taken in the State of Ohio, and delivered to me near Lewisburg, Mason County, Ky.

THO'S H. WILLIAMS.

August 4, 1853.

18

Am I to argue that it is wrong to make men brutes, to rob them of their liberty, to work them without wages, to keep them ignorant of their relations to their fellow men, to beat them with sticks, to [lash] their flesh with a [whip], to load their limbs with irons, to hunt them with dogs, to sell at auction, to [break up] their families, to knock out their teeth, to burn their flesh, to starve them into obedience to their masters? Must I argue that a system marked with blood is wrong? No — I will not.

A speech to citizens of Rochester, New York on July 4, 1852

Which statement best summarizes the argument made by Frederick Douglass in this speech?

F The national government has an obligation to protect slaves. [Citi 22(B)]

G Some have falsely accused slaveowners over how slaves were treated.

H It is obvious to all who care to look that the system of slavery is wrong.

J Some slaves do not mind their treatment at the hands of their masters.

---

19 Which statement best describes the economic differences between the North and the South in the period prior to the Civil War?

A The Northern economy had significant manufacturing, while the [Econ 12(A)]
Southern economy was almost exclusively agricultural.

B Jobs on plantations attracted more European immigrants to the South than the North

C Transportation systems were less developed in the North than in the South

D The Southern economy was more diversified than the Northern economy.

20

| The Emergence of the Abolitionist Movement | Henry David Thoreau's action against the U.S. government | John Brown's raid on Harper's Ferry, Virginia |

Using the information shown in the boxes, what did these developments have in common?

F They established public education for all Americans. [Cult 24(A)]

G They introduced fairer voting procedures for state officials.

H They led to a continuation of slavery in the United States.

J They sought changes to end slavery.

21   How did the Texas War for Independence differ from the U.S.-Mexican War?

    A   One involved fighting Mexico for independence, the other did not.   `Hist 6(C)`

    B   One led to an eventual increase in the land area of the United States, the other led to a surrender of land.

    C   One began as a border dispute with Mexico, the other involved France.

    D   One began over the issue of slavery in the West, the other involved a border dispute.

22   The Supreme Court ruling in *Dred Scott v. Sanford* (1857) had an important effect on life in the United States because the decision —

    F   prohibited slavery in lands west of the Mississippi River   `Govt 18(C)`

    G   gave full citizenship to all enslaved persons

    H   denied Congress the power to regulate slavery in the territories

    J   allowed for the importation of enslaved persons for ten years

23   During the 1840s, many abolitionists were against the annexation of new Western territory because they —

    A   feared the admission of new slave states   `Cult 24(A)`

    B   wanted to limit the power of the national government

    C   were concerned with the legal rights of Native American Indians

    D   supported an isolationist foreign policy

24   One effect of the rise of sectionalism, the growing disagreement over states' rights, and the issue of slavery was —

    F   the formation of the Whig Party   `Hist 8(B)`

    G   increasing tensions between the North and the South

    H   an end to the conflict over the extension of slavery in the territories

    J   a permanent compromise between the North, South, and West

25   Which issue did the Missouri Compromise, the Compromise of 1850, and the Kansas-Nebraska Act all concern?

    A   The extension of slavery in the western territories   `Citi 21(C)`.

    B   The placement of tariffs on foreign imports.

    C   The need for internal improvements in transportation.

    D   The distribution of frontier lands to small farm owners.

26   Which statement best explains the main reason why many Irish immigrants decided to migrate to the United States in the nineteenth century?

    F   They came in search of gold and silver.   `Cult 23(A)`

    G   They came because of religious wars in Ireland.

    H   They came as a result of the Irish Potato Famine.

    J   They came to convert American settlers to Catholicism.

27   With which policy is Congressman John Quincy Adams most closely associated?

    A   theory of nullification   **C**   "Manifest Destiny"   `Hist 7(D)`

    B   support of anti-slavery petitions   **D**   "popular sovereignty"

Name _____

CHAPTER 13

THE CIVIL WAR, 1861–1865

TEKS COVERED IN CHAPTER 13

- **History 1A** Identify the major eras and events in U.S. history through 1877, including [the] Civil War, and describe their causes and effects.
- **History 1B** Explain the significance of the following dates: 1861–1865, Civil War.
- **History 7C** Analyze the impact of slavery on different sections of the United States.
- **History 8A** Explain the roles played by significant individuals during the Civil War, including Jefferson Davis, Ulysses S. Grant, Robert E. Lee, and Abraham Lincoln, and heroes such as Congressional Medal of Honor recipients William Carney and Philip Bazaar.
- **History 8B** Explain the central role of the expansion of slavery in causing sectionalism, disagreement over states' rights, and the Civil War.
- **History 8C** Explain significant events of the Civil War, including the firing on Fort Sumter; the battles of Antietam, Gettysburg, and Vicksburg; the Emancipation Proclamation; Lee's surrender at Appomattox Court House; and the assassination of Abraham Lincoln.
- **History 8D** Analyze Abraham Lincoln's ideas about liberty, equality, union, and government as contained in his first and second inaugural addresses and the Gettysburg Address and contrast them with the ideas contained in Jefferson Davis's inaugural address.
- **Geography 10A** Locate places and regions directly related to major eras and turning points in the United States during the 19th century.
- **Economics 12A** Identify economic differences among different regions of the United States.
- **Economics 12C** Analyze the causes and effects of economic differences among different regions of the United States at selected times.
- **Government 17B** Explain constitutional issues arising over the issue of states' rights, including the Civil War.
- **Citizenship 21A** Identify different points of view of political parties and interest groups on important historical issues.
- **Citizenship 22A** Analyze the leadership qualities of elected and appointed leaders of the United States, such as Abraham Lincoln.
- **Citizenship 22B** Describe and evaluate the contributions of significant political, social, and military leaders of the United States.
- **Culture 24A** Describe and evaluate the historical development of the abolitionist movement.
- **Culture 26A** Identify examples of American art, music and literature that reflect society in different eras such as the "Battle Hymn of the Republic"....

In this chapter, you will learn how Americans endured their greatest test since independence — the Civil War. More Americans died in the Civil War than in any other conflict. The war ignited an issue that had been festering for years: the disagreement between free and slave states over the power of the federal government to prohibit slavery in territories that were not yet states. From 1861 to 1865, brother fought brother in many families over this issue and over the right of a state to withdraw from the Union. After four years of fighting, the war brought an end to slavery and firmly established the supremacy of the federal government over the states.

— IMPORTANT IDEAS —

A. The expansion of slavery, which in turn led to increased sectionalism and disagreement over states' rights, played the central role in causing the Civil War. Democrats divided and nominated two candidates to the Presidency. As a result of this split, Republican candidate **Abraham Lincoln** won the election. Because of Lincoln's reputation as an opponent of slavery, South Carolina seceded. Five other states seceded before Lincoln's inauguration.

B. **Jefferson Davis** became President of the Confederacy. In his Inaugural Address, Davis claimed Southern states had the right to secede.

C. In his **First Inaugural Address**, Lincoln pledged not to attack slavery in the South, but warned that he would act to preserve the Union, by force if needed.

D. When Lincoln tried to reinforce **Fort Sumter** in April 1861, South Carolina fired on the fort. The **Civil War** began. Lincoln called on all states to contribute militia to put down the rebellion. Virginia and three more Southern states seceded and joined the Confederacy.

E. Both sides thought the war would end quickly. The North failed in its early attempts to take Richmond. The North had a large population, more industry, more money, and a larger navy than the South. Lincoln adopted the "**Anaconda Plan**," attempting to strangle the South with a naval blockade. Southerners had gifted military leaders like **Robert E. Lee**. Confederate leaders felt they were fighting to preserve their way of life, even though this meant denying freedom to others (the slaves).

F. Lincoln took all needed steps for pursuing the war, including a naval blockade of the South, **conscription**, use of paper money, and limited censorship.

G. General Lee led Southern forces into the North in 1862, but they were stopped at the **Battle of Antietam**.

H. Soon after, Lincoln issued the **Emancipation Proclamation**, declaring slaves in states still in rebellion on January 1, 1863, would be free. This did not extend to border states still in the Union. Lincoln hoped the Emancipation Proclamation would give the war a moral purpose and would prevent Britain and France from allying with the South.

I. In the summer of 1863, Lee's march northward was stopped at the **Battle of Gettysburg**. In his **Gettysburg Address**, Lincoln argued the war had become a struggle to see if the system of democracy could survive.

J. The same week, General **Ulysses S. Grant** took **Vicksburg**, giving the North control of the Mississippi River. General **William T. Sherman** marched from the West across Georgia to the sea, destroying crops, towns, and farms.

K. Lincoln was re-elected in 1864. In his **Second Inaugural Address**, he focused on slavery and the need to take a conciliatory approach at the war's end.

L. In April 1865, General Lee surrendered to General Grant at **Appomattox Court House**. This brought the Civil War to an end. A few weeks later, President Lincoln was assassinated by **John Wilkes Booth**.

KEY TERMS AND PEOPLE IN THIS CHAPTER

- Election of 1860
- Civil War
- Abraham Lincoln
- Confederate States of America
- Jefferson Davis
- Lincoln's First Inaugural
- Fort Sumter
- Robert E. Lee

- "Anaconda Plan"
- Conscription (*Draft*)
- Battle of Antietam
- "Battle Hymn of Republic"
- Emancipation Proclamation
- Battle of Gettysburg
- Gettysburg Address
- Battle of Vicksburg

- William Carney
- Ulysses S. Grant
- William T. Sherman
- Philip Bazaar
- Election of 1864
- Second Inaugural Address
- Appomattox Court House
- John Wilkes Booth

ESSENTIAL QUESTIONS

- What was the central role of slavery in causing the Civil War?
- What specific events led to the outbreak of the conflict?
- What were the contrasting visions of Lincoln and Jefferson Davis?
- What were the main turning points of the war?
- What roles did individuals play in determining the outcome of the war?

THE CIVIL WAR BEGINS

THE ELECTION OF 1860

By the late 1850s, deep divisions existed among Americans over the future of the nation, and especially over the institution of slavery. Slavery played a central role in increasing sectionalism and in causing the disagreements that led to the Civil War. Two regions of the country were on different paths of development: the South increasingly relied on slave labor to grow more cotton for factories in the North and overseas, while the North depended on free labor. As Abraham Lincoln had foretold in 1858: "A house divided against itself cannot stand." The nation could not long continue half slave and half free.

Lincoln as he looked after winning the 1860 election.

In the Presidential election of 1860, the Republican Party nominated **Abraham Lincoln**. "Honest Abe" ran on a platform that opposed the extension of slavery in the territories.

Democrats could not agree on a candidate. Northern and Southern Democrats chose separate candidates. The split in their party allowed Lincoln to win the election with only 39% of the popular vote. Lincoln did not campaign in the South, and not surprisingly, did not win a single Southern state.

BIRTH OF THE CONFEDERACY

When Lincoln won the election, Southerners were outraged. South Carolina immediately seceded from the Union. Six other Southern states followed South Carolina's example by seceding before Lincoln took office. These included Texas, where a statewide convention decided on secession on February 1, 1861. Despite the opposition of Governor Sam Houston, Texas voters approved the secession on February 23rd. Meanwhile, in the months before Lincoln's inauguration, President **James Buchanan** took no action.

The seceding states formed the **Confederate States of America**. Their point of view was best expressed by **Jefferson Davis**, who was elected President of the Confederacy. He delivered his Inaugural Address in February 1861. Davis argued that the seceding states were acting on principles found in the Declaration of Independence. The South's secession illustrated "the idea that government rests upon the consent of the governed, and that it is the right of the people to alter or abolish a government whenever it becomes destructive of the ends for which it was established." The Southern states "merely asserted a right which the Declaration of Independence defined to be inalienable." While defending their own freedom, Davis overlooked the fact that Confederates were denying freedom to others — their slaves.

Jefferson Davis

Davis emphasized that the South had no aggressive designs on the North. Since the South's economy was primarily agricultural — growing and exporting cotton — and the North's interests were industrial, Davis did not believe there were any grounds for conflict. But if the North attacked the South, Davis warned the new Confederacy would be prepared.

ACTING AS AN AMATEUR HISTORIAN

In part of his Inaugural Address, Davis said the following:

"As a necessity, not a choice, we have resorted to separation, and henceforth our energies must be devoted to the conducting of our own affairs, and perpetuating the Confederacy.... If [the North] shall permit us to pursue our separate political career, my most earnest desire will have been fulfilled. For purposes of defense, the Confederate States under ordinary circumstances may rely upon their militia; but it is deemed advisable in the present condition of affairs, that there should be a well instructed, disciplined army, more numerous than would be usually required...."

What is Davis telling the Northern states in this part of his Inaugural Address?

LINCOLN'S FIRST INAUGURAL ADDRESS

Three weeks after Davis spoke, Lincoln responded to the challenge posed by the secession in his **First Inaugural Address**. Lincoln reassured Southerners that he would not interfere with slavery in the South. But he warned that the Constitution was based on the idea that "the Union of these states is perpetual" and that "no state can lawfully get out of the Union." Thus, he would do his utmost to preserve the Union, by force if necessary. He denied Jefferson Davis' claim that Southern states had a lawful right to leave it. He further stated that even if the Constitution were taken to be a simple contract, it could not be legally cancelled without an agreement between all the states, both North and South. He saw the Union as a union of people, not of states.

March 1861, Lincoln delivers his First Inaugural Address.

ACTING AS AN AMATEUR HISTORIAN

When Lincoln delivered his Inaugural Address, thousands came, not just to see the new President, but to hear what he had to say about the crisis facing the nation. Part of his address was a direct appeal to the seceding Southern states:

"… In your hands, my dissatisfied fellow countrymen, not in mine, is the momentous issue of civil war. The government will not assail you. You can have no conflict, without being yourselves the aggressors. You have no oath registered in Heaven to destroy the government, while I shall have the most solemn one to 'preserve, protect and defend' it…. We are not enemies, but friends. We must not be enemies. Though passion may have strained, it must not break our bonds of affection. The mystic chords of memory, stretching from every battlefield and patriot grave, to every living heart and hearthstone, all over this broad land, will yet swell the chorus of the Union, when again touched, as surely they will be, by the better angels of our nature."

★ What message was Lincoln giving to Southern states in his address?

★ How did his views on the Union differ from those of Jefferson Davis?

★ Why did Lincoln state he would not challenge slavery where it existed?

FIRING ON FORT SUMTER

Fort Sumter was a federal fort in Charleston Harbor, South Carolina. The garrison of federal troops stationed there was running out of food and supplies and had no way of obtaining these onshore after South Carolina seceded.

In a move to preserve national unity, President Lincoln refused to surrender the fort to South Carolina. He ordered a relief expedition to resupply the fort. On April 12, 1861, Confederate forces fired on Fort Sumter, and the **Civil War** began. Although no casualties were caused by the firing on the fort, one Union soldier was killed during the surrender ceremony when a cannon backfired.

Fort Sumter, S.C., April 4, 1861, under the Confederate flag.

On April 15, 1861, President Lincoln asked each state to provide militia to help suppress the rebellion. His request led four more Southern states, including Virginia, to join the Confederacy. Lincoln sent federal troops to border states, such as Missouri and Maryland, to make sure they stayed loyal to the Union. West Virginians formed a new state rather than secede.

U.S. During the Civil War, 1861–1865

UNION (FREE STATES)
BORDER STATES LOYAL TO UNION
CONFEDERATE STATES OF AMERICA

ACTING AS AN AMATEUR HISTORIAN

Some timelines help us to understand the unfolding of key events. Historians may place a series of complicated events on a timeline, not to memorize them, but simply to understand them better.

THE OUTBREAK OF THE CIVIL WAR

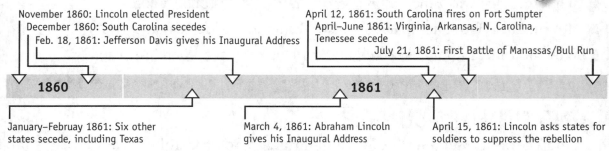

November 1860: Lincoln elected President
December 1860: South Carolina secedes
Feb. 18, 1861: Jefferson Davis gives his Inaugural Address

April 12, 1861: South Carolina fires on Fort Sumpter
April–June 1861: Virginia, Arkansas, N. Carolina, Tenessee secede
July 21, 1861: First Battle of Manassas/Bull Run

1860   1861

January–February 1861: Six other states secede, including Texas

March 4, 1861: Abraham Lincoln gives his Inaugural Address

April 15, 1861: Lincoln asks states for soldiers to suppress the rebellion

Carefully study the events on this timeline. Then select two events on the timeline and explain how the first of these events may have affected the second.

APPLYING WHAT YOU HAVE LEARNED

★ Could the Civil War have been avoided, or was it inevitable? Explain.

★ Imagine that you are President Lincoln in 1861. Write a short speech to the Southern states to convince them not to secede from the Union.

ACTING AS AN AMATEUR HISTORIAN

Look at the following four viewpoints on the causes of the Civil War. Three of them are from primary sources from the time of the Civil War. The fourth one provides the views of a modern historian.

Stephens Confederate Vice-President

Thomas Jefferson's ideas rested upon the assumption of the equality of races. This was an error.... Our new government is founded upon exactly the opposite idea; its foundations are laid, its cornerstone rests, upon the great truth that the [African American] is not equal to the white man; that slavery — subordination to the superior race — is his natural and normal condition.

— *Alexander Stephens, Confederate Vice-President March 1861.*

Sumner's Speech

[T]here are two [causes] to this war. One is slavery and the other is state rights. If slavery were out of the way, there would be no trouble from state rights. The war is for slavery, nothing else. [The South] seeks to install this barbarism as the truest civilization. Slavery is declared to be the 'corner-stone' of their new [structure].

— *Republican Senator Charles Sumner, in a speech delivered in July 1863.*

Lincoln's Speech

My object in this struggle is to save the Union,.... If I could save the Union without freeing any slave I would do it, and if I could save it by freeing all the slaves I would do it; and if I could save it by freeing some and leaving others alone I would also do that.... I here state my purpose ... and I intend no modification of my often expressed personal wish that all men everywhere could be free.

— *President Abraham Lincoln in a speech delivered in August 1862*

A Modern Historian

If the North fought to uphold the justice, power and authority of the federal government, the opposite, many assume, must be that the South fought for the power of the states. But the equation did not balance in that way: the North did not fight at first to end slavery, but the South did fight to protect slavery. It is vital that we grasp this truth....

— *Edward Ayers, Professor of History, University of Richmond, April 2011*

Based on these viewpoints, write a short essay of one page on the central role of slavery in causing the Civil War. Refer to at least two of these documents in your essay.

LEARNING WITH GRAPHIC ORGANIZERS

Complete the graphic organizer below on the causes of the Civil War. Explain the role each of these causes played in contributing to the outbreak of the Civil War:

Sectionalism

What was it? _____

_____

_____

Its role in leading to the Civil War:

_____

_____

_____

_____

_____

States Rights

What was it? _____

_____

_____

Its role in leading to the Civil War:

_____

_____

_____

_____

_____

CAUSES OF THE CIVIL WAR

The Central Role of Slavery

What was it? _____

_____

Its role in leading to the Civil War:

_____

_____

_____

_____

_____

Election of Abraham Lincoln

What was it? _____

_____

Its role in leading to the Civil War:

_____

_____

_____

_____

_____

THE COURSE OF THE WAR

For the next four years, Americans were engaged in the bloodiest conflict in their history. Southerners were fighting to defend their independence and preserve their way of life, even though this included denying freedom to others — the slaves. Northerners fought to maintain national unity. Later, they also fought in order to end the system of slavery.

BALANCE SHEET ON THE EVE OF WAR

When the war began, the North enjoyed several important advantages over the South:

THE NORTH vs. THE SOUTH

Population. The North's population was 22 million in 1860, compared to only six million free citizens in the South.

Transportation. The North had a superior transportation system with more railroads, canals, ports, and roads.

Resources. The North had more factories and grew more food. The South was primarily rural and agricultural. It produced mainly cotton and cash crops to be sold to others. The South lacked manufacturing centers.

Leadership. Jefferson Davis, President of the Confederacy, lacked the political skills of President Lincoln. However, the South appeared to have superior military leadership in the early years of the war, with commanders such as General Lee.

Naval Power. The South had few war ships, while the North had a powerful navy, which blockaded Southern ports and helped in the Mississippi campaign. This naval power would prove decisive.

Although the North had superior wealth and resources, Southerners thought they had one very important advantage: they were fighting to defend their own way of life.

APPLYING WHAT YOU HAVE LEARNED

Categorize the advantages and disadvantages of the North and the South during the war as either political, economic, or social.

WARTIME STRATEGIES

Northerners adopted a long-term strategy, first suggested by General Winfield Scott, that was aimed at strangling the South. Because the North hoped to surround and strangle the South like a giant anaconda snake, this plan became known as the **"Anaconda Plan."** President Lincoln ordered a naval blockade of the Confederacy that was practically unchallenged. His objectives were to prevent Southerners from receiving supplies from Europe, to block Southern states from exporting cotton, to prohibit the South from importing war materials, and to thwart the creation of a Confederate navy.

Lincoln also sent Union forces to take control of the Mississippi River in the West, in order to split the Confederacy in two. Lincoln hoped to use the greater resources of the North to challenge the South on several fronts at once.

The South's Strategy. Although the North was stronger, white Southerners were motivated to fight to uphold their way of life. The South's strategy was a defensive one. They did not need to attack the North — just survive. Northern attacks would be met by Confederate citizens defending their homes. The plan sought to show the world that

General Winfield Scott first proposed this plan.

Southerners were fighting in self-defense. Like a century earlier, they looked to European allies for support. Southerners hoped Northerners would soon tire of the war and accept Southern independence. Southerners also believed that they had more military experience. In General **Robert E. Lee** (1807–1870), they had the most respected military commander on either side. Lincoln had even asked Lee, a West Point graduate and officer in the U.S.-Mexican War, to lead Northern troops. However, when Virginia seceded, Lee felt he had to fight on the side of his home state.

LINCOLN'S LEADERSHIP

Throughout the war, President Lincoln displayed his own great talents of leadership. Lincoln appointed the best advisers to his Cabinet, even when they disagreed with him. He sought to reassure the South to prevent the secession, even though this failed. Lincoln showed firmness in going to war when the South fired on Fort Sumter. Lincoln persevered in the war even when the North failed to obtain a quick victory and it appeared that the war would last for a long time. He took all the steps he felt necessary to support the war effort, including **conscription** (*required military service*), the naval blockade of the South, the use of paper money, and arrests of suspected rebel sympathizers in the North. Lincoln even fired several generals in his search for a military leader who could bring the war to a successful conclusion.

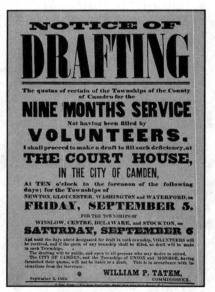

A recruiting poster from the North.

EARLY CAMPAIGNS

In the early part of the war, both sides hoped for a quick victory. Geography played a key role in the conflict. Washington, D.C. and **Richmond**, Virginia, the capital of the Confederacy, were only a short distance from one another. Northerners hoped that by capturing the Confederate capital at Richmond, the war would be quickly over.

Name _____

In July 1861, a Union army of 30,000 soldiers marched towards Richmond but was defeated at the **Battle of Manassas** (*also called the Battle of Bull Run*). General **"Stonewall" Jackson** and other Confederate leaders, commanding 22,000 soldiers, forced the Union army to retreat. Jackson displayed remarkable skill on the battlefield, which inspired his soldiers. He was widely regarded as one of the best Confederate commanders. Later in the war, he was accidentally shot by Confederate troops returning from battle.

"Stonewall" Jackson (1824–1863)

After some early successes, Jefferson Davis and Robert E. Lee decided that the best way to end the war was to invade the North. In late 1862, Lee's forces crossed into Maryland, a border state with slavery that they thought would be sympathetic. Confederate and Union forces fought a major battle at Antietam Creek. At the **Battle of Antietam** (*also known as the Battle of Sharpsburg*), six thousand soldiers were killed in just one day — the bloodiest day of the war. Lee retreated to Virginia, but to Lincoln's disappointment, Union leaders failed to pursue his forces.

APPLYING WHAT YOU HAVE LEARNED

Why were more battles fought in the South than in the North?

LEARNING WITH GRAPHIC ORGANIZERS

Complete the graphic organizer below. Describe the North's advantages and strategy.

The North's Advantages over the South	The North's Strategy in Fighting the War

THE COURSE OF THE CIVIL WAR

The South's Strategy for Fighting the War

Leadership Characteristics on each Side	Early Campaigns in the Civil War

ACTING AS AN AMATEUR HISTORIAN

Julia Ward Howe

By the start of the Civil War, "John Brown's Body" had become a popular marching song of the Union Army. One day, **Julia Ward Howe** watched as Union soldiers marched off to war singing "John Brown's Body." Howe believed the tune needed better words. In 1861, she "scrawled the verses almost without looking at the paper." "**The Battle Hymn of the Republic**" first appeared in a magazine as a battle song for the republic. Before long, the entire nation was inspired by her hymn and singing her words based on the old tune. Below are the first and fifth stanzas of "The Battle Hymn of the Republic":

Mine eyes have seen the glory of the coming of the Lord:
He is trampling out the vintage where the grapes of wrath are stored;
He hath loosed the fateful lightning of His terrible swift sword:
His truth is marching on.

He has sounded forth the trumpet that shall never call retreat;
He is sifting out the hearts of men before His judgment-seat:
Oh, be swift, my soul, to answer Him! be jubilant, my feet!
Our God is marching on.

★ Explain the meaning of these two stanzas in your own words.

★ Research the "Battle Hymn of the Republic" on the Internet. Read how these words have been interpreted by historians and see how your interpretation matches those.

EMANCIPATION PROCLAMATION (1862)

President Lincoln did not originally believe he had the power to end slavery. However, as the war progressed, he believed he should do so if it would help save the Union. Lincoln used the victory at Antietam as the occasion for announcing the **Emancipation Proclamation**. The death toll was now so great that Lincoln wanted to give the war effort a greater moral purpose. Frederick Douglass and other abolitionists were urging him to use the war as an opportunity to end slavery. Lincoln also wanted to prevent Britain and France, which opposed slavery, from taking sides with the South. Finally, he wanted to prevent Southern States from using black troops for combat and to keep border states, such as Missouri, from deserting the North for the South.

The Emancipation Proclamation, issued in September 1862, pledged to free slaves in all states still in rebellion at the beginning of 1863. It did not affect the loyal border states. Lincoln issued it on the basis of his emergency wartime powers. It was the most controversial document of Lincoln's Presidency. The announcement of the Proclamation met with both hostility and jubilation in the North. On approving it, Lincoln remarked, "I never, in my life, felt more certain that I was doing right, than I do in signing this paper."

ACTING AS AN AMATEUR HISTORIAN

The Emancipation Proclamation declared:

> "That on the first day of January, 1863, all persons held as slaves within any State or part of a State, the people whereof shall then be in rebellion against the United States, shall be forever free; and the Executive Government of the United States, including the military and naval authority, will recognize and maintain the freedom of such persons, and will do no act to repress such persons, [from] their actual freedom."

Why was Lincoln so certain that he was "doing right"?

The Emancipation Proclamation had two important immediate effects. First, it disrupted the Confederacy's agricultural economy, as slaves fled plantations. Second, it ended all chances of British or French intervention. The British and French governments had been very sympathetic to the Confederate States, which supplied them with cotton. However, the Emancipation Proclamation cast the North on the moral high ground as the emancipator of slaves, struggling against the pro-slave Confederacy. Slavery was condemned by both Britain and France.

Draft Riots. In 1863, the United States government passed a "draft" law requiring men to serve in the army. The draft was unpopular among many Northerners. In July 1863, **draft riots** broke out in New York City, protesting the law. Angry mobs attacked abolitionists and an African-American children's orphanage in New York City. Many rioters blamed African Americans for the draft.

Anti-draft rioters attack the Colored Orphans Asylum in New York City.

1863: THE TURNING POINT OF THE WAR

As the war continued, the South was slowly being strangled by the Northern naval blockade. Southern cotton piled up on docks without being shipped. Union ships also captured Southern cities along the Mississippi River.

The Battle of Gettysburg. In the summer of 1863, Confederate commander Robert E. Lee moved north in a bold attempt to cut off Washington, D.C. from the rest of the Union. Union and Confederate armies met at Gettysburg, Pennsylvania. After three days of heavy fighting, Lee retreated. The battle was the turning point of the war. Lee's army suffered heavy casualties and was never again able to take the offensive against the North. Lincoln later gave his most famous speech, the **Gettysburg Address**, at the site of the battle.

THE GETTYSBURG ADDRESS

Lincoln was invited to the battlefield of Gettysburg in 1863 to dedicate a cemetery to the Union soldiers who had died there. He spoke for only two minutes. Simply and eloquently, Lincoln explained the meaning of the Civil War to the 20,000 people who had come to see him.

ACTING AS AN AMATEUR HISTORIAN

By the third year of bloodshed, Lincoln began to feel that the war was being fought not just to preserve the Union but to test the system of democracy itself. The purpose of the war was to see if the American experiment in democracy, launched in 1776, could survive. Lincoln told his listeners that those who had sacrificed their lives had already made holy the ground where they were buried. The best that those still living could do was to continue with the terrible task that the fallen soldiers had died for:

Lincoln stands to deliver the Gettysburg Address.

> "The world will little note, nor long remember what we say here, but it can never forget what they [the soldiers who died] did here. It is for us the living, rather, to be dedicated here to the … great task remaining before us — that from these honored dead we take increased devotion to that cause for which they gave the last full measure of devotion — that we here highly resolve that these dead shall not have died in vain — that this nation, under God, shall have a new birth of freedom, and that government of the people, by the people, for the people, shall not perish from the earth."

★ What did Lincoln see as the "great task remaining"?

★ Why do you think this speech is one of the most famous in American history?

The Battle of Vicksburg. Meanwhile, Union forces had captured New Orleans and were slowly working their way up the Mississippi River in order to divide the South in two. Vicksburg was located on top of a 200-foot bluff, allowing the Confederacy to control movement along the Mississippi River. In the spring of 1863, General **Ulysses S. Grant**'s armies focused on taking **Vicksburg** to trap the Confederate army. The day after the Battle of Gettysburg, Vicksburg surrendered after a 47-day siege.

The Battle of Vicksburg

A **siege** is a military operation in which an army surrounds a city and cuts it off from all outside supplies in order to force it to surrender. Faced with starvation because of the seige, Vicksburg residents had been forced to eat rats, shoe leather, and weeds. The constant hammering of Union siege artillery drove many of the citizens of Vicksburg into caves dug into the hillsides. Grant's victory effectively cut the Confederacy in half, sealing the fate of the Confederacy.

Fort Wagner Assault. In 1863, **William Carney** (1840–1908) took part in an assault on Fort Wagner, which covered the approach to Charleston Harbor in South Carolina. The assault was one of the first major battles in the Civil War in which the Union army used African-American soldiers. For his acts of bravery, Carney later became the first African American to be awarded the Congressional Medal of Honor.

William Carney

Grant Takes Command. Lincoln was so pleased with Grant's success at Vicksburg that he placed him in charge of all Union forces. Unlike earlier commanders, Grant made his goal the total destruction of Confederate forces. He also waged war on the economic resources of the South, which supported its army. Grant sent General **William T. Sherman** with a Union army across Georgia. Sherman captured and destroyed much of Atlanta. He then marched to Savannah to further divide the Confederacy. As Sherman's army moved through the South, they tore up railroads, cut telegraph lines, and burned down farms, businesses, and villages in his "**March to the Sea.**" His army lived off the land — his troops had few supplies of their own and ate what they could seize. (*See map on page 267*).

General Ulysses S. Grant

Fort Fisher Assault. Late in 1864, General Grant ordered an assault on Fort Fisher, a Confederate stronghold that protected trading routes in North Carolina. In January 1865, **Philip Bazaar**, born in Chile, was an ordinary seaman aboard the *USS Santiago de Cuba*. Bazaar and five other crew members carried dispatches during the battle while under heavy Confederate gunfire. Bazaar became the first Hispanic-American to be awarded the Congressional Medal of Honor.

APPLYING WHAT YOU HAVE LEARNED

General Sherman ordered his army to destroy everything it encountered. They burned farms, livestock, plantations and villages. "War is cruelty," he wrote, "and you cannot refine it." In his "March to the Sea," General Sherman destroyed civilian as well as military property. In your opinion, was such destruction justified?

Name _____

LEARNING WITH GRAPHIC ORGANIZERS

◆ Complete the graphic organizer below. Describe each of the topics listed:

Julia Ward Howe's "The Battle Hymn of the Republic"	The Issuance of the Emancipation Proclamation

KEY EVENTS IN THE CIVIL WAR

Battle of Gettysburg	Battle of Vicksburg

◆ Complete the graphic organizer by briefly identifying each of these individuals:

William Carney	Ulysses S. Grant	Philip Bazaar

THE PRESIDENTIAL ELECTION OF 1864

As 1864 approached, Lincoln's chances for reelection appeared uncertain. Since Andrew Jackson, no President had been reelected for a second term. Lincoln had become subject to widespread criticism for his handling of the war. Union armies had suffered a long string of losses, and many blamed these failures on Lincoln's strategy. Other voters in the North were outraged by the Emancipation Proclamation, claiming it went too far.

Lincoln's main opponent, **George McClellan**, had been the commander of the Union Army at Antietam. In the campaign, Republicans accused Democrats of disloyalty. Republican newspapers and speakers charged Democrats with wishing to preserve slavery just when the North seemed to be on the verge of victory. With the recent Union victories, especially the capture of Atlanta, President Lincoln was able to win re-election in 1864.

Candidate	Party	Popular Vote	Percent	Electoral Vote
Abraham Lincoln	National Union	2,218,388	55%	212
George McClellan	Democratic	1,812,807	45%	21

LINCOLN'S SECOND INAUGURAL ADDRESS

Meanwhile, Lincoln's ideas had shifted again in the last months of 1864. The focus of Lincoln's **Second Inaugural Address** (1865) was not on the nature of the Union, but on the sin of slavery. Southern slave owners, Lincoln declared, had been willing to make war on the Union rather than to give up their slaves.

ACTING AS AN AMATEUR HISTORIAN

The heavy costs of the war, Lincoln believed, were God's punishment on both the North and South for centuries of slavery — "every drop of blood drawn from the lash shall be paid by another drawn from the sword." Despite this condemnation of slavery, Lincoln ended his speech on a note of national reconciliation:

"One-eighth of the population were colored slaves…. These slaves constituted a peculiar and powerful interest. All knew that this interest was somehow the cause of the war. To strengthen, perpetuate, and extend [slavery] was the object for which the insurgents would [end] the Union even by war, while the Government claimed no right to do more than to restrict the territorial [growth] of it…. With malice toward none, with charity for all … let us strive to finish the work we are in, to bind up the nation's wounds … to do all which we may achieve and cherish a just and lasting peace among ourselves and with all nations."

★ What did Lincoln now say was the underlying issue of the Civil War?

★ What was Lincoln's attitude towards the future treatment of the South?

THE WAR COMES TO AN END

The devastation caused by Union armies in the South caused many Confederates to lose hope. General Lee's army slowly dwindled. By late 1864, half of his soldiers had deserted to return home to protect their families.

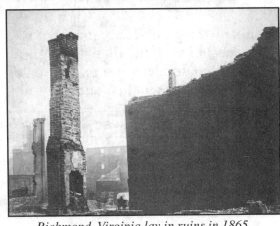

Richmond, Virginia lay in ruins in 1865.

Grant marched south with a Union army towards Richmond. In April 1865, Richmond, the capital of the Confederacy, fell to Union armies. A few days later, Lee met Grant at **Appomattox Court House**, Virginia. Under the terms of the agreement, the officers and men of Lee's army surrendered and were pardoned. All Confederate arms were collected by Union troops as captured property. Both generals signed the document of surrender. The war was finally over.

Lincoln's Assassination. Less than a week after the surrender, President Lincoln was **assassinated** on April 15, 1865, in Washington, D.C. It was exactly four years after his call to put down the rebellion. Lincoln was shot in the back of the head by the actor **John Wilkes Booth**, who thought Lincoln was a tyrant. Lincoln died the next day. Had Lincoln lived, he was prepared to forgive the South and to work together as Americans dedicated to a system of

government based on liberty, equality, and unity. Lincoln's greatest achievement was his ability to energize and mobilize the nation by appealing to its highest ideals, while acting "with malice towards none."

APPLYING WHAT YOU HAVE LEARNED

★ Rewrite one or two paragraphs of the Gettysburg Address using your own words.

★ Look for photographs of the war by noted photographer Matthew Brady and other primary documents on the Internet. Write a paragraph describing three items you found during your research.

★ Use resources from your school library or Internet to write a brief biography of Abraham Lincoln, Robert E. Lee, Ulysses S. Grant, William T. Sherman, William Carney, or Philip Bazaar.

LEARNING WITH GRAPHIC ORGANIZERS

Complete the graphic organizer below contrasting three of Abraham Lincoln's most important speeches with the Inaugural Address of Jefferson Davis. For each speech, briefly summarize its main ideas and include a famous line from the speech. Be sure to consider their ideas on liberty, equality, and government.

Davis' Inaugural Address

Main Ideas: _____
_____
_____
_____
_____

Quotation: _____
_____
_____

Lincoln's First Inaugural Address

Main Ideas: _____
_____
_____
_____
_____

Quotation: _____
_____
_____

MAJOR SPEECHES BY JEFFERSON DAVIS AND ABRAHAM LINCOLN

Gettysburg Address

Main Ideas: _____
_____
_____
_____
_____

Quotation: _____
_____
_____

Lincoln's Second Inaugural Address

Main Ideas: _____
_____
_____
_____
_____

Quotation: _____
_____
_____

Name _____

CHAPTER 13 CONCEPT MAP

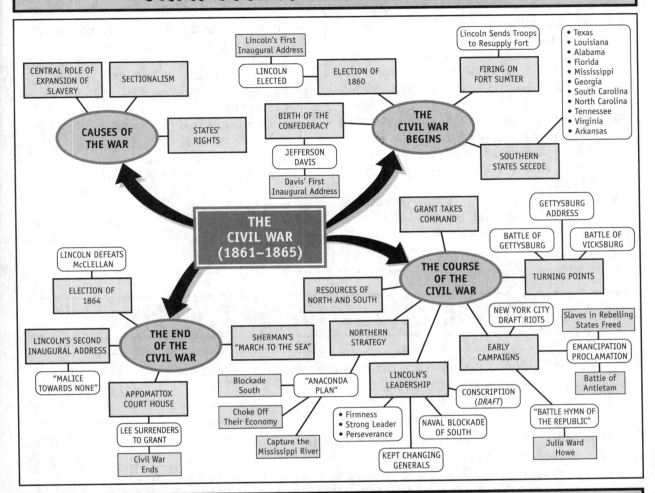

CHAPTER STUDY CARDS

Causes of the Civil War

★ **Central Role of the Expansion of Slavery.** Abolitionists in the North thought slavery should be ended.
  - Southerners feared Northerners would try to abolish slavery.
  - Debate over extension of slavery in West.
  - Breakdown of Compromise.
  - Election of Lincoln.

★ **Sectionalism.** The existence of slavery in the South encouraged sectional differences.

★ **States' Rights.** People disagreed on the right of a state to withdraw from the Union.

Highlights of the Civil War

★ **North's Strategy.** "Anaconda Plan."
  - Naval blockade of Southern ports.
  - Capture control of the Mississippi River.

★ **Main Events of the War (1861–1865).**
  - Firing on Fort Sumter (1861).
  - Battle of Antietam (1862).
  - Emancipation Proclamation (1862).
  - Battle of Gettysburg (1863).
  - Battle of Vicksburg (1863).
  - Sherman's "March to the Sea."
  - Appomattox Court House. Lee surrenders.

Significant Individuals in the Civil War

★ **Julia Ward Howe.** Wrote "Battle Hymn of the Republic" in 1861.

★ **Jefferson Davis.** President of the Confederate States of America.

★ **Robert E. Lee.** Commander of the Confederate forces during the Civil War.

★ **Ulysses S. Grant.** Commander of Union forces during the Civil War.

★ **William Carney.** Took part in attack on Fort Wagner. First African American to get Medal of Honor.

★ **Philip Bazaar.** Hispanic seaman who aided the Union victory. Received the Medal of Honor.

Key Speeches by Lincoln

★ **Lincoln-Douglas Debates, 1858 (see Chapter 12).**

★ **First Inaugural Address, 1861.**
  • Reassured South but stated he would act to preserve Union, by force if needed.

★ **Emancipation Proclamation, 1862.**
  • Freed all slaves in rebelling states.
  • Kept France and Britain out of the war.
  • Met demands of abolitionists.

★ **Gettysburg Address, 1863.**
  • Raised the purpose of the Civil War to the continued survival of democracy.

★ **Second Inaugural Address, 1865.**
  • Focus was on the end of slavery and trying to bind the wounds that were caused by the Civil War.

CHECKING YOUR UNDERSTANDING

1

> A house divided against itself cannot stand. I believe this government cannot endure permanently half slave and half free.
>
> — *Abraham Lincoln, 1858*

According to this statement from the Lincoln-Douglas debates, Lincoln believed that —

A   slavery should be permitted in the North   `Hist 8(B)`
B   sectional differences over slavery threatened to destroy the Union
C   the Southern states should be allowed to secede
D   a permanent compromise with the South on slavery was possible

EXAMINE **the question.** This question asks you to interpret a statement from the Lincoln-Douglas debates of 1858. Begin by carefully reading the quotation to see what it says. RECALL **what you know.** The Lincoln-Douglas debates took place after the *Dred Scott* decision. Lincoln felt that slavery was threatening to overwhelm the United States. APPLY **what you know. Choice A** is wrong since Lincoln never wanted slavery to spread. **Choice C** is wrong because Lincoln did not want to let the South secede. **Choice D** is also wrong. Lincoln offered to compromise but believed the compromise would not last — the country "cannot endure permanently" if slavery continues in the South. The best answer is **Choice B** since Lincoln believed that sectional differences over slavery were threatening the Union.

Name _____

Now try answering some additional questions on your own.

2   Which two individuals received a Congressional Medal of Honor for their service to
the nation in the Civil War?
    F   Jefferson Davis and Robert E. Lee   Hist 8(A)
    G   William Carney and Philip Bazaar
    H   Stonewall Jackson and Hiram Rhodes Revels
    J   Dred Scott and Stephen Douglas

3   What was the most important advantage the North had during the Civil War?
    A   unified popular support for the war effort   Econ 12(C)
    B   superior military leadership
    C   economic aid from Great Britain and France
    D   greater human and economic resources

4   What warning did Abraham Lincoln give the South in his First Inaugural Address?
    F   He would act to end slavery.   Hist 8(D)
    G   He would act to keep the South dependent on the North.
    H   He would act to preserve the Union.
    J   He would act to protect the freedom of the seas.

5
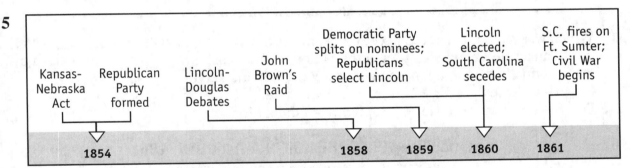

Based on the information in the timeline, which statement is accurate?
    A   John Brown's raid immediately led to the attack on Fort Sumter.   Hist 8(B)
    B   Lincoln was the first elected Democratic President.
    C   Most Southern states had seceded before Lincoln was elected.
    D   South Carolina seceded in the same year that Lincoln was elected.

6   Which would be considered a major cause of the Civil War?
    F   Northern states objected to high tariffs.   Hist 8(B)
    G   Southern states wanted to allow the importation of African slaves.
    H   Southern states claimed the right to secede from the Union.
    J   Democrats demanded a recount of votes in the election of 1860.

7   Which argument did President Lincoln use to oppose the secession of the Southern states in his First Inaugural Address?

A   Slavery was not as profitable as Southerners believed.

Hist 8(D)

B   The government was a union of the people as a whole and not of states.

C   Southern states did not permit their people to vote on secession.

D   As President, he had to defend the nation against foreign invasions.

8

> With malice toward none, with charity for all, with firmness in the right as God gives us to see the right, let us strive on to finish the work we are in, to bind up the nation's wounds, to care for him who shall have borne the battle and for his widow and his orphan, to do all which may achieve and cherish a just and lasting peace among ourselves and with all nations.
>
> — *Abraham Lincoln, Second Inaugural Address, March 4, 1865*

This speech by President Lincoln reveals his strong support for —

F   a new peace treaty with Great Britain

Hist 8(D)

G   universal male suffrage

H   a fair and generous peace

J   harsh punishment for Confederate leaders

9   Which was an immediate result of Abraham Lincoln's election to the Presidency in 1860?

A   Kansas and Nebraska joined the Union as free states.

Hist 8(B)

B   A constitutional amendment was adopted to end slavery.

C   Missouri entered the Union as a slave state.

D   Several Southern states seceded from the Union.

10

RESOURCES OF THE NORTH AND SOUTH, 1861
(expressed as percentages of their total)

Resource	North	South
Total Population	71%	29%
Factories	85%	15%
Farmland	65%	35%
Railroad Miles	71%	29%
Bank Deposits	78%	22%

Which conclusion can be drawn from the chart?

F   More people lived in the South than in the North.

Econ 12(A)

G   The South grew more crops than the North.

H   Transportation was more developed in the South than in the North.

J   The North was more industrialized than the South.

11 Which of the following was a major result of the Civil War?   `Govt 17(B)`

   A States now had the right to secede from the Union.

   B The power of the federal government was strengthened.

   C The South could collect tariffs on imports.

   D The judiciary became the most powerful branch of the federal government.

12

SELECTED BATTLES OF THE CIVIL WAR, 1861–1865

Year	Battle	Description
1861 • April • July	Fort Sumter, South Carolina Bull Run, Virginia	Union forces surrender at Charleston. Union army routed by Confederates.
1862 • Sept. • Dec.	Antietam, Virginia Fredericksburg, Virginia	First major Union defeat of Lee Lee halts Union advance to Richmond.

1863   • May
        • July
        • July
	Chancellorsville, Virginia
	 Vicksburg, Mississippi
	 Gettysburg, Pennsylvania
		Lee defeats Union. Lee invades North.
		 Grant captures Vicksburg. Lee's invasion
		 North halted, Lee retreats.

1864 • Sept.	Atlanta, Georgia	Sherman's "March to the Sea"
1865 • April	Appomattox, Virginia	Lee surrenders to Grant; Civil War ends.

Based on the information in the chart, why was the war more destructive in the South than in the North?   `Hist 8(C)`

   F Most major battles took place in the South.

   G The South lacked the support of major European allies.

   H The South's resources were not as great as those in the North.

   J The South's economy was too weak to support a long war.

---

13 The tariff issue of 1832 and the secession of the Southern states in the 1860s were similar in that both concerned the constitutional issue of —   `Govt 17(B)`

   A states' rights

   B representation in Congress

   C popular sovereignty

   D republicanism

14

> This war is not being waged on our part ... for the purpose of conquest or interfering with the rights of established institutions of the states, but to defend and maintain the supremacy of the Constitution, and to preserve the Union.

Which individual held the beliefs expressed in this quotation?   `Hist 8(D)`

   F John Brown

   G Abraham Lincoln

   H Jefferson Davis

   J Robert E. Lee

15 Which statement describes an economic difference between the North and South in the period just before the start of the Civil War?

A   The South's economy was more diverse than the North's.

B   More European immigrants went to the South than to the North.

C   Transportation was more advanced in the South than in the North.

D   The South was agricultural; while the North was agricultural and industrial.

Econ 12(A)

16

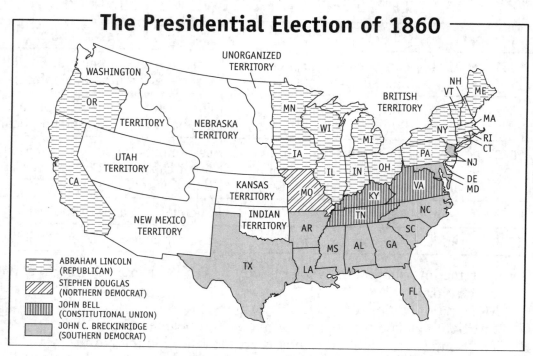

The Presidential Election of 1860

Based on the information in the map, which states supported the candidacy of John Breckinridge (Southern Democrat) in the Presidential election of 1860?

F   Texas (TX) and Florida (FL)

G   Missouri (MO) and Delaware (DE)

H   Kentucky (KY and Ohio (OH)

J   California (CA) and Oregon (OR)

Geog 10(A)

17 According to the map, the election results of 1860 most clearly illustrate the concept of —

A   nullification

B   federalism

C   sectionalism

D   republicanism

Hist 8(B)

18 Which conclusion can be drawn from the information in the map?

F   Breckinridge won more states in 1860 than did Lincoln.

G   Breckinridge's greatest support came from Southern voters.

H   Voters in the Utah Territory supported candidate John Bell.

J   Lincoln's strongest support came from Kentucky, Virginia and Tennessee.

Geog 10(B)

19 "He hath loosed the fateful lightning of His terrible swift sword, His truth is marching on." In which nineteenth-century song are these words found?

   A "Battle Hymn of the Republic"   **C** "America the Beautiful" `Cult 26(A)`

   B "Star Spangled Banner"   **D** "God Bless America"

20

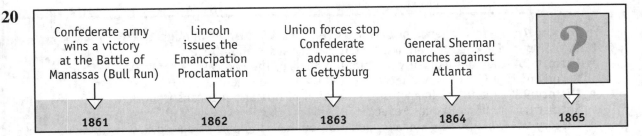

Confederate army wins a victory at the Battle of Manassas (Bull Run)	Lincoln issues the Emancipation Proclamation	Union forces stop Confederate advances at Gettysburg	General Sherman marches against Atlanta	?
1861	1862	1863	1864	1865

Which event belongs in the box in this sequence of events?

   F The Kansas-Nebraska Act is passed in Congress. `Hist 1(B)`

   G Jefferson Davis named President of the Confederacy.

   H General Robert E. Lee surrenders his forces at Appomattox Court House.

   J John Brown captured at Harpers Ferry attempting a slave uprising.

21 Which is the best description of Abraham Lincoln's leadership qualities?

   A He was unable to communicate his ideas effectively. `Citi 22(A)`

   B He refused to listen to opposing points of view.

   C He sought to compromise but did not shy away from using force.

   D He lacked military experience, which made him ineffective in wartime.

22 Despite the North's superior resources, the South won many battles. The Civil War lasted four years, from 1861 to 1865. Which might help to explain these developments?

   F The North was more dependent on foreign aid than the South. `Citi 22(B)`

   G The Underground Railroad was important to the Southern cause.

   H Guided by capable leaders like Robert E. Lee, white Southerners were fighting to maintain their way of life.

   J Personal wealth was a key factor in determining the outcome of the war.

23 How did Jefferson Davis and Abraham Lincoln disagree on the nature of the federal union?

   A Davis believed the states should replace the Constitution with new Articles of Confederation, while Lincoln disagreed. `Hist 8(D)`

   B Davis believed slavery should be extended throughout the United States, while Lincoln wanted slavery limited to the South.

   C Davis believed sovereign states had the right to legally leave the Union, while Lincoln opposed this claim.

   D Davis believed agricultural and industrial regions could not remain in the same Union, while Lincoln believed the South needed to industrialize.

THE
RECONSTRUCTION ERA

TEKS
COVERED IN
CHAPTER 14

- **History 1A** Identify the major eras and events in U.S. history through 1877, including ... Reconstruction, and describe [its] causes and effects.
- **History 9A** Evaluate legislative reform programs of the Radical Reconstruction Congress and reconstructed state governments.
- **History 9B** Explain the impact of the election of African Americans from the South such as Hiram Rhodes Revels.
- **History 9C** Explain the economic, political, and social problems during Reconstruction and evaluate their impact on different groups.
- **Geography 10A** Locate places and regions directly related to major eras and turning points in the United States during the 19th century.
- **Geography 11B** Describe the positive and negative consequences of human modification of the physical environment of the United States.
- **Economics 12A** Identify economic differences among different regions of the United States.
- **Economics 12C** Analyze the causes and effects of economic differences among different regions of the United States at selected times.
- **Economics 13B** Identify the economic factors that brought about rapid industrialization and urbanization.
- **Government 16B** Describe the impact of the 13th, 14th, and 15th amendments.
- **Citizenship 21A** Identify different points of view of political parties and interest groups on important historical issues.
- **Citizenship 22B** Describe the contributions of significant political, social, and military leaders of the United States such as ... Susan B. Anthony.
- **Culture 23D** Analyze the contributions of people of various racial, ethnic, and religious groups to our national identity.
- **Culture 24B** Evaluate the impact of reform movements, including ... the labor reform movement.
- **Culture 26B** Analyze the relationship between the arts and continuity and change in the American way of life.
- **Science, Technology, and Society 27C** Explain how technological innovations brought about economic growth such as ... the construction of the Transcontinental Railroad.
- **Science, Technology, and Society 28B** Identify examples of how industrialization changed life in the United States.

In this chapter, you will learn about the period of American history immediately following the Civil War. During the Reconstruction Era, Southerners experienced military occupation by the North. African Americans, liberated from slavery, began voting and participating in political life. New economic relationship were forged, and most freedmen became sharecroppers or tenant farmers. In the West, the end of the Civil War was followed by completion of the first Transcontinental Railroad, the forced relocation of American Indian tribes to reservation lands, and the opening of the Great Plains to ranchers and farmers. In the North, these years witnessed the rise of heavy industry, the organization of early trade unions, increased immigration, and growing urbanization.

— IMPORTANT IDEAS —

A. During the **Reconstruction Era**, Southern states needed to rebuild their economies and to be re-admitted into the Union.

B. Lincoln sought to treat the South leniently by asking 10% of its voters to take an oath of allegiance and have the state ratify the **Thirteenth Amendment**. When he was assassinated, the next President, **Andrew Johnson**, sought to follow Lincoln's plan by treating the South leniently, pardoning former Confederates.

C. One of the biggest issues facing the South was the fate of the freedmen. Despite experiments during the war, the freedmen were not given their own land. The federal government set up the **Freedmen's Bureau**, with offices throughout the South, to help the freedmen adjust and to set up schools to educate them.

D. Southern state legislatures created "**Black Codes**," based on older slave codes. These limited the civil rights and freedom of movement of the freedmen.

E. **Radical Republicans** in Congress were outraged by the Black Codes. They passed the **Civil Rights Bill**, granting freedmen their civil rights. This act later became the **Fourteenth Amendment**. Congress also passed **Military Reconstruction**, dividing the South into districts governed by the army. Former Confederate leaders lost their political rights, while the freedmen were given the right to vote.

F. Congress impeached President Johnson. He was "impeached" (*accused*) by the House of Representatives, but the Senate failed to remove him from office.

G. During Reconstruction, three amendments were added to the Constitution. The **Thirteenth Amendment** abolished slavery. The **Fourteenth Amendment** made all those born in the United States into U.S. citizens, and guaranteed all citizens the "equal protection of the laws" and "due process" in actions by state governments. The **Fifteenth Amendment** prohibited denial of voting rights on the basis of race.

H. During Reconstruction, freedmen, **carpetbaggers**, and **scalawags** held power in Southern governments. For the first time, African Americans could vote and participate in political life. Some were elected to government posts. **Hiram Rhodes Revels** became the first African American elected to Congress. Reconstruction governments built roads, schools, and took steps towards racial equality. Reconstruction ended in 1877 when President Rutherford B. Hayes withdrew federal troops from the South. Rutherford had promised to withdraw these troops to win disputed electoral votes. Not long after Northern troops were withdrawn, Southern states passed segregation laws in the 1880s.

I. Southerners also developed a new economy during Reconstruction. Many former slaves became tenants or **sharecroppers**, giving a share of their crops to the landowner. New industries developed in the South, especially in larger cities.

J. This period also saw the opening of the **Great Plains** to settlement in the West. The completion of the **Transcontinental Railroad** (1869) helped develop the West.

K. The **Indian Wars** forced Indians onto government reservations, while the widespread massacre of the buffalo on the Great Plains destroyed their food supply.

L. The Civil War provided a great stimulus to industrial production in the North. New banking laws and higher tariffs helped Northern industries to expand. Immigration from Europe stimulated the growth of Northern cities, while workers organized into **trade unions** for higher wages and better working conditions.

KEY TERMS AND PEOPLE IN THIS CHAPTER

- Reconstruction
- "Black Codes"
- Freedman's Bureau
- Radical Republicans
- Civil Rights Act
- Thirteenth Amendment
- Fourteenth Amendment
- Fifteenth Amendment
- Tenure of Office Act
- Carpetbaggers
- Scalawags
- Hiram Rhodes Revels
- Sharecropping
- "New South"
- Transcontinental Railroad
- Indian Wars
- National Labor Union
- Knights of Labor

ESSENTIAL QUESTIONS

- What problems faced the nation during Reconstruction?
- What was the impact of the 13th, 14th and 15th Amendments?
- How well did Reconstruction governments in the South succeed?
- What factors promoted the opening of the Great Plains following the Civil War"?
- How was the North transformed by further industrial growth?

THE SOUTH: RECONSTRUCTION

The Civil War had preserved the Union and abolished slavery. The Union victory established the supremacy of the federal Constitution over states' rights and demonstrated that states did not have the right to secede from the Union. However, this victory came at the cost of enormous human suffering and 600,000 dead.

The **Reconstruction Era** (1865–1877) refers to the period after the Civil War, especially in the South. After the war was over, the first major issue confronting the national government was how the Southern states were to be admitted back into the Union. A bitter power struggle developed between the President and Congress over which branch should determine the conditions for admission.

PRESIDENTIAL PLANS FOR RECONSTRUCTION

President Lincoln believed that to rebuild national unity, Southern states should be treated leniently. He felt the Southern states had never really left the Union. Lincoln therefore sought to mend the nation's wounds as rapidly as possible and ignored punishing the South. Once ten percent of a former Confederate state's voters took an oath of allegiance to the Constitution and ratified the Thirteenth Amendment ending slavery, Lincoln was prepared to admit representatives from that state back into Congress.

The looming battle between Lincoln and Congress over Reconstruction never occurred. In 1865, only a few days after the South surrendered, Lincoln was assassinated. The new President, **Andrew Johnson**, was from the border state of Tennessee and lacked President Lincoln's stature and authority.

Initially, Congress believed Johnson would not be lenient on the South. Johnson made wealthy planters write personal letters for clemency. One Senator remarked about Johnson: "I thank God that you are here. Lincoln had too much of the milk of human kindness to deal with these darn rebels. Now they will be dealt with according to their just deserts." But in the end, President Johnson followed Lincoln's plan of lenient treatment. Johnson was especially sympathetic to poor Southern whites. He recognized newly formed Southern state governments and pardoned most rebel leaders. Many Southern states then elected former Confederate leaders for seats in the new Congress.

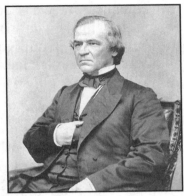

Portrait by Matthew Brady of President Andrew Johnson.

THE "BLACK CODES"

Another problem facing the South was how to deal with the millions of freed slaves, known as **freedmen**. During the war, the Union army had even given some freed slaves land in the Sea Islands of South Carolina and Georgia as an experiment. Congress established the **Freedmen's Bureau** to help the freed slaves with food, clothing and medical care. Some of these agents were former Northern veterans, empowered to settle disputes between the freedmen and their former masters. The

A Freedmen's Bureau school.

bureau also searched for lost family members, made slave marriages legal, opened schools to teach former slaves to read and write, and organized to demand their civil rights. The new Southern states were slow to extend voting rights to the freedmen. Some freedmen called for Southerners to give them their own land and tools —"20 acres and a mule" — but Southern governments refused to do so.

Instead, Southern states passed "**Black Codes**," based on older "**Slave Codes**," in order to regulate the lives of the freedmen. The aim of these codes was to preserve traditional Southern society despite the abolition of slavery. For example, the "Black Codes" made it illegal for freedmen to hold public office, to travel freely or to serve on juries. Any freedman found without a job could be fined and jailed.

THE CONGRESSIONAL PLAN FOR RECONSTRUCTION

Many Northerners were outraged at the election of rebel leaders and the passage of the Black Codes. Congress refused to recognize the new Southern governments. The **Radical Republicans**, a group of Northern Congressmen, wanted freedmen to be granted full political equality. They passed a **Civil Rights Bill**, which guaranteed freedmen's rights. To ensure that this legislation would not be held unconstitutional by the Supreme Court, they then rewrote the Civil Rights Bill as the **Fourteenth Amendment**. (You will learn more about this amendment later in this chapter.)

In 1867, Congress also passed the **Reconstruction Act** to deal with how the Southern states would be governed. The Reconstruction Act established direct military rule over former Confederate states until new governments could be formed. The act divided the Confederate states into five military districts. Federal troops helped register African Americans as voters, while former Confederate leaders were excluded from voting.

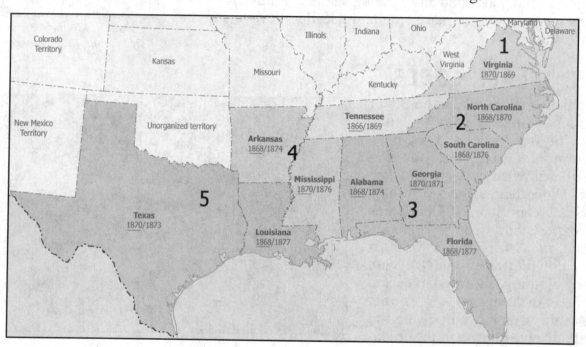

THE POLITICS OF RECONSTRUCTION

President Johnson opposed the Congressional program, believing that only the President should determine the conditions for the readmission of Southern states. The Radical Republicans in Congress believed that they should have this power. They were also quite suspicious that Johnson, a Southerner from Tennessee, was overly sympathetic to the South.

The hostile relations between Johnson and the Radical Republicans in Congress quickly affected Reconstruction policies. Congress sent the military into the South to carry out its Reconstruction policy, but President Johnson, the Commander-in-Chief, was opposed to it.

THE IMPEACHMENT OF PRESIDENT JOHNSON

Even before 1867, a number of Radicals had called for Johnson's removal, fearing that Reconstruction could never be successful so long as he remained in office. To enforce its program, Congress passed the **Tenure of Office Act**, limiting the President's power to dismiss his own Cabinet members. Johnson refused to obey this law, which he believed was unconstitutional. When Johnson dismissed his Secretary of War, Congressional leaders moved to remove Johnson from office through the process of **impeachment**. Under the Constitution, this process

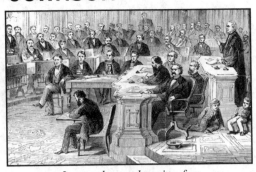

Impeachment hearing for President Andrew Johnson.

involves two steps. Johnson was first impeached (*accused*) by the House of Representatives. Next, the process moved to the Senate, where the Radical Republicans fell one vote short of removing Johnson from office.

THE GRANT PRESIDENCY

Shortly after the attempt to remove Johnson from office, **Ulysses S. Grant** (1869–1877), the Republican candidate, was elected President. Although Grant had been a brilliant general, his administration was characterized by weak Presidential leadership and widespread corruption at the national and local levels. His two terms in office coincided with the rest of Reconstruction.

THE CIVIL WAR AND RECONSTRUCTION AMENDMENTS

Following the Civil War, the Radical Republicans in Congress introduced three new Constitutional amendments: the Thirteenth, Fourteenth, and Fifteenth Amendments, known as the **Civil War** or **Reconstruction Amendments**. Their purpose was to abolish slavery, provide citizenship to the freedmen, and guarantee their civil and political rights.

THE THIRTEENTH AMENDMENT (1865)

"Neither slavery nor involuntary servitude, except as a punishment for crime whereof the party shall have been duly convicted, shall exist within the United States, or any place subject to their jurisdiction."

Lincoln's Emancipation Proclamation has been called a hollow document since it "freed no slaves." The Proclamation only freed persons held as slaves in rebelling states. Lincoln realized that as President, he had no legal grounds to single-handedly end the institution of slavery. He recognized that the Emancipation Proclamation needed to be followed by a constitutional amendment in order to guarantee the abolition of slavery. Passed in 1865, the **Thirteenth Amendment** abolished slavery throughout the nation, confirming the intent of the Emancipation Proclamation.

THE FOURTEENTH AMENDMENT (1868)

> *"All persons born or naturalized in the United States, and subject to the jurisdiction thereof, are citizens of the United States and of the State wherein they reside. No State shall make or enforce any law which shall abridge the privileges or immunities of citizens of the United States; nor shall any State deprive any person of life, liberty, or property, without due process of law; nor deny to any person within its jurisdiction the equal protection of the laws."*

As you learned earlier, although the Thirteenth Amendment abolished slavery, it failed to give slaves equal protection under the law. The Supreme Court had ruled in *Dred Scott* that slaves were not citizens, but property. After the Civil War ended, many Southern states passed Black Codes, which denied the freed slaves their civil rights. The Radical Republican Congress passed the Civil Rights Act in response to the Black Codes, and quickly proposed its terms as a Constitutional amendment.

The **Fourteenth Amendment** granted U.S. citizenship to all former slaves. It said that states must provide all citizens with "due process of law" and "equal protection of the laws." It also prohibited state governments from denying any citizen their rights to a fair trial. In effect, the Fourteenth Amendment allowed federal courts to protect individual rights from acts by state governments. It also stated that no one in the former Confederate government could be a member of the federal government. Finally, it said that all debts incurred by the United States to fight the Confederacy were to be paid, but none of those incurred by the Confederacy. Before being re-admitted into the Union, Southern states were forced to ratify this amendment.

The Fourteenth Amendment made freedmen citizens, while the Fifteenth Amendment gave them the vote.

THE FIFTEENTH AMENDMENT (1870)

> *"The right of citizens of the United States to vote shall not be denied or abridged by the United States or by any State on account of race, color, or previous condition of servitude."*

The **Fifteenth Amendment**, the last of the Civil War Amendments to be ratified, was designed to close the last means being used by white Southern leaders to deny civil rights to newly-freed, former slaves. This amendment guaranteed voting rights to former slaves. Women reformers were disappointed when this amendment gave voting rights to male freedmen but not to women. Native American Indians also did not receive any rights under any of these amendments.

One special motive behind the Fifteenth Amendment was the Republican desire to secure its power base in both the North and the South for future elections. African-American voters were expected to support Republicans. Ratification of the amendment actually had little effect in the South, since terrorism and special hurdles to voting were later used to prevent African Americans from voting once Reconstruction ended.

APPLYING WHAT YOU HAVE LEARNED

★ Which plan for Reconstruction — that of Lincoln, Johnson or the Radical Republicans — would you have favored? Debate these plans with your class.

★ Compare the impeachment of President Andrew Johnson with the more recent impeachment of President Bill Clinton. When do you think impeachment of a President is justified?

★ Make a poster explaining the Civil War Amendments in your own words.

Women reformers, who had been key to the abolitionist movement, were greatly disappointed when the Fifteenth Amendment guaranteed the right to vote for freedmen, but not for women. In 1872, **Susan B. Anthony** was arrested for illegally leading a group of women to vote in Rochester, New York, in the Presidential election. An all-male jury found her guilty of the election laws. The judge ordered Anthony to pay a $100 fine — which she refused to pay.

ACTING AS AN AMATEUR HISTORIAN

U.S. History   Search

Susan B. Anthony asked to say a few words before Judge Ward Hunt passed his sentence. She told the court:

"Your Honor, all forms of law are made by men, interpreted by men, administered by men, in favor of men, and against women. Your verdict of guilty against a citizen for the exercise of 'that citizens' right to vote,' is simply because that citizen was a woman and not a man. But, yesterday, that same man declared it a crime punishable with a fine and imprisonment, for you or me to give a cup of cold water, a crust of bread, or a night's shelter to a fugitive as he was making his way to Canada. Every man or woman in whose veins coursed a drop of human sympathy violated that wicked law, [regardless] of consequences, and was justified in so doing.... [N]ow women, to get their voice in this government, take it. I have taken mine, and mean to take it at every possible opportunity."

★ What historic comparison did Susan B. Anthony make to prove her point?

★ Later that night, Anthony wrote in her diary that the trial was "the greatest judicial outrage history has ever recorded!" Why do you think she felt that way?

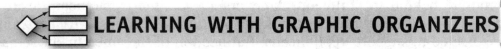 LEARNING WITH GRAPHIC ORGANIZERS

Complete the graphic organizer below by describing what each of these amendments did and what problem or problems each addressed.

POLITICS OF RECONSTRUCTION PRESIDENTS

President Andrew Johnson

Why was Johnson distrusted: _____
_____

Actions by Congress: _____
_____

President Ulysses Grant

Grant's claim to recognition: _____
_____

Features characterizing him: _____
_____

Complete the graphic organizer below by describing what each of these amendments did and what problem or problems each addressed.

CIVIL WAR AND RECONSTRUCTION AMENDMENTS

Thirteenth Amendment

Problem addressed:
_____
_____
_____

What it did: _____
_____
_____
_____
_____
_____

Fourteenth Amendment

Problem addressed:
_____
_____
_____

What it did: _____
_____
_____
_____
_____
_____

Fifteenth Amendment

Problem addressed:
_____
_____
_____

What it did: _____
_____
_____
_____
_____
_____

THE SOUTH UNDER RECONSTRUCTION

Before the Civil War, there were virtually no African-American office holders in the South, and only a few were able to vote in some Northern states. The defeat of the Confederacy was seen by the African-American community as an opportunity to demand their legal and political rights, especially the right to vote. During the first years of Reconstruction, African-Americans held state and local conventions throughout the South to protest their unfair treatment and to demand the right to vote and equality before the law.

As Republicans took control of all Southern governments and state legislatures changes began to occur. One of the most significant changes that Reconstruction brought about was the participation of African Americans in the South's political, economic and social life.

AFRICAN AMERICANS IN OFFICE IN THE SOUTH

State	State Legislators	U.S. Senators	U.S. Congressmen
Alabama	69	0	4
Arkansas	8	0	0
Florida	30	0	1
Georgia	41	0	1
Louisiana	87	0	1
Mississippi	112	2	1
North Carolina	30	0	1
South Carolina	190	0	6
Tennessee	1	0	0
Texas	19	0	0
Virginia	46	0	0

After Congress enacted the Civil Rights Act, former Confederates were barred from voting or holding office. Instead, freedmen, so-called **carpetbaggers** (*Northerners who went South*) and **scalawags** (*Southerners who had sided with the North during the Civil War*) held political power in the Southern states. The Congressional plan for Reconstruction dramatically altered politics in the South. More than 700,000 freedmen could suddenly vote.

The first African Americans to serve in Congress, during Reconstruction.

The era witnessed some 2,000 African Americans holding public office, from the local level up to the U.S. Senate. However, as the chart above indicates, most of the participation was at the local and state level.

Reconstruction was a first step in correcting the many injustices done to African Americans since colonial times. Republican governments came to power in each Southern state. African Americans held positions of authority in Southern governments for the first time. New state constitutions established free statewide public school systems, open to African Americans as well as to whites. Reconstruction governments built new hospitals, orphanages, roads, and railroads. They banned racial discrimination.

Representative of the changes taking place in the South was the election of **Hiram Rhodes Revels**. He became the first African American to serve in the U.S. Congress. Born in North Carolina, Revels attended college in the North and became a minister. He helped raise two regiments of African Americans during the Civil War. During Reconstruction, he moved to Mississippi, where he served in local and state governments before being elected as a U.S. Senator in 1870. In the Senate, he spoke on behalf of racial equality and amnesty for former Confederates. Senator Charles Sumner, a Radical Republican, spoke of the importance of Revels' election: "The Declaration was only half established by Independence. The greatest duty remained ahead. In assuring the equal rights of all, we complete the work."

Hiram Rhodes Revels
(1827–1901)

THE SHARECROPPING SYSTEM

Following the war, plantation owners in the South faced a dilemma. Even if a family still owned a large amount of land, they could not farm it by themselves: they needed workers. The Southern economy was in such shambles that in many instances landowners lacked the money to buy seed and farm implements, much less to hire laborers. To deal with the South's economic problems, plantation owners and freedmen developed the system of **sharecropping** as a replacement for slavery. Former plantation owners provided livestock, tools, and land to former slaves in exchange for a share of their crop. Other former slaves became tenant farmers, paying rent for use of the land.

A group of sharecroppers
work the land raising cotton.

These arrangements soon developed into a new means of oppression of the freedmen. The larger plantations even printed their own paper money as an advance to their tenant farmers against the following year's crop, rather than giving them real cash. Plantation money could only be used at plantation stores, which often charged high prices for basic necessities.

THE "NEW SOUTH"

The term "New South" is used to describe the emergence of a modern, industrial South. The South moved away from plantation culture and could no longer rely on slave labor. Northerners came to the South to help rebuild towns and cities, put down new rail lines, and develop new industries, including cotton and steel mills. The introduction of new farming methods increased yields. New crops, like fruits and vegetables, were added to old staples like cotton, tobacco, rice, and sugar. With financial support from the North, industrial expansion in the South began. A shift in population began to take place. People began moving from farms into Southern cities in search of jobs. This encouraged the growth of Atlanta and other large Southern cities.

The most significant change was the introduction of textile mills. Starting in the early 1880s, capitalists from the North saw the South as a great opportunity to invest in building textile mills. They were drawn to the region by the fact that they could pay Southern mill workers half what they would have to pay workers in Northern mills.

In general, prosperity in the New South benefited landlords and factory owners, and bypassed poor whites and African Americans. Sharecroppers and low-wage factory workers across the region continued to face a life of poverty.

THE END OF RECONSTRUCTION

In 1872, Congress passed the **General Amnesty Act**, which allowed most former Confederates to vote and hold office. Congress also ended the Freedmen's Bureau. In 1873, the U.S. Supreme Court handed down a decision dealing with the Fourteenth Amendment. The Court decided that the amendment's protection of a citizen's "privileges and immunities" was to be narrowly defined. This opened the door to many of the abuses African Americans would suffer at the hands of restored Southern state governments.

The Presidential election of 1876 had a disputed outcome that played a surprising role in bringing Reconstruction to an end. Democrat **Samuel J. Tilden**, a former governor of New York, won the popular vote but fell one electoral vote short of being the winner. Results were disputed in Oregon and three Southern states. Republican **Rutherford B. Hayes** struck an agreement to withdraw federal troops still stationed in the South and to end Reconstruction in exchange for support from Southern Congressmen for the disputed electoral votes against his rival Tilden.

Rutherford B. Hayes
1822–1893

In 1877, Reconstruction officially came to an end. Northern troops withdrew and home rule was restored to Southern state governments. Former Confederate leaders were once again allowed to serve in public office. State legislatures quickly moved to bar African Americans from the political process. Most white Southerners resented their treatment at the hands of the Radical Republicans and sought to take power back. As a result, for decades to come the South gave its political support almost entirely to the Democratic Party, becoming known as the "**Solid South**."

After Reconstruction, Northerners appeared to lose interest in the South and freedmen lost most of their newly won rights. The **Ku Klux Klan**, founded in 1866 by ex-Confederate soldiers, was a secret fraternal organization. The "KKK" used acts of terrorism — including murder, lynching, arson, rape, and bombing — to oppose the granting of civil rights to African Americans. Federal legislation destroyed the Klan in 1872, but similar organizations arose to take its place.

Political cartoon showing the fear generated by the KKK over African Americans.

Since African Americans were also still dependent on white Southern landowners for their economic survival, they remained vulnerable. After Reconstruction ended, Southern state governments then passed a series of laws **segregating** whites from blacks in schools and other public facilities. These laws sent the message that African Americans were inferior to whites and should be kept in their place.

African-American leaders such as **Booker T. Washington**, author of the book *Up From Slavery*, and **W.E.B. DuBois**, founder of the N.A.A.C.P., spoke out against these injustices. But it would take another 80 years before these conditions were reversed by the Civil Rights Movement of the 1960s and the efforts of leaders like Dr. Martin Luther King, Jr.

ACTING AS AN AMATEUR HISTORIAN

★ Write a skit showing relations between a freedman and his former master during the Reconstruction Era.

★ Use the Internet or school library to conduct research on one of the Southern states during the Reconstruction Era. Write a brief report on the problems faced by people in that state, and how they tried to overcome their problems.

★ Use the Internet to research Booker T. Washington and W.E.B. DuBois. Although both were African-American leaders, they had differing approaches as to how African Americans should approach the future. Describe their different responses to segregation and the oppression of African Americans in the nation.

LEARNING WITH GRAPHIC ORGANIZERS

Complete the graphic organizer below by describing some of the key institutions and developments during the period of Reconstruction.

Freedmen's Bureau	"Black Codes"	Reconstruction Acts

KEY DEVELOPMENTS DURING RECONSTRUCTION

Impeachment Trial	Sharecropping System	"New South"

THE WEST: THE LAST FRONTIER

The end of the Civil War also saw the opening of the "Last Frontier" — the Great Plains.

THE SETTLEMENT OF THE FRONTIER

The American **frontier** has generally been defined as the line separating areas of settlement from "unsettled" wilderness territory. From another point of view, the American frontier marked the dividing line between areas where Native Americans lived and areas where more technologically advanced peoples lived. Since the arrival of the first colonists, the American frontier had moved slowly westwards. By the end of the Civil War, American settlers occupied the mid-Western prairies and had a foothold along the Pacific coast. Between these two lines was a vast expanse of territory.

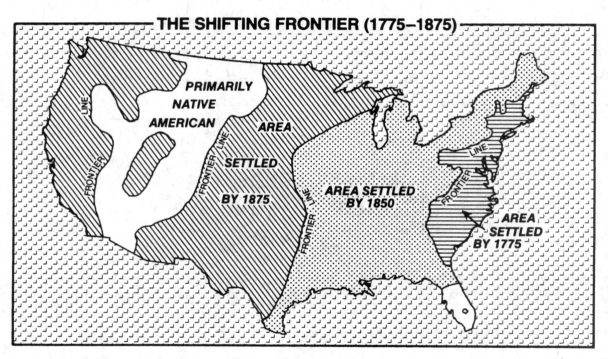

THE SHIFTING FRONTIER (1775–1875)

Much of this last frontier consisted of the Great Plains, home to millions of buffalo and the American Indian tribes who lived off their food and hides. From about 1860 to 1890, these herds of buffalo were destroyed, the Plains Indians were forced onto reservations, and the Great Plains were divided into farms and ranches.

THE IMPACT OF THE TRANSCONTINENTAL RAILROAD

The extension of the railroads was one of the principal factors behind the settlement of the Great Plains. Before the Civil War, Northerners and Southerners could not agree on a route for a Transcontinental Railroad. After the South seceded, it was clear that the route would go through the North. After the war, separate crews of engineers and laborers worked from California eastward and from the middle of the country westward.

Name _____

In laying the track, they had to cut through the high mountains of the Sierra. The two halves of the Union Pacific-Central Pacific Transcontinental Railroad were connected in 1869 at Promontory Point, Utah. After the completion of the first Transcontinental Railroad, trunk lines were soon built, which connected to the main transcontinental line. Sharp-shooters on the railroads killed off many of the buffalo.

Completion of the Transcontinental Railroad at Promontory Point, Utah.

Impact of the Transcontinental Railroad. Completion of the railroad greatly changed the nation. Products from the West, such as coal and minerals, could be shipped to the East. Ranchers and farmers also shipped their cattle and grain to Eastern markets. The railroad united East and West. Passengers and freight could now reach the West Coast in a matter of days instead of months, and at one-tenth the cost. Settlers rushed to live on lands once considered desert wasteland.

Chinese Immigrant Workers. Many of the laborers working on the Transcontinental Railroad on the California side were Chinese immigrants. Disorder and poverty in China drove many of them to emigrate to California. These immigrants received from $26 to $35 a month for a 12-hour day, 6-day work week, and they even had to provide their own food and tents. Their crews of laborers performed dangerous tasks, like making tunnels through mountains. The number of workers from China rose to a high of 12,000 in 1868, making up about 80 percent of the railroad construction workforce.

THE IMPACT OF GEOGRAPHY ON AMERICAN HISTORY

When gold was discovered in California in 1848, those struck by gold fever had either to sail around South America, to sail to Central America (*which could be crossed by land*), or to take a horse-drawn coach or wagon across the mountains and prairies of the United States. Even before the Civil War, Americans realized the need for a Transcontinental Railroad — but were divided on the route. Southerners proposed a route through Utah and Nevada. Amer-

California gold miners.

icans rightly suspected the choice of the route would have an important impact on economic development. During the Civil War, the Northern route was chosen. Completion of the Transcontinental Railroad opened the Great Plains to settlement.

THE PLAINS INDIANS

Native Americans, also known as American Indians, once occupied all of the entire United States. The advancing line of settlement, and diseases from Eurasia like smallpox, severely reduced their population and pushed them westward. The continuous demand for resources and Western lands would greatly change the life of American Indians, who through a series of treaties and government actions continued to be displaced from their ancestral lands.

Tribes such as the Sioux, lived by hunting the millions of buffalo that grazed the Great Plains. However, completion of the Transcontinental Railroad and the arrival of settlers created pressure to remove the Plains Indians from these lands.

One of the most severe limitations on the Plains Indians was the disappearance of the buffalo. These tribes depended on the buffalo for their sustenance — food and clothing. At one time, fifteen million buffalo had roamed the Great Plains. From 1871 to 1873, hide hunters sought out the hides of buffaloes — leading to three million hides being harvested

A mountain of buffalo skulls collected by white hunters.

annually. When Congress was called upon to halt the indiscriminate slaughter and extermination of the buffalo, it turned a blind eye. By 1883 most of the buffalo herds were eliminated.

THE "INDIAN WARS"

Expansion into the Great Plains and mountain regions by miners, ranchers and settlers led to a growing number of conflicts with the American Indian tribes in the West. From the 1840s to the 1880s, the U.S. military fought several battles, usually in the form of small skirmishes, in an effort to clear routes to the West for white settlers and to establish government control over this vast territory.

Native American warriors were no match for federal troops.

During these "Indian Wars," the U.S. Army defeated the Plains Indians and forced them onto reservations. Most of the federal troops in the West had battle experience learned in fighting during the Civil War. The technological superiority of these troops made successful resistance by the Indian tribe nearly impossible. Government reports estimate that as many as 45,000 Indians and 19,000 U.S. troops and settlers were killed in these wars. Faced with extermination or moving to government reservations, most Indians chose to move.

Name _____

CHAPTER 14: The Reconstruction Era   **301**

THE RESERVATION SYSTEM

There were well over 1,000 tribes in existence prior to the formation of the United States. Many of those tribes disappeared after the introduction of new diseases and the forced implementation of the reservation system. By 1869, the Transcontinental Railroad was completed. The expansion of railroad lines throughout the nation made tribal lands in the West even more desirable. From 1830 to 1890, the U.S. government followed a policy of pushing Indian tribes from their traditional lands onto government reservations in the West.

A Nez Perce reservation in Idaho 1899

Once an Indian tribe submitted to federal authority, its members were moved to a reservation. Reservation lands were usually smaller than the traditional tribal lands and often consisted of undesirable land. The federal government promised the Indians food, blankets, and seed, but this policy clashed with tribal customs, since most Indians were traditionally hunters, not farmers.

For most American Indians, life on the reservation was extremely difficult. Although tribes were permitted to create their own tribal councils and courts, most of them living on the reservation suffered from poverty, malnutrition, low standards of living, and low rates of economic development.

Not only had their tribes lost their traditional lands, but it was often impossible to maintain their traditional lifestyles in a confined reservation area. Starvation was not uncommon, and life in such close quarters often helped to spread diseases. Indians were encouraged to wear non-Indian clothing and learn to read and write English. Children were sent to reservation schools, where Christian missionaries sought to convert them and persuade them to give up tribal spiritual beliefs. Some were sent to far-off boarding schools, where they were taught to look down on tribal rites and traditions.

Luther Standing Bear

ACTING AS AN AMATEUR HISTORIAN _____

Some historians claim that American Indians were treated unfairly by the federal government. Conduct your own research on this topic. Then write a brief "position paper" — a report in which you inform others of your position — on whether you agree or disagree with this claim.

THE NORTH: AMERICA'S "SECOND INDUSTRIAL REVOLUTION"

While the Civil War destroyed the economy of the South, it actually provided a tremendous stimulus to the economy of the North. Manufacturers supplied uniforms, rifles, cannons, processed foods and other supplies to the Union army. During the Civil War, the federal government also passed legislation creating a national banking system, enabling it to borrow money to pay for the war, and began issuing paper money. Without the Southern states to block legislation, Northerners also raised tariffs to protect Northern manufacturers.

At the end of the war, Northern manufacturers adapted their factories and workshops to civilian needs. The introduction of the **Bessemer process** in the 1850s made steel production easier. The laying of thousands of miles of railroad track created an immense demand for iron and steel. New railroad lines also connected resources, factories, and centers of population. The sewing machine, invented in 1846, was coming into wider use, while the first oil well was drilled in Pennsylvania in 1859. Some historians call this rise of heavy industry the "Second Industrial Revolution."

In 1855, Henry Bessemer developed a new method of making steel.

Urbanization. The rise of industry also led to increased urbanization. The increased number of jobs, along with advances in technology and transportation encouraged people to migrate to cities. Northeastern and Midwestern cities mushroomed in size.

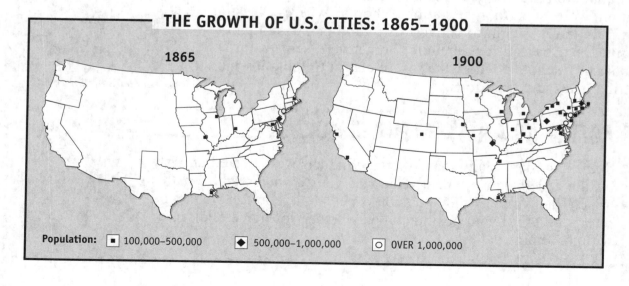

THE GROWTH OF U.S. CITIES: 1865–1900

1865

1900

Population: ■ 100,000–500,000 ◆ 500,000–1,000,000 ◉ OVER 1,000,000

Immigration. Industrial growth also led to increased immigration. The development of ocean-going passenger vessels made the journey to America easier, cheaper, and faster for many immigrants. Immigrants continued to come from Germany and Ireland, but they were now joined by newcomers from Italy, Russia, Austria-Hungary, and Poland.

ORIGINS OF THE LABOR MOVEMENT

One of the main reasons for the rapid economic growth of the North following the Civil War was the increasing exploitation of industrial workers. Gains in industrial productivity were made at terrible costs to workers. Working conditions at factories were often hazardous. Employers hired the cheapest possible laborers. Immigrants were willing to work for low wages. Factories often employed women and children at especially low pay.

The 1860s saw the emergence of labor as an organized force in the United States. A **trade union** is an association of workers who act together in making demands to employers for higher wages and better working conditions. The earliest unions were also mutual assistance societies. Members contributed part of their wages to create a fund to help members who became sick or died. Trade unions were formed on a national scale between 1861 and 1866. The first attempt to unite all trade unions into a single federation took place in 1866, with the formation of the **National Labor Union**. However, in 1872 this union disbanded because of internal friction.

In 1869, the National Labor Union was succeeded by the **Knights of Labor**. By 1886, they had grown into a national organization with more than 700,000 members. Their policies pushed for state and national laws to improve conditions. The Knights demanded an 8-hour work day, higher wages, safety codes in factories, an end to child labor, and equal pay for women. They backed restrictions on immigration, which they saw as competition for their jobs.

Anti-union cartoon showing a competent worker supporting an incompetent one on his back.

APPLYING WHAT YOU HAVE LEARNED

★ In what ways did the further growth of industry contribute to the birth of a national labor movement at this time?

★ Were labor unions justified in opposing immigration to the United States? Explain your answer.

★ Why do you think the initial public reaction was hostile to labor unions?

ART, MUSIC, AND LITERATURE IN THE POST-CIVIL WAR PERIOD

The period after the Civil War also produced art, music and literary works of great worth and striking individuality.

ART IN AMERICA

Among the best known American artists of this period were James McNeill Whistler, Thomas Eakins, and Winslow Homer. **James McNeill Whistler** (1835–1933) moved to Europe where he was influenced by modern French painters. His famous portrait of his mother emphasizes composition and tone. **Winslow Homer** (1836–1910) is known for paintings featuring scenes of the sea, boats, and coastlines. **Henry Ossawa Tanner** (1859–1937) emerged as one of the first important African-American painters. His paintings gave accurate depictions of his subjects.

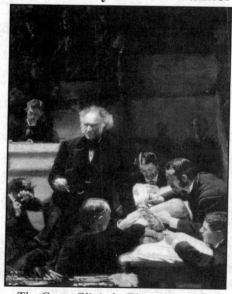

Thomas Eakins (1844–1916) was a realist painter, recognized for his portraits, usually of friends, family, or people in the arts, sciences, and medicine. *The Gross Clinic* is often considered his finest painting. It shows Dr. Gross performing surgery on a young man, while the patient's mother woman cringes in the corner. Depicted in a surgical amphitheater, the viewer appears to occupy a seat alongside Gross' students.

This period also saw the emergence of painters whose focus was on the American West. **Frederick Remington** (1861–1909), **Charles Russell** (1864–1926), and **George Catlin** (1776–1872) painted and sculpted cowboys, Native American Indians, and landscapes in romanticized scenes of life in the Old West.

The Gross Clinic by Thomas Eakins.

AMERICAN LITERATURE

After the Civil War, America began to take its modern shape as a pluralistic, industrialized, and commercial society. During this period two of the nation's greatest poets flourished. **Walt Whitman** (1819–1892) wrote *Leaves of Grass*, in which he used a free-flowing verse and lines of irregular length to celebrate both nature and urban life. **Emily Dickinson** (1830–1886) is considered one of the most original 19th-century American poets. She is praised for her innovative style with its broken rhyming, use of dashes, and random capitalization. Her work was so unconventional that little of it was published in her lifetime.

Born in Missouri, **Mark Twain** (1835–1910) was the first major American writer born away from the East Coast. Two of his masterpieces, *Adventures of Tom Sawyer* and *Adventures of Huckleberry Finn*, chronicled life along the Mississippi River. His fictional characters spoke like real people and sounded distinctively American, using local dialects, newly invented words, and regional accents. His honest and candid approach revealed what life was really like for many African-Americans along the Mississippi. As he grew older, his writings came to express the sad view that all human motives were selfish. Today, he is best remembered as a humorist who used sharp wit, comedy, and exaggeration to attack false pride and self-importance.

Mark Twain

AMERICAN MUSIC

The music of America is the culmination of many different styles that have grown and changed over the years. American music has been especially influenced by both African and European musical styles.

Slave spirituals and work songs grew in popularity after the Civil War. Chamber music and parlor songs were also quite popular in many American homes during this period. **Stephen Foster** (1826–1864) was a noted composer whose songs were uniquely American in theme, characterizing a love of home, work, politics, battlefields, slavery and plantation life. His songs included "My Old Kentucky Home," and "Oh! Susana."

In these years, most small towns in America had an amateur brass or wind band. Many of these bands originated in the military. Brass bands were especially popular in parades. **John Philip Sousa** was a key early composer, who composed many marches. He is most famous for *The Stars and Stripes Forever*.

John Philip Sousa (1854–1932)

ACTING AS AN AMATEUR HISTORIAN

Select one of the artists, writers, or musicians mentioned in this section. Research that individual's work on the Internet or at your school or local library.

Then write a brief report, specifically referring to at least two of that individual's works. Explain how those works are representative of this period in United States history.

LEARNING WITH GRAPHIC ORGANIZERS

Complete the graphic organizer indicating some of the major developments that took place in the West and North.

Building of the Transcontinental Railroad
_____
_____
_____
_____
_____
_____
_____
_____
_____
_____

The Growth of Organized Labor
_____
_____
_____
_____
_____
_____
_____
_____
_____
_____

War's Effect on Northern Industry
_____
_____
_____
_____
_____
_____
_____
_____
_____

The Emergence of New Technologies
_____
_____
_____
_____
_____
_____
_____
_____
_____

Name _____

CHAPTER 14 CONCEPT MAP

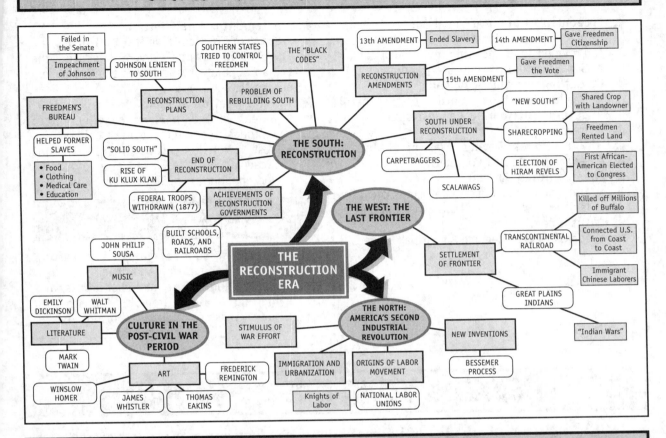

CHAPTER STUDY CARDS

The Politics of Reconstruction Plans

★ **Lincoln's Plan.** Sought lenient treatment of South: 10% of voters swear allegiance to Constitution, state would be readmitted.

★ **Johnson's Plan.** Allowed Southern state governments to be make up of former Confederates. States passed "Black Codes" which restricted freedmen's rights.

★ **Radical Reconstruction Plan.** A group of Congressmen sought to punish the South.
- **Reconstruction Act** imposed harsh treatment with military rule in South.
- **Civil Rights Act** and Fourteenth Amendment gave rights to freedmen.
- **Impeachment.** Radical Republicans tried but failed to impeach President Johnson.

Civil War Amendments

To be readmitted to the Union, each Southern state had to approve these amendments:

★ **Thirteenth Amendment (1865).** Abolished slavery in the nation.

★ **Fourteenth Amendment (1868).** Guaranteed states give citizens basic civil rights and equality, including "due process of law" and "equal protection of the law."

★ **Fifteenth Amendment (1870).** Gave the right to vote to former slaves (but not women).

Despite these amendments, Southern states deprived African American of their rights when Northern troops withdrew in 1877.

Reconstruction In South

★ **Freedmen's Bureau.** Federal agency to help former slaves.
  • Provided food, clothing and health care.
  • Set up schools to educate freedmen.
★ **Carpetbaggers and Scalawags.**
  • Northerners took control of Southern governments during Reconstruction with freedmen.
★ **Hiram Rhodes Revels.** Was first African American elected to Congress.
★ **Sharecropping System.**
  • Freedmen occupied plantation owner's land in exchange for landowner getting a share of the crop.
  • Served to keep freedmen in virtual "slavery."

The West: Opening Great Plains

★ **Settlement of the Frontier.**
★ **Impact of Transcontinental Railroad.**
★ **The "Indian Wars."** Severely reduced the Indian population and forced them onto reservations. .
★ **The Reservation System.**
  • Defeat in Indian Wars, construction of railroads forced relocation of tribes.
  • Reservation life was difficult. Indians faced poverty, low standards of living, and challenges to their tribal traditions.

The North: Second Industrial Revolution

★ Civil War stimulated growth of nation's industries, immigration and cities.
★ New technologies, like Bessemer Process and laying railroad lines, promoted industry.
★ Period saw rise of national labor unions.

CHECKING YOUR UNDERSTANDING

1 What was the primary goal of Radical Republican legislative reform programs?
   A   to establish equality under the law for freedmen
   B   to restore white Southern representation in Congress
   C   to honor military leaders of the Confederacy
   D   to prevent African-American land ownership

`Hist 9(A)`

EXAMINE **the question.** This question tests your knowledge of the legislative reform program of the Radical Republicans in Congress. RECALL **what you know.** You should recall that after the Civil War, Radical Republicans had control of Congress. They believed slavery had been a moral evil and wanted to help the freedmen while punishing the South. APPLY **what you know. Choice B** is wrong because they did not aim at restoring white Southern representation in Congress. **Choice C** is wrong because they did not honor Confederate leaders. **Choice D** is also wrong, since they wanted to promote, not prevent, African-American land ownership. The best answer is **Choice A.** Both the Civil Rights Bill and Fourteenth Amendment tried to give freedmen equality under the law.

Now try answering some additional questions on your own.

2

POPULATION OF SELECT WESTERN CITIES, 1860–18

Name of City	Population in 1860	Population in 1890
Denver, Colorado	2,603	106,713
Omaha, Nebraska	1,883	140,352
Portland, Oregon	2,874	46,385
San Francisco, California	56,802	298,997

Source: *Population Abstract of the United States*

Using this table, what conclusion can be drawn about the effect of the Transcontinental Railroad on these Western cities?

F   These cities became corrupt and crime-ridden.   STS 27(C)
G   Their populations increased greatly.
H   Most Native American Indians relocated to these cities.
J   The railroad had little impact on these cities.

---

3   Which statement describes an important aspect of the Radical Republican plan for the reconstruction of state governments after the Civil War?

A   Southerners should be made to pay for their rebellion.   Hist 9(A)
B   The Union should be restored as quickly as possible.
C   The freedmen should have to purchase their freedom.
D   The freedmen should not be prevented from voting.

4   Which best describes one way in which industrialization changed life in the United States following the Civil War?

F   Low cost goods became more available.   STS 28(B)
G   Slave labor was still permitted in factories in the South.
H   There was an increased reliance on the domestic system in the Northeast.
J   Technological innovations made immigrant labor unnecessary.

5   The Thirteenth, Fourteenth, and Fifteenth Amendments to the Constitution dealt primarily with —

A   the rights of workers to form labor unions   Govt 16(B)
B   protecting the rights of women
C   the rights of formerly enslaved people
D   limiting the rights of former Confederate leaders

6   Susan B. Anthony was best known for her efforts to —

F   prohibit the manufacture and sale of alcohol
G   form labor unions   Citi 22(B)
H   obtain the right to vote for women
J   expose government corruption

7 What is the main idea of this cartoon from the Reconstruction Era?

The "Strong" Government, 1869–1877

Source: J. A. Wales, *Puck*, May 12, 1880 (adapted)

Hist 9(C)

A Southern society was oppressed by Radical Republican policies.

B Military force was necessary to stop another Southern secession.

C United States soldiers forced women in the South to work in factories.

D Sharecropping was an economic burden for women after the Civil War.

8 What impact did the election of Hiram Rhodes Revels have on American society during Reconstruction?

Hist 9(B)

F It exposed the dangers of free elections in the South.

G It pressured Radical Republicans to support women's suffrage.

H It confirmed that African Americans could participate fully in political life.

J It convinced the U.S. Congress to ban the importation of slaves.

9

URBANIZATION, RAILROAD MILEAGE, AND INDUSTRIALIZATION

	1860	1870	1880	1890
Urban Population (millions)	6.2	9.9	14.1	22.1
Percent of U.S. Population in Cities	20%	25%	28%	35%
Cities Over 10,000 in Population	93	168	223	363
Railroad Mileage (thousands)	30.6	52.9	93.3	166.7

Source: Gary Fields, *Communications, Innovations, and Networks*

Based on the table, what was one effect of industrialization on the United States in the decades following the Civil War?

STS 28(B)

A People began to move away from cities to rural areas.

B The urban population remained about the same.

C The number of cities with more than 10,000 people grew rapidly.

D The rate of expansion of railroad lines began to decline.

10 Which group in the United States presented the strongest opposition to increased immigration in the period following the Civil War?

F steel-producing industrialists

G steamship company owners

H organized labor

J recent immigrants

Cult 24(B)

11

> We may be asked … why we want [the right to vote]. I will tell you why we want it. We want it because it is our right, first of all. No class of men can, without insulting their own nature, be content with any deprivation of their rights. We want it again, as a means for educating our race…. By depriving us of suffrage, you affirm our incapacity to form an intelligent judgment respecting public men and public measures; you declare before the world that we are unfit to exercise the [vote], and by this means lead us to undervalue ourselves, to put a low estimate upon ourselves, and to feel that we have no possibilities like other men….
>
> — *Frederick Douglass, Speech before the Massachusetts Anti-Slavery Society, April 1865*

In this excerpt, Frederick Douglass argues that —

A   the freedmen in the South should not fall victim to new forms of slavery   `Citi 21(A)`

B   the freedmen should be treated like other citizens with full voting rights

C   the freedmen should be given land, tools and animals as repayment for slavery

D   the freedmen in the South require the protection of the North

---

12   After the Civil War, the most common occupations for freedmen were—

F   sharecroppers and tenant farmers   `Econ 12(C)`

G   factory owners and teachers

H   skilled artisans and mechanics

J   miners and soldiers

13   Which of the following best describes the impact of the Fifteenth Amendment?

A   Slavery was abolished in several "Border States."   `Govt 16(B)`

B   All U.S. citizens were guaranteed the "equal protection" of the laws.

C   For the first time, large numbers of African Americans were able to participate in American political life.

D   Congress was given the power to develop uniform rules for new immigrants.

14   Immediately after the Civil War, which action by white Southern legislators most enraged Northern Congressmen?

F   enacting the "Black Codes"   `Hist 9(C)`

G   granting voting rights to African Americans

H   forcing African Americans to move to the North

J   refusing to let African Americans participate in the sharecropping system

15   What was the economic impact of the Transcontinental Railroad on the United States immediately following the Civil War?

A   It brought about the manufacture of safer products.   `STS 27(C)`

B   It promoted a decrease in European immigration.

C   It limited the abuses of the larger railroad companies.

D   It led to an expansion of trade between the East and West Coasts.

16 What characteristic was shared by the Irish workers who helped build the Erie Canal in 1825 and the Chinese laborers who helped construct the Transcontinental Railroad in 1869?

    F   They communicated to one another in English.   `Cult 23(D)`

    G They were warmly welcomed into American society for their valuable contribution.

    H They endured difficult working conditions at moderate pay to construct transportation routes that were the marvel of their age.

    J   They were mainly prisoners forced to accept their conditions of work.

17 Following the Civil War, the federal government most encouraged the westward settlement of the United States by —

    A   making low-interest loans to settlers   `Econ 12(C)`

    B   paying Western farmers to grow crops

    C   relocating American Indian tribes to reservations

    D   honoring American Indian territorial claims

18 Which statement most accurately portrays the policy of the U.S. government toward American Indian tribes on the Great Plains after the Civil War?

    F   The Plains Indians were encouraged to retain their customs.   `Hist 9(C)`

    G The Plains Indians were forced to move from their tribal lands onto reservations.

    H Settlers were taught to respect American Indian tribal cultures.

    J   Management of American Indian affairs was shifted to the state governments.

19 What was the main reason many former Confederates joined the Ku Klux Klan during the Reconstruction Era?

    A   to support the arrival of new industries in the South   `Hist 9(C)`

    B   to eliminate the new system of sharecropping

    C   to prevent the freedmen from exercising their rights

    D   to encourage European immigrants to settle in the South

20 Which of the following was a direct result of the Civil War?

    F   the emergence of the United States as an imperialist power   `Econ 12(C)`

    G the rapid growth of industry in the North

    H the elimination of Southern "Jim Crow" laws

    J   the end of the sharecropping system

21 Which goal was shared by the National Labor Union and the Knights of Labor?

    A   to help Northern industrialists increase their production   `Cult 24(B)`

    B   to help spread modern manufacturing techniques to the New South

    C   to promote immigration of skilled workers from Asia and Europe

    D   to organize workers to demand better conditions from employers

22 Which of the following developments came last?

    F   The buffalo population started to decrease.   `Econ 12(C)`

    G The Great Plains Indians were forced on to reservations.

    H Settlers felt they could now safely move to the Great Plains.

    J   U.S. troops fought a number of battles with the Plains Indians.

23 The "Compromise of 1877" brought an end to Reconstruction by providing for—

   A   the resignation of President Rutherford B. Hayes   `Hist 1(A)`

   B   the removal of federal troops from Southern states

   C   the introduction of the system of sharecropping

   D   a stricter enforcement of the 14th Amendment

24 Which was a result of the completion of the Transcontinental Railroad in 1869?

   F   It ended the need for overseas trade with Europe.   `STS 27(D)`

   G   It led to a decline in settlers moving to the West.

   H   It reduced the influence of businesses on the U.S. economy.

   J   It created a more unified national economy for sharing resources.

25 Which was a direct result of the growth of industry in the North and Midwest following the Civil War?

   A   a decline in the number of urban factories.   `STS 28(B)`

   B   a movement of people from rural areas to cities

   C   a decline in the number of goods that people bought

   D   a sharp increase in the price of manufactured goods

26 What was the impact of the Fourteenth Amendment on the power of state governments?

   F   It reduced the power of the President over the states.   `Govt 16(B)`

   G   It increased the power of state governments over their citizens.

   H   It allowed the federal government to restrict the actions of state governments.

   J   It prevented Congressional interference with states' rights.

27

> We mean to make things over,
> we are tired of toil for naught,
> With but bare enough to live upon,
> and never an hour for thought;
> We want to feel the sunshine,
> and we want to smell the flowers,
> We are sure that God has will'd it,
> and we mean to have eight hours.
> We're summoning our forces
> from the shipyard, shop and mill,
>
> Chorus.
> Eight hours for work, eight hours for rest,
> eight hours for what we will!
> Eight hours for work, eight hours for rest,
> eight hours for what we will!
>
> — I.G. Blanchard, "Eight Hours," 1878

In the decades following the Civil War, the ideas expressed in these lyrics reflected the goals of which group in American society?

   A   labor union members   `Cult 24(B)`

   B   plantation owners

   C   sharecroppers

   D   businesses owners

CHAPTER 15

A PRACTICE FINAL
IN GRADE 8
SOCIAL STUDIES

Now that you have completed the chapters in this book, you are ready to take a final practice test to see your progress. Before you begin, look at some tips for taking such tests:

Answer All the Questions. Don't leave any questions unanswered. There is no penalty for guessing. Answer all questions, even if you're only guessing!

Use the "E-R-A" approach. _Examine the Question_, _Recall What You Know_, and _Apply What You Know_ to answer each question.

Use the Process of Elimination. When answering a multiple-choice question, certain choices are either irrelevant, lack a connection to the question, or are inaccurate statements. Eliminate these choices, then choose the best response that remains.

Read the Question Carefully. If a word in the question is unfamiliar, try to break it down into words that are familiar. Look at the prefix (_start of the word_), root, or suffix (_ending_) for clues to the meaning of the word.

1   Which event demonstrated that citizens sometimes disobey government policies when they feel they are being treated unfairly?

   A   Boston Tea Party   `Citi 20(B)`
   B   ratification of the Constitution
   C   annexation of Texas
   D   War of 1812

2   What advice did President George Washington give to the nation in his Farewell Address of 1796?

   F   A new and weak nation should ally itself with stronger nations.   `Hist 5(E)`
   G   European countries should not try to establish new colonies in the Western Hemisphere.
   H   The United States has the right to intervene in Latin America if necessary.
   J   Americans should avoid permanent alliances with other nations.

3

London Gazetteer	Boston Intelligencer
·1607·	·1775·
Settlers Establish Colony at Jamestown	**Declaration of Independence Announced**

Charleston Courier	Harper,s Weekly
·1787·	·1861·
New U.S. Constitution Drafted	**Civil War Comes To An End**

In which two newspapers are the headlines correctly dated?

A   Boston Intelligencer and Charleston Courier

B   London Gazetteer and Harper's Weekly

C   Boston Intelligencer and Harper's Weekly

D   London Gazetteer and Charleston Courier

Hist 1(B)

4

"... the right of the people to keep and bear arms, shall not be infringed."
— *Second Amendment*

"No soldier shall, in time of peace be quartered in any house, without the consent of the owner ..."
— *Third Amendment*

"Excessive bail shall not be required, nor excessive fines imposed, nor cruel and unusual punishments inflicted."
— *Eighth Amendment*

What do all three of these amendments have in common?

F   They promote the idea of equal rights for minorities.

G   They protect individuals against actions by the federal government.

H   They strengthen the power of the federal government

J   They safeguard the right of individuals to criticize the federal government.

Citi 19(B)

5

MAJOR JOB CATEGORIES IN THE UNITED STATES, 1840

NORTH

Manufacturing

27%

Farming

63%

4%

6% Trading

Other

SOUTH

Manufacturing
Trading 2%
8%
Other 2%

Farming

88%

WEST

Manufacturing

14%

Trading 2%
Other 3%

Farming

81%

Which conclusion can be logically drawn from these pie charts?

A   Manufacturing was the major occupation in the South.

B   In the North, most people were employed in commerce.

C   Jobs in shipping and craftsmanship dominated the South.

D   A larger percentage of people worked in manufacturing in the North than in the South or West.

Geog 10(B)

6   Which historic document granted freedom to enslaved peoples living in the Confederacy?

F   Articles of Confederation

G   Bill of Rights of 1791

H   Monroe Doctrine

J   Emancipation Proclamation

Hist 8(C)

7   How are prices determined in a free enterprise system?

A   by government officials

B   by tradition

C   by the interaction of producers and consumers

D   by military leaders

Econ 14(B)

8   According to the Declaration of Independence, which of the following is an "unalienable right" to which all Americans are entitled?

F   the right to personal liberty

G   the right to vote in elections

H   the right to own your own home

J   the right to a public education

Citi 19(A)

9   Americans sought to obtain control of New Orleans in 1803 so that —

A   Western farmers could ship goods through the Erie Canal

B   Western ranchers could drive cattle to railroad stops

C   Western farmers could ship goods down the Mississippi River

D   Miners could reach California more easily

Geog 10(C)

10

> The history of the present King of Great Britain is a history of repeated injuries and usurpations, all having in direct object the establishment of an absolute tyranny over these States.
>
> — *The Declaration of Independence (1776)*

The authors of the Constitution intended to prevent a repetition of the situation described in the statement above by —

F providing for the separation of powers   `Govt 15(C)`
G forbidding Congress to raise an army
H creating a national executive
J allowing Constitutional amendments

11

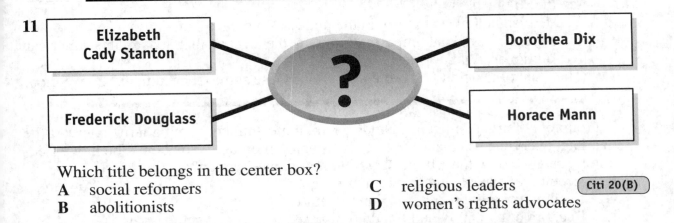

Which title belongs in the center box?

A social reformers   **C** religious leaders   `Citi 20(B)`
B abolitionists   **D** women's rights advocates

12

Macon, Georgia	Richmond, Virginia
• November, 1837 •	• September, 1837 •
Reward of $25 for run-away Negro man. He was brought from Florida, has a wife near Mariana, and probably will attempt to make his way there.	Ran away from the subscriber, Ben. He ran off without any known cause, and I suppose he is aiming to go to his wife, who was sold off last winter.

The two notices shown above appeared in Southern newspapers. Based on this information, what conclusion can be drawn about slavery?

F Slaves were protected and well cared for by their masters.   `Hist 7(B)`
G Slave owners usually recovered run-away slaves.
H Slave owners separated enslaved families based on their own needs.
J Slaves were better treated than Northern factory workers.

13

The liberty of an Englishman is a phrase [so familiar] that I will not define its meaning, but will say what it cannot mean — an exemption from taxes imposed by the British Parliament. Nor is there any charter that ever granted such a privilege to any colony in America. — *S. Jenyms, Member of Parliament (1765)*	Exemption from the burden of taxes we have not ourselves passed must be a principle of every free state. Without this right there can be no liberty, no happiness, and no security! — *New York General Assembly (1776)*

What conclusion could a historian draw from examining these two primary sources about the American Revolution?

A   Differences of opinion existed about the right of Parliament to tax the colonists.   `Citi 21(A)`

B   The British believed strongly in the policy of mercantilism.

C   New York played an important role in the events that led to the American Revolutionary War.

D   The issue of taxation was settled by compromise at the Constitutional Convention.

14   A group of American citizens attends a public meeting concerning tariff rates. At the meeting, everyone has a chance to express an opinion on the matter. Which two freedoms guaranteed by the Bill of Rights apply to this situation?

F   freedom of speech and freedom of religion   `Citi 21(B)`

G   freedom of religion and the right to petition

H   freedom of assembly and freedom of speech

J   freedom of assembly and freedom of the press

15   Which development most encouraged Irish immigration to the United States in the mid-nineteenth century?

A   religious persecution against Irish Protestants   `Cult 23(A)`

B   a famine in Ireland from the failure of the potato crop

C   the failure of a series of political revolutions aimed at unifying the country

D   the need for a workforce to work on the Transcontinental Railroad

16   What was the main goal of the Women's Rights Movement after the Seneca Falls Convention in 1848?

F   to allow women to join labor unions   `Cult 24(B)`

G   to gain the right to vote for women

H   to expand the number of women managers

J   to increase the pay of women workers

17 Based on the map, which of the following statements is true?

A New England colonies grew rice and tobacco.

B Pennsylvania and New Jersey were noted for their fur products.

C Georgia and North Carolina were major producers of shipping supplies.

D New York and Massachusetts were centers for the production of milled grain.

Econ 12(A)

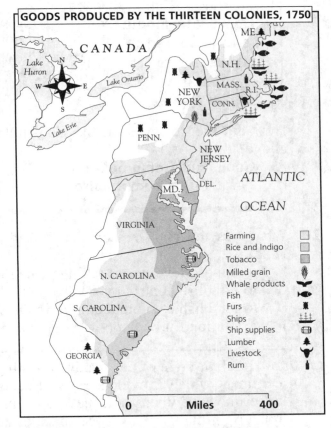

GOODS PRODUCED BY THE THIRTEEN COLONIES, 1750

Farming
Rice and Indigo
Tobacco
Milled grain
Whale products
Fish
Furs
Ships
Ship supplies
Lumber
Livestock
Rum

0   Miles   400

18 What motivated British colonists to come to North and South Carolina and Georgia?

F to find gold and silver

G to escape religious persecution

H to escape poverty and obtain land

J to trade furs with the natives

Hist 2(B)

19 The Mayflower Compact (1620) was an important step in the development of American democracy because it —

A promoted respect for self-government

B created the first colonial courts

C established freedom of religion

D granted all males the right to vote

Hist 3(B)

20 How did the War of 1812 promote the rise of industry in the Northeast?

F Hamilton's financial plan created a national system of credit.

G Cut off from British trade, Americans bought more goods from American manufacturers.

H Without Southern representatives in Congress, Northerners were able to pass high tariffs.

J Napoleon preferred to import American, rather than British, goods into France.

Econ 13(A)

21

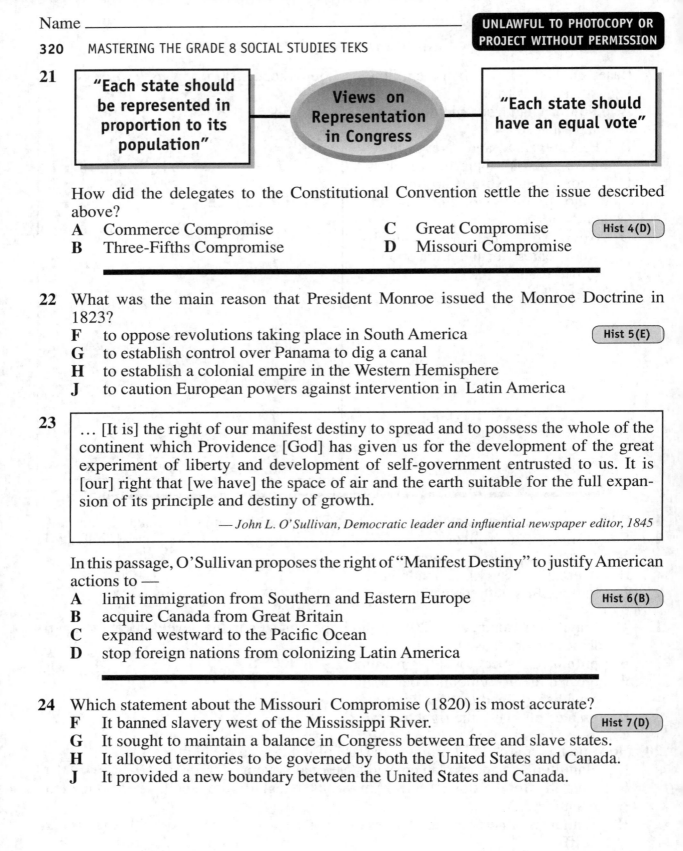

"Each state should be represented in proportion to its population"

Views on Representation in Congress

"Each state should have an equal vote"

How did the delegates to the Constitutional Convention settle the issue described above?

A Commerce Compromise   **C** Great Compromise   `Hist 4(D)`
B Three-Fifths Compromise   **D** Missouri Compromise

---

22 What was the main reason that President Monroe issued the Monroe Doctrine in 1823?

F to oppose revolutions taking place in South America   `Hist 5(E)`
G to establish control over Panama to dig a canal
H to establish a colonial empire in the Western Hemisphere
J to caution European powers against intervention in Latin America

23

> … [It is] the right of our manifest destiny to spread and to possess the whole of the continent which Providence [God] has given us for the development of the great experiment of liberty and development of self-government entrusted to us. It is [our] right that [we have] the space of air and the earth suitable for the full expansion of its principle and destiny of growth.
>
> — *John L. O'Sullivan, Democratic leader and influential newspaper editor, 1845*

In this passage, O'Sullivan proposes the right of "Manifest Destiny" to justify American actions to —

A limit immigration from Southern and Eastern Europe   `Hist 6(B)`
B acquire Canada from Great Britain
C expand westward to the Pacific Ocean
D stop foreign nations from colonizing Latin America

---

24 Which statement about the Missouri Compromise (1820) is most accurate?

F It banned slavery west of the Mississippi River.   `Hist 7(D)`
G It sought to maintain a balance in Congress between free and slave states.
H It allowed territories to be governed by both the United States and Canada.
J It provided a new boundary between the United States and Canada.

25 Which factor helped the North to defeat the South in the Civil War?

    A   The South had more enslaved persons than the North.   `Hist 8(C)`

    B   The North had a more powerful navy than the South.

    C   Northerners were fighting to preserve their way of life.

    D   Britain was an important trading partner of the South.

26 During Reconstruction, what belief was shared by Radical Republicans in Congress?

    F   Freedmen should be granted equal civil rights.   `Hist 9(A)`

    G   Former Confederate states should return the Union quickly.

    H   The North and South should take equal responsibility for the Civil War.

    J   Political and social reforms should not be forced on Southern states.

27

> … With malice toward none, with charity for all, with firmness in the right as God gives us to see the right, let us strive on to finish the work we are in, to bind up the nation's wounds, to care for him who shall have borne the battle and for his widow and his orphan, to do all which may achieve and cherish a just and lasting peace among ourselves and with all nations.
>
> — *Abraham Lincoln, Second Inaugural Address, March 4, 1865*

This statement reveals President Abraham Lincoln's support for —

    A   a new peace treaty with Great Britain   `Hist 8(D)`

    B   voting rights for all adult males

    C   a fair and generous peace with the Southern states

    D   harsh punishment for all former Confederate leaders

28 In the 1760s, the British system of mercantilism was opposed by many American colonists because it —

    F   placed quotas on immigration   `Hist 4(A)`

    G   discouraged the export of raw materials to England

    H   placed restrictions on colonial trade

    J   encouraged colonial manufacturing

29 Under Chief Justice John Marshall, the U.S. Supreme Court strengthened its authority by —

    A   applying judicial review to state and federal laws   `Govt 18(A)`

    B   changing the operation of the Electoral College

    C   increasing the number of Justices on the Court

    D   expanding the freedoms included in the First Amendment

30 Which conclusion can best be drawn from the information on the map?
F   Slavery did not exist in New York in 1775.
G   There was a greater number of slaves in Pennsylvania than in Georgia in 1775.
H   In 1775, slaves were a greater proportion of the population in the South than in the North.
J   In 1775, slaves made up more than half of Georgia's population.

Geog 10(B)

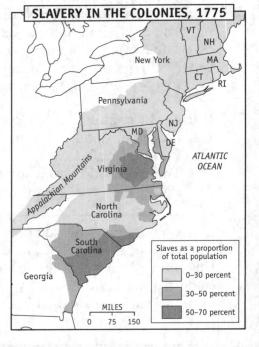

31

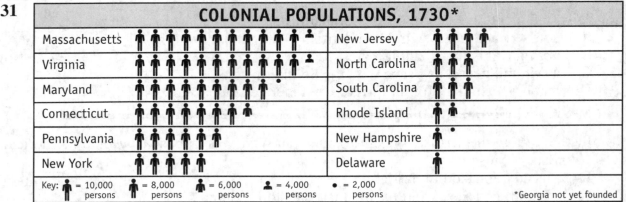

Source: *Historical Statistics of the United States*

Which conclusion about the British colonies in 1730 can be drawn from the information in the pictograph?
A   Two of the most heavily populated colonies were in the South.   Geog 10(B)
B   The colonial population grew rapidly after 1730.
C   The colony of Maryland was the most populous.
D   The first colony established in the Americas was Massachusetts.

32 During the Reconstruction Era (1865–1877), the Civil War Amendments were proposed and ratified to grant African Americans —
F   new educational opportunities   Govt 16(B)
G   complete economic and social equality
H   financial compensation for past injustices
J   the basic rights of citizenship

33

Article I, Section 1

All legislative powers herein granted shall be vested in a Congress....

Article II, Section 1

The executive power shall be vested in a President of the United States of America.

Article III, Section 1

The judicial power of the United States shall be vested in one Supreme Court.

Which Constitutional principle is illustrated in the above diagram?

Govt 15(D)

A   checks and balances
B   "unwritten constitution"
C   federalism
D   separation of powers

34 What was the significance of the Northwest Ordinance?

F   It prevented the extension of slavery into the Louisiana Territory.   Hist 6(A)
G   It established a loose confederation of newly independent states to deal with common problems.
H   It established procedures for the admission of territories into the Union as new states once they reached a certain population.
J   It allowed former Confederate states to be readmitted into the Union after each state's voters took an oath of allegiance to the U.S. Constitution.

35 Which argument did Federalists use in favor of adopting the Constitution?

A   Territories should be admitted as states on equal terms.   Govt 17(A)
B   A bill of rights is needed to protect individual liberties.
C   A stronger government will better protect America from outside enemies.
D   Americans cannot long survive half slave and half free.

36 Which was a characteristic of the system of free enterprise that developed in the United States in the nineteenth century?

F   high rates of taxation   Econ 14(A)
G   minimal government involvement in the economy
H   lack of respect for property rights
J   government protection of labor organizations

37 The Stamp Act (1765) placed a tax on every newspaper, book, and legal document in the British colonies. Which description of the Stamp Act is written from the viewpoint of a member of the British Parliament?

A Britain has the right to tax the colonists to repay debts made   Hist 4(A)
       in their defense.
B The Stamp Act is unfair since it was enacted without the consent of the colonists.
C The colonists should not be forced to pay a tax that they strongly oppose.
D The Stamp Act is likely to provoke a war between Britain and its colonies.

38 Early in the nineteenth century, supporters of high protective tariffs believed they would strengthen the American economy by —

F promoting free trade   Hist 5(B)
G limiting industrial jobs
H encouraging American manufacturing
J expanding global interdependence

39

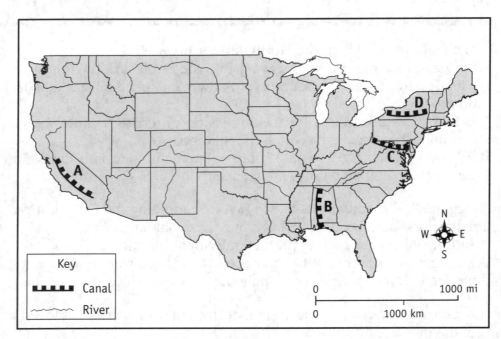

Key
▪▪▪▪▪ Canal
⌇⌇⌇⌇ River

0   1000 mi
0   1000 km

Which letter on the map shows the location of the Erie Canal?

A Letter A   **C** Letter C   Geog 10(A)
B Letter B   **D** Letter D

40 How did the American victory in the U.S.-Mexican War (1846–1848) contribute to the later outbreak of the Civil War?

F It resulted in the election of Abraham Lincoln.   Hist 6(C)
G It ended the ban on slavery in Northern states.
H It raised the issue of whether territories acquired in the war should permit slavery.
J It led the Mexican government to encourage Southern states to secede.

41 What was the main purpose for creating a process to amend the U.S. Constitution?
- **A**   to allow the different branches of government to cooperate   `Govt 16(A)`
- **B**   to permit the national government to adapt to changing needs
- **C**   to allow for the gradual expansion of democracy
- **D**   to prevent any one branch of government from becoming too tyrannical

42

> I see nothing wrong in the maxim that to the victor belong the spoils.
>
> — *William L. Marcy*

Under such a system, President Andrew Jackson sought to —
- **F**   limit the term of office of the Presidency   `Hist 5(F)`
- **G**   extend the charter for the national bank
- **H**   replace existing officeholders with members of his own party
- **J**   stop one branch of government from becoming too powerful

43 What was a major weakness of the Articles of Confederation?
- **A**   The Congress had too many different powers.   `Govt 15(B)`
- **B**   It failed to provide legal rights to male property owners.
- **C**   State governments held the most important powers.
- **D**   All three branches of the government shared equal powers.

Use the chart and your knowledge of social studies to answer the following question.

44   **ERIE CANAL: BEFORE AND AFTER ITS CONSTRUCTION**

Characteristic	Before Construction of the Erie Canal (1820)	After Construction of the Erie Canal (1850)
Population	Rochester: 1,502 people	Rochester: 36,403 people
	Buffalo: 2,112 people	Buffalo: 42,261 people
Cost to ship 1 ton of goods from Buffalo to NYC	$90–$125	$10
Average Travel Time from Buffalo to NYC	10 to 12 days	4 days
Rank of New York City as a Seaport	The fifth largest seaport in the nation	The busiest seaport in the nation

Based on the information in this chart, what economic impact did construction of the Erie Canal have?
- **F**   It limited the number of immigrants entering the country.   `STS 27(B)`
- **G**   It led to the formation of national labor unions.
- **H**   It increased urbanization and reduced shipping costs.
- **J**   It raised the cost of shipping manufactured goods to the West.

45

> "Now jest take this gal and whip her; you've seen enough to know how."
>
> "I beg Mas'r's [master's] pardon," said Tom, "hopes mas'r won't set me at that. It's what I ain't used to — never did — and can't do it, no way possible."
>
> "Ye'll learn many things ye never did before. I'm done with ye!" said Legree, taking up a cowhide and striking Tom a heavy blow across his cheek, and following up the hit with a shower of blows.
>
> "There!" he said, as he stopped to rest. "Now will ye tell me ye can't do it?"
>
> "Yes, mas'r" said Tom, raising his hand to wipe the blood that trickled down his face. "I'm willin' to work night and day, and work while there's still life and breath in me; but I can't feel it right to do this; and mas'r, I never shall do it — *never!*"

Adapted from Harriet Beecher Stowe, Uncle Tom's Cabin.

Using this excerpt, how did the publication of this book by Harriet Beecher Stowe promote the abolitionist movement?

Cult 24(A)

A   by encouraging the expansion of slavery in new territories
B   by depicting the brutality and inhumanity of slavery
C   by offering to buy slaves from Southern plantation owners
D   by making Southern state governments restrict plantation owners

46

> They would erect a shed, sufficiently large to protect 5,000 people from the wind and rain…. Ten, twenty and sometimes thirty ministers of different denominations would preach day and night, four and five days together….

— Peter Cartwright (1856)

What is Cartwright describing in this passage?

Cult 25(B)

F   the Salem witchcraft trials
G   the inauguration of Andrew Jackson
H   the Second Great Awakening
J   the Underground Railroad

47   What has been an important impact of the First Amendment?

Cult 25(C)

A   Each state has been able to establish its own state religion.
B   Americans of all religions have been able to live in harmony.
C   People are free to say anything they wish, even if it harms others.
D   People have been unable to teach their religious beliefs to their children.

48

> Whitney could not have foreseen the ways in which his invention would change society for the worse. The most significant of these was the growth of slavery. While it was true that the cotton gin reduced the labor of removing seeds, it did not reduce the need for slaves to grow and pick the cotton. In fact, the opposite occurred. Cotton growing became so profitable for the planters that it greatly increased their demand for both land and slave labor.
>
> — *The Eli Whitney Museum*

According to this passage, what was an important effect of Eli Whitney's invention of the cotton gin in 1793?

F   American slavery died out.

G   Slavery spread throughout the South along with the cultivation of cotton.

H   British manufacturers began using Egyptian cotton.

J   The farming of cotton expanded to Northern states.

STS 27(A)

49   Which of these paintings is representative of the Hudson River School?   Cult 26(A)

A

C

B

D

50 Which was an important reason for the spread of factories in America in the early-nineteenth century?

    F   They made greater use of skilled labor.   `Econ 13(B)`

    G   They had access to resources from the Great Plains.

    H   Their machines could be driven by steam and water power.

    J   Factory machines cost less than looms under the domestic system.

51 What was the primary goal of President Jackson's policy toward the Cherokee Indians?

    A   to improve their educational opportunities   `Hist 5(G)`

    B   to force them to move west of the Mississippi River

    C   to encourage them to take a fuller role in American society

    D   to establish a program to grant them U.S. citizenship

52 What was an important effect of the Transcontinental Railroad on the United States?

    F   It opened the Great Plains to western settlers.   `STS 27(C)`

    G   It led to the Proclamation Line, closing western lands to settlement.

    H   It led to the passage of the Indian Removal Act, forcing Indian tribes to move west of the Mississippi River.

    J   It brought about unrest in Kansas and Nebraska over the future of slavery.

EVALUATE YOUR RESULTS

After you take and score this test, you should evaluate your results. On the chart below mark incorrect answers with an (**X**) next to those questions. Then look to see which TEKS those questions assessed. For example, if you missed Question 1, you would see that it tested Citizenship 20(C). Then you should review that topic in this book. The TEKS covered by each chapter can be found on the first page of the chapter.

#	X	TEKS	#	X	TEKS	#	X	TEKS	#	X	TEKS
1		Citi 20(B)	14		Citi 21(B)	27		Hist 8(D)	40		Hist 6(C)
2		Hist 5(E)	15		Cult 23(A)	28		Hist 4(A)	41		Govt 16(A)
3		Hist 1(B)	16		Cult 24(B)	29		Govt 18(A)	42		Hist 5(F)
4		Citi 19(B)	17		Econ 12(A)	30		Geog 10(B)	43		Govt 15(B)
5		Geog 10(B)	18		Hist 2(B)	31		Geog 10(B)	44		STS 27(B)
6		Hist 8(C)	19		Hist 3(B)	32		Govt 16(B)	45		Cult 24(A)
7		Econ 14(B)	20		Econ 13(A)	33		Govt 15(D)	46		Cult 25(B)
8		Citi 19(A)	21		Hist 4(D)	34		Hist 6(A)	47		Cult 25(C)
9		Geog 10(C)	22		Hist 5(E)	35		Govt 17(A)	48		STS 27(A)
10		Govt 15(C)	23		Hist 6(B)	36		Econ 14(A)	49		Cult 26(A)
11		Citi 20(B)	24		Hist 7(D)	37		Hist 4(A)	50		Econ 13(B)
12		Hist 7(B)	25		Hist 8(B)	38		Hist 5(B)	51		Hist 5(G)
13		Citi 21(A)	26		Hist 9(A)	39		Geog 10(A)	52		STS 27(C)